CAMEROON'S PREDICAMENTS

PeterTse Angwafo

Langaa Research & Publishing CIG
Mankon, Bamenda

Publisher:
Langaa RPCIG
Langaa Research & Publishing Common Initiative Group
P.O. Box 902 Mankon
Bamenda
North West Region
Cameroon
Langaagrp@gmail.com
www.langaa-rpcig.net

Distributed in and outside N. America by African Books Collective
orders@africanbookscollective.com
www.africanbookcollective.com

ISBN: 9956-792-38-1

Table of Contents

Introduction

It was Saturday 24th March 2007 and the time was about 5 O'clock when I arrived at the Texaco petrol station, Ngomgham Mankon to refuel my vehicle. I had spent almost the whole day on the farm and by the time I arrived at the station, I was completely exhausted and very hungry. In addition to the work that I did in the farm, my exhaustion was caused by the bumpy and dusty road that rattles through the hills and valleys from Alabukam to the petrol point. I decided to get some for food and then rest for a while before heading home. Adjacent the Petrol station is the popular 'Mushroom' Bar that I am very familiar with. I moved there to buy food for myself. In front of the bar was the make-shift food kiosk owned by one Patricia. Patricia was about 52 years old and sold assorted food items. I will talk a bit about this lady later. I ordered a dish of rice and stew from Patricia. I had just started eating when a young man of about 30 years and about 1.76 meters tall, and dressed in the uniform of the Cameroon People Democratic Movement (henceforth CPDM) party, hurried in and also ordered *Corn Fufu* and *Jama jama* for 500 Frs. This guy gobbled all the food in gulps and within the next 5 minutes his plate was completely empty. Ngang, as I later on got his name pulled out 450 Frs instead of 500 Frs from his pocket and handed the money to Patricia. Noticing that the money was less by 50 Frs, Patricia frowned at Ngang and told him to complete the money or else he could not leave the premises. Ngang pleaded to no avail saying that he had no money on him.

In what was to be a protracted quarrel and drama, Patricia insisted that Ngang must pay the money to the last Franc because he was a member of the CPDM-the party with lots of money, the party that has siphoned the state coffers, and the party that has ruined the Cameroonian economy. 'Are you not the people who have rendered me poor?' she asked. Ngang told her that despite his support for the CPDM, there is nothing that he gains from the party. In a rhetorical manner Patricia asked to know where Ngang has kept his own share of the money that the CPDM ministers have 'stolen'. 'You must give me the 50 Frs, I did not spend all night burning myself with fire only for CPDM people to come and eat for nothing', Patricia insisted. Again, Ngang informed Patricia that it is the President and the Beti that have money not the Anglophones. Interestingly, Patricia wondered aloud why Ngang, an Anglophone, could militate in the CPDM. 'The leaders, those people, Paul Biya and you people have killed this contri!!!' she lamented. 'Look at that boy he is a graduate and he cannot have a job (pointing at a passer-by), are you not a member of the CPDM gang? Why are you also complaining? I beg give me my 50 Frs'.

As the drama unfolded my hunger vanished and I had forgotten that there was food placed in front of me. I was in no hurry to go home any more. I became interested and followed the discussion with keen interest. Noticing that Patricia would not allow Ngang to go, I decided to intervene and paid the 50 Frs which Patricia graciously received before releasing Ngang. For about thirty minutes no customer visited Patricia's kiosk and the food was still there gazing at her. Considering that it was already a few minutes to six PM, I wondered if she sold all the food before it was dusk. Could this also be the source of her frustration? That is the question I could not find an answer to.

Each year on March 24th, the CPDM party commemorates the anniversary of the party.[1] The anniversary is always an

---

[1] March 24th 1985 is the day the Cameroon National Union (CNU) party was transformed into the CPDM at the Ordinary Congress of the party in Bamenda.

opportunity for the party to 'take stock and recount their "achievements" and also to strengthen party structures at the grass roots'.[2] However, such anniversaries have also been known for their lavish, extravagances and conspicuous consumptions and ostentatious displays of wealth. Because the CPDM offers political and economic leverage, non members and militants of the party alike often use the arena to enjoy the booty and spoils of the party in the form of gifts and money. It is common knowledge that during such events, money, gifts and food are distributed to so-called 'militants'. Informed by such ideas, Patricia found it difficult to understand why Ngang was unable to buy food for 500 Frs.

Back to the lady, Patricia was a very popular lady in town and I knew her as a vocal and staunch supporter of one of the prominent football clubs in town-PWD[3] Bamenda for decades. Patricia was not associated with a job of any sort and seemed to have taken supporting PWD as a job. Her close association with players and coaches earned her the nickname of the 'wife of PWD'. Others called her 'Mrs. PWD,' after all, Patricia was not married and hadn't a child. It was after Patricia retired from her job as a supporter that she started the food business. One could infer from her utterances that she was not a supporter of the CPDM though it was difficult to cipher to which party she belonged. She hadn't a home of her own and had returned to occupy her father's house at Alakuma after he died in 1978. I learnt that Patricia also died in November 2012, unexpectedly.

Mushroom bar on the other hand was (and still is) a popular bar in the Ngomgham neighbourhood in Mankon

---

[2] Speech delivered by Cletus Anye Matoya, Vice President of the CPDM for Mezam 1 Section during the 2012 party anniversary celebrations at the Bamenda Congress Hall

[3] The team is owned by the Public Works Department, an institution which is in charge of road construction hence the name PWD Bamenda Social Club

known for selling bush meat and roasted fish, considered as delicacies by most people. Apart from selling drinks, the bar is also an information pool where news or the latest gossips in town are always available. It is here that programmed and impromptu datings take place and the bar also offers an opportunity for businessmen to exhibit wealth especially in the evenings and during week-ends. So the bar attracts people of all walks of life and even idling ladies go there to shop for men. The availability of a television room at Mushroom bar also attracts sport fans interested in watching local and European football matches. The bar also creates an arena of social autonomy and opportunity that relieve the lives of people deeply affected by the drudgery of unemployment, poverty and the painful constraints of an ethnically and politicized country. This bar also serves as a thermometer and constitutes a meeting point where the political temperature in the country is measured. Visitors of Mushroom bar appear to be very knowledgeable and informed about what is happening around them and even around the country. Whatever information one gets from Mushroom bar is always confirmed by politicians and newspaper reports. The rise to prominence of this bar is also linked to its proprietor- a retired school teacher and a quarter head known for his politeness and good services. Mushroom bar has remained a social node around which people revolve.

Going back to Patricia, I noticed that in less than 20 minutes, she shifted a simple matter of 50 Frs, to talk about her life and frustrations, but also about the predicaments of the country. It was like Ngang simply gave her an opportunity to regurgitate what she had been stomaching for a long time. Otherwise, one would not understand why an issue of 50 Frs could degenerate and take such unexpected and unprecedented proportions. The problems of Cameroon seemed to be embedded in the 50 Frs saga which Patricia used to express her frustrations and feelings about the state of the nation. I realised that Patricia's encounter with Ngang reflects the daily lives and occurrences that one finds everywhere in town. Patricia's story also constitutes the collective experiences, discourses and memories of many Cameroonians that are (re)narrated everywhere and at anytime in towns, cities, villages, at work places, in buses, at funerals, in churches and where there are gatherings. Informed by previous encounters and experiences with other Cameroonians, I became intrigued by Patricia's yearning for relief and decided to investigate this phenomenon of complaining.

Although the constitution of Cameroon allows for freedom of expression, Cameroonians seem to have, instead, opted to adopt the freedom of complaining. With such attitudes, everyone including the President of the republic complains about everything in the country.[4] Though seemingly a non-event, the narrative on Patricia and Ngang is loaded and embedded with lots of problems which I set out to investigate. Some of the key problems raised by Patricia include; leadership crisis, embezzlement, unemployment, poverty, politics of belonging, and especially the feeling of marginalisation by Anglophones. Just as I observed in the pronouncements of Patricia, these issues are interrelated and interdependent and the effect of one predicates the cause of the other. In the course of organising the work for this book, I decided to include other problems which are directly related and interconnected. The decision to write this book entitled *Cameroon's Predicaments* has been inspired by this culture of complaining and my personal experiences, conversations and interactions with Cameroonians.

---

[4]In his end of year message to the nation on the 31st of December 2013, more than presenting his program or vision for 2014, President Biya raised lots of complaints even against his own ministers.

Cameroon is a country with a triple colonial legacy, having been colonised by the Germans, and later by the French and British after the Germans were defeated in 1916 during the Second World War. For 54 years of its existence, the country has had only two Heads of state. Ahmadou Ahidjo was the pioneer president who ruled from 1960 to 1982. He was followed by Paul Biya who took over and is still in power today. The origins and upbringing of Ahidjo are unclear but he was born in Garoua in 1924 of a Fulani mother of slave descent (Astagabdo Ada Kano Garoua), who died in Garoua on February 16, 1983.The identity of his father is uncertain. He may have been one Youssoufou, and Ahidjo may have known him briefly inasmuch as Youssoufou is supposed to have died in 1929, when Ahidjo was only five. Other schools of thought hold that Ahidjo's father was a Sierra Leonean, a former soldier in Britain's colonial army, who passed through Cameroon shortly after the end of the First World War (See Gros 2003: 34). Ahidjo was a Muslim who attended Quranic School. In 1932 he went to primary school and obtained his First School Leaving Certificate in 1938. In 1942 Ahidjo joined the civil service as a radio operator for a postal service. Ahidjo dominated the political landscape of Cameroon, first from 1958 to 1960 as Prime Minister, then from 1960to 1982 as President. Why the French chose Ahidjo is a frequently asked question .There were clever, better educated, and even sometimes, 'brilliant' men of the south but Ahidjo was preferred as a puppet of the French (ibid 37).

He experienced a rebellion in the 1960's from the Union des Populations de Cameroun (UPC) who considered his regime as a neo-colonial creation and the combined French and Cameroonian forces massacred between 300,000 and 400,000 persons and its key leaders, while other members went into exile. A true genocide! (Gros 2003: 44). Ahidjo's rule in Cameroon was dictatorial and very cruel. In 1972, he created an unpopular constitution which ended the autonomy of British Cameroon and established a unitary rule.

On 4th November 1982, although he resigned ostensibly for health reasons, it is generally believed that his French doctor 'tricked' him about his health and he was succeeded by Prime Minister Paul Biya. Paul Biya was a Christian from the South and not a Muslim from the north like himself and this was a surprise. Biya became head of state but Ahidjo maintained the chairmanship of the CNU, a situation that generated conflicts and rivalry between the two. In 1983, the first coup attempt took place but because of the military Biya held on to power. The rife between the two continued until Ahidjo resigned as the head of the CNU party and went into exile. While Ahidjo was in exile, he was sentenced to death in absentia in February 1984, along with two others for fermenting the coup plot of June 1983.Although Ahidjo denied involvement in another violent but unsuccessful coup of 6th April 1984, it was widely believed by Biya and his supporters that the coup was orchestrated by him. In the remaining years of his life, Ahidjo lived between France and Senegal. He died in Dakar on 30th November 1989 and was buried there. He was however officially rehabilitated by the amnesty law in December 1991.[5]

The federal structures created in 1961 were abolished, and a unitary and highly centralised system of government was put in place with a new constitution in 1972. In 1966, all hitherto political parties unified to form a single party- the Cameroon National Union (CNU). With everything drifting towards a unitary form of government, power became centralised and concentrated in the hands of one man- the President of the republic. At independence, there was no freedom of speech or of movement and the press was seriously gagged. However, in the 1960s and 1970s the country enjoyed relative economic

---

[5] See : http://en.wikipedia.org/wiki/Ahmadou_Ahidjo accessed 25/03/2013

growth from self reliant efforts and improvements in agricultural development. Unfortunately, the country went into economic slumber in the 1980s and this was highly attributed to mismanagement and corruption. This led to massive retrenchments of workers, salary cuts, and high rates of unemployment, poverty, and migrations among others.

The clamour for democratisation and economic liberalisation in the 1990s by Cameroonians met with stiff resistance from the government and led to serious political stalemate and impasse. This almost crumbled an already ailing economy which forced the government to succumb to such demands and a return to multiparty politics. In 1990, the 'liberty' and communication laws were promulgated and this paved the way for multiparty politics.[6] In the highly contested multiparty elections of 1992, Paul Biya was declared the winner. Since then Paul Biya has won all subsequent elections and his party the CPDM has always enjoyed an absolute majority in parliament. By 1996, another constitution was promulgated but its implementation was to be done 'progressively'. For the past 17 years, the country has been using two constitutions- the 1972 constitution and portions of the 1996 constitution. All through, elections were organised by the Ministry of Territorial Administration and Decentralization until an electoral code gave birth to the present election body - Elections Cameroon (ELECAM). However, appointments into this body are still done by the president singlehandedly. There seems to be a growing feeling among Cameroonians that there is too much concentration and personalisation of political power in the country, which has been counterproductive to the development of the country.

---

[6] See, Degree N0 90/52 of 19th December 1990 relating to freedom of mass communication generally referred to as the 'liberty laws' guaranteeing certain basic human and civil rights in Cameroon.

The book has been written in a simple and straight forward manner for easy understanding. In chapter one, I try to identify the problems plaguing the country. I acknowledge that we cannot understand Cameroon's geo-politics without examining the colonial encounters or contexts that gave birth to the state of Cameroon and the colonial legacies that were inherited and the cord that has continuously tied the colonisers to the colonised. First, the creation of the Cameroon state was exogenous with institutions superimposed over pre-existing political structures and inherited by domestic but Westernised elites at independence (Englebert 2000: 1822). Implicitly, African inheritance elites 'were bequeathed the colonial state but not the colonial power that forced it and kept it together *(ibid)*. Beyond the short-term legitimacy which they may have derived from the anti-colonial nationalist movements or the charisma of their personality, African independence elites soon discovered how little power they had inherited. One of the major challenges they had was competing loyalties. Politicians and citizens alike came to conceive of the post colonial African state not so much as the outcome of a social contract or an instrument of collective action based on common 'ideological convictions' but as an 'alien institution' which had 'nothing to do with you and me'. The state therefore, became either a potential resource to be appropriated, or a possible instrument of the domination of other groups to be resisted. In short, Africa has the highest proportion of countries where the process of state creation was exogenous to their societies and where colonial values were at variance with local ones and so were not only ambiguous but generated more problems than solutions.

In Chapter two, I try to demonstrate that the main problem that Cameroon suffers from is the lack of committed leadership. This is more worrisome because the two Presidents of Cameroon have been products of colonial rule and have tended to foster colonial laws and policies. They have been blamed for the economic woes of the country such as; mismanagement, corruption and embezzlement and for instituting political tribalism and nepotism. National integration, which originally was designed in the early years of independence to give Cameroonians a feeling of belonging, has in practice been replaced by ethnicisation of politics (Nkwi and Nyamnjoh 1997: 99). The introduction of ethnicity in the 1996 constitution has ushered in the politics of belonging, representation and at the same time that of exclusion. Everything in the public sphere in Cameroon is, first of all, interpreted along ethnic lines which reinforces the notion of 'outsiders and insiders'. Intra-party and inter-party competition for political power is based on inter-ethnic competition. Consequently, there is gross marginalisation, politics of belonging and exclusion, especially towards the management and distribution of resources of the nation and this has resulted in the imbalance of development. This has not only led to perpetual tensions, frustration, misery and deprivation but a growing state of insecurity. Cameroonians seem to have lost hope in their leaders and state institutions. I also examine the configurations of the different political parties and have concluded that in Cameroon, adherence to a political party depends on how much gains one can make from the party and is not based on any contributions, ideology or party philosophy.

Chapter three documents the chronic problem of unemployment which seems to be at the centre of issues that I am talking about. In the 1980s and early 1990s, Cameroon was hit by an economic crisis and this led to a very high rate of unemployment and salary cuts. Today, Cameroon has one of the highest rates of youth unemployment in sub Saharan

Africa.[7] Since political parties are created along ethnic lines, recruitments into the public service also follow the same sequence. Those regions and people who are considered hostile to the regime in place are hardly given consideration in recruitment opportunities. Selective development and recruitment have become a way of life and collective interest or the policy of equity is not the hall mark of the state policy. Again, the old hardly go on retirement therefore, the youth do not have access to jobs and the public service. I argue that instead of seeing the youth as the workforce of the nation, African youth Dolby (2006: 38), are increasingly seen by the old as a threat to their positions who need to be checked by the state. In this way, the *present* is often postponed to the *future* with the illusion that the youth are 'leaders of tomorrow'-the tomorrow that has never come. According to the 2005 population census, 54% of the population of Cameroon is made of youth.[8] As I try to explain, each of the problems produces an effect which generates another problem. For instance, unemployment causes other social problems such as poverty, corruption and criminality.

Chapter four discusses the social problems of poverty, corruption and bribery that have a direct correlation, and I argue that poverty is an upshot of unemployment generated by the economic crisis. Poverty generates multifold negative effects on the population and also prevents the population from having access to basic necessities of life. The majority of Cameroonians cannot afford houses, potable water, electricity, a balanced diet and good clothing to name a few. Although the country has made positive strives in the educational sector, (one of the highest literacy rates in the continent); less than

---

[7] 15.8% of youths between the ages of 18 and 25 years are unemployed and 70% of youths are underemployed CRTV news cast 7/2/2014

[8] Those between the ages of zero to 40 years. The 2005 statistics is the most recent and available official figures in Cameroon and there is little doubt if the percentage of youth has changed today.

20% of graduates find employment within their first five years after graduation. Because the main employer is the public service, there is little or no access into the public service. Consequently, the few available opportunities have been commoditised and only the rich can negotiate and mediate access through corruption and bribery. As Balogun (2007: 248) demonstrates in a similar study on corruption and bribery in Nigeria, bribery was once a shameful deed, but it appears to have become a legitimate way of conducting business at police checkpoints, passport and immigration offices, customs long rooms, tax collection and motor licensing offices, electricity connection and billing departments, town planning agencies, and mortuaries! This is evident by the high number of top government officials convicted of embezzlement and corruption. To paraphrase Balogun (2007: 248), the grossly mismanaged Cameroon Ship Yard-*Chantier Naval* has gone into crisis several times and the Cameroon Airlines has gone into liquidation. Even the remodelled Cameroon Air Corporation (Camair-Co) is notorious for not settling its bills and having its aircraft impounded by foreign creditors.

In chapter five, I discuss the problem of criminality and violence. These problems are interlaced with those of unemployment and given the inaccessibility of the youth to the very few jobs available; the majority of them indulge in a variety of criminal activities in order to survive. Contrary to popular opinion that criminality is caused by unemployment; I argue that unemployment only leads to a propensity to commit crimes. The reasons why people commit crimes cannot be explained by unemployment alone. If unemployment was the cause of criminality, how, then, do we explain the phenomenon of corruption orchestrated by those who are employed and have access to state resources? However, hardly a day goes by without a criminal offence being reported, be it armed robbery, burglary, arson or theft. I have intentionally treated corruption as a separate chapter because most of those involved in it are those who have access to state resources and live in affluence. I therefore consider corruption and bribery as elite and special crimes that need special attention. Generally, there is a high incidence of violence associated with burglary, armed robbery and assaults. I try to show that most of these crimes are committed with the complicities of law officers and politicians. They use political corruption to acquire finances, which they in turn use to maintain themselves in power.

Chapter six treats the phenomenon of transnational migration which most of the unemployed youth see as a means to seek greener pastures and as a solution to joblessness and poverty. The migration of Cameroonians to Europe, USA and the Asian continents is referred to as 'bushfalling'. Constrained by the dwindling economic fortunes, most Cameroonians consider the streets of the industrialised countries flooded with money. Paradoxically, the dream of travelling abroad hardly conforms to the yearnings and expectations of the migrants. Most often, their ambitions and expectations are stalled by rigorous and difficult immigration laws and other forms of cultural shocks which leave them stranded, and frustrated. Many migrants are either repatriated or they indulge in unorthodox means to survive. The crucial problem is that of brain drain as Cameroon intelligentsias migrate in search of better working conditions and salaries. The anxiety and desire to travel abroad has not spared any social category of Cameroonians. For example, playing football seems to offer one of the best opportunities as the immigration laws are more simple and flexible towards footballers. Here, I emphasise that the regime of the bush faller creates new forms of social hierarchies and identities. I also try to show how these migrants appropriate this *bushfallerness*.

Chapter seven, tackles the 'Anglophone problem' that has been high on the agenda of the English speaking

Cameroonians for some time now. The division of German Kamerun between the French and the British in 1916 ushered in a polarised country along Francophone and Anglophone lines and was to produce an everlasting scar. First of all, the French took two thirds and the British only had one third. This gave a numerical advantage (both in space and population) to the Francophones who gradually used it for the domination or marginalisation of their Anglophone counterparts. Since 1961, Anglophones have systematically been relegated to second class fiddles. As Gros (2003: xviii) states, 'rightly or wrongly, Anglophones in Cameroon today, or at least their elite, feel that they are second-class citizens of a country dominated by Francophones'. According to the constitution of Cameroon, the country is bilingual with French and English being the two official languages, unfortunately, there is no law that ensures the proper implementation of this bilingualism. In the public sphere, French enjoys a prestigious position while English is relegated to the periphery. French and English which ought to be an asset for Cameroonians have been reduced to mere liabilities. I argue that the 'Anglophone problem' is socially constructed to prevent the English speaking Cameroonians from occupying the public sphere thereby, also preventing them from having access to the human and natural resources of the state. Despite complaints and protests made by Anglophones against their marginalisation, Francophones have remained indifferent, adopting a culture of silence.

The next chapter sets out to examine the social problems of insecurity, disorder and rising levels of moral decadence. It may not be an exaggeration to consider Cameroon as a lawless country, yet the country is often seen to have some of the best laws. Presently, Cameroon is governed by a pluralistic legal system where two constitutions co- exist side by side. This gives room for the powers that be to manipulate and (mis)interpret the laws according to their whims and caprices.

This makes it difficult for the common man to seek legal redress, especially as the legal system is controlled by the powerful. Cameroon has often been referred to as an island of peace in a turbulent Central African Sub-region, but embedded in this peace are ethnic tensions, disorder and growing inequalities.

Chapter nine focuses on what I refer to as the 'waithood syndrome' which is simply an exploration of the various tactics that the regime in place uses to keep people and 'things' on hold or the late application or execution of state agenda. This has conditioned Cameroonians, in most cases, to stop reasoning and has rendered them unable to initiate or complete their own plans. Consequently, be it in private or in public, everything in Cameroon is either kept on hold or never executed on time, what Mbiti (1990) refers to as 'African concept of time' or what Cameroonians call 'blackman time or African time'. The inability to do 'things' or execute projects on time has had tremendous negative impacts on the social and economic development of Cameroon.

Chapter ten is a synthesis of the book. I try to stitch the entire work together and to show that Cameroon has not yet attained the level of nationhood as ethnic cleavages and considerations supersede national interests. Since its independence, the country seems not to have had a national development policy or a philosophy. Additionally, the development path is determined by the president who favours some areas and regions at the detriment of others. For instance, there is no systematic and planned electoral calendar for the alternation of power in the country. There is, therefore, the urgent need for an acceptable due process through which people can compete for and occupy public spaces. The various chapters interlock at various levels and are shaped by antagonistic economic and political interests between groups and elites, demographic pressures, resource competition and hierarchical state policies that have not devolved power to lower levels (Abbink and De Bruijn 2011: 2). Finally, I have attempted to explain that Cameroon's development agenda seems to have no ideological basis.

The book ends with concluding reflections in Chapter eleven, where I have also provided some suggestions that are not an end but simply the starting point to solve these problems. It should be born in mind that this work is just my modest contribution to identify the many structural and social problems that Cameroon and most African countries are facing. Cameroonians and those interested in contemporary African studies will also find this book useful. It is therefore hoped that politicians and social scientists can exploit it for better governance and the social well-being of Cameroonians. It would be too presumptuous for anyone to think that this work has provided solutions to the problems of Cameroon. Far from it!

Methodology of data collection

The data for this work was collected from both primary and secondary sources. In the former, discussions, interviews, observations and personal experiences have been very relevant. It is common place in Cameroon for people to discuss daily chores which include not only their own activities but also national events; which very often are intertwined in politics and economics. In most instances, I triggered the discussions in order to have insights into issues. In such discussions, the salient issues raised were noted and contributions were made as a strategy to keep the discussions going. I also adopted the non participant observation method as in Patricia's case with Ngang has demonstrated. I was able to gather huge data through this method. Structured interviews were also used to gather data from key persons such as Politicians, students, traders, trade union leaders, civil servants, traditional rulers amongst others. Finally, as a Cameroonian, my personal experiences in the system also provided useful insights that helped in explaining and analysing most of the issues discussed in the book. I have also relied on newspapers, magazines and the use of the internet. In some cases, news reports from the Cameroon Radio and Television Corporation (CRTV), *Cameroon Calling* and *luncheon date* programs provided useful information.

Most of the empirical data collected has been corroborated and crossed checked with secondary sources. The African Studies Centre at Leiden University was very resourceful as I was able to get secondary sources with particular emphasis on published works on Cameroon. However, references from relevant issues were extrapolated from other countries or continents that were useful in elucidating the issues raised for better understanding.

Chapter 1

In the Beginning

Introduction

This chapter explores the colonial enterprise and the circumstances that led to the creation of the modern state of Cameroon. It analyses the role played by the different colonial expansionists who, because of their capitalist and mercantilist tendencies, partitioned the African continent with rancour to the various ethnic groups and local communities. An abundance of scholarly work has been written on the colonial encounter as being essentially exploitative. The main objective of this chapter therefore, is to show, through Cameroon, how colonial powers used different tactics and strategies to exploit and rape the economic potentials of the African continent. I continue to argue that most of the post-colonial problems that Africa and Cameroon are facing today were created by the colonialists. Secondly, those who took over at independence were in most cases opportunists that were hand –picked and since they were unfamiliar with the laws and policies that were handed to them, they instead created more problems; some of which have been haunting the country for over 50 years since independence. I also note that despite the rich human and economic potentials that Cameroon has, the country is still in an economic quagmire because of nefarious laws and bad management.

Cameroon, like most African states is a creation or an invention of colonial rule which started in 1884 with the Berlin conference.[1] Before 1884, the region, which later became the

---

[1] The Berlin Conference was held to partition Africa among European nations and this was done perhaps with the exception of Ethiopia. The rest

protectorate of Germany, comprised of many indigenous polities varying in size and administrative systems (Chem-Langee1999: 88).[2] In pre-colonial times, the societies they now comprise were often organized along different lines- some were acephalous (stateless) while others had evolved into kingdoms (Englebert 2000: 1823). It should be known, however, from the onset that even these kingdoms had not developed into states as is the case today. This has been elucidated and explained by Egbo et al (2010: 5) thus:

> In many parts of Africa, for most of their known history and until only a century or so ago, people contrived to live together in recognisable political communities without powerful bureaucracies, without standing armies, sometimes without a single national language, without cities, without modern industry and without the degree of centralized government which most people today would probably regard as necessary for the definition of a state. It may even be argued that many of the political entities of pre-colonial Africa which historians have called states like old Mali and Old Kongo were hardly states at all in any modern definition of the word…

Colonisation therefore altered the nature and concept of the state in Africa. Following the scramble and partition of Africa by European powers, this territory became a German colony and was known as Kamerun. The colony derived its name from River Wouri where the Portuguese traders found a great variety of prawns in 1472 and called it 'Rio dos Cameroes' 'meaning river of prawns (Neba 1987: 2;Ngome 1985;LeVine 1963: 266). It is from this version that other colonial powers

---

of the continent was divided arbitrarily without linguistic or ethnic considerations.

[2] There are about 250 ethnic groups and languages in Cameroon that co-exist with French and English as official languages

involved in the territory later on gave different spellings to it.[3] Against slaves, palm oil and ivory, the Portuguese, Dutch, French and the British merchants exchanged gun powder, silk, spirits, and tobacco for animal skins, gold, diamond, and beads with the local people (Warnier 1975: 299; Warnier 1995: 331; Davidson 1963: 58). The trade in human beings as the principal article to serve as Slaves in plantations of the New World had become very lucrative to these European nations as far back as 1517 (Neba1987). As Stock (2004: 29) notes, prior to the 19th century, European knowledge of Africa was virtually confined to the coast. The coastal towns served as entrepots for the shipment of slaves and goods from the hinterlands to the New World.

The conclusions of the Berlin West Africa Conference, however, gave European imperial powers the green light to partition Africa, and so Africa was divided amongst European nations according to their whims and caprices. The arbitrary partitioning did not take into account the conglomerations of ethnic groups, which were split into two or more colonies. Colonialism, which essentially ensured that some groups that, had dissimilar cultures and religions were brought together under a central government, also ensured the emergence of ethnic divisions and rivalries (see Egbo et al. 2010:8). The Ejagham, for instance, were divided between Cameroon and Nigeria; the Wolof and Serers between Senegal and Gambia; the Banyang also divided between Cameroon and Nigeria and the Yoruba between Nigeria and (Dahomey) Benin Republic. These arbitrary colonial and even postcolonial administrative boundaries have been a major source of contestation and tension even in post-independent Africa (Nyamnjoh and Awasom 2008: 2; Egbo et al 2010; 8; Nkwi 2011: 1).

German occupation of Kamerun did not last following the outbreak of the First World War in 1914. After the defeat of

---

[3]The Germans spell it Kamerun, the French, Cameroun and the British, Cameroon.

the Germans in 1916 by the allied forces, they lost German Kamerun and the territory was then shared unequally between the French and the British with the former taking 2/3 and the latter 1/3. The part handed to the British was known as British Cameroons.[4] The road covered by the two Cameroons to achieve independence and later reunification can never be fully told if the history of the people is not taken back from 1916. This is because during the same time, the Germans who had formed a protectorate over the territory since 1884 were jointly attacked by Britain and France following the outbreak of the First World War (Ngum 2013: 51). France and Britain administered their respective spheres of Cameroon as mandated territories of the League of Nations between 1922 and 1945 (Ngoh 2004: 1).

Although German occupation of Cameroon was short lived, they laid the foundation for what Le Vine (1963: 267) refers to as the 'social overhead capital' of modern Cameroon. In fact, they relied on the use of slave labour and migrant labourers that were used to lay the foundation and contributed immensely towards what Cameroon is today. Their contributions in the development of plantations and structures which the state of Cameroon is still using today include the construction of communication and transport facilities and the development of wharves and docks at Douala, Kribi, Tiko and Victoria.[5]

The Political Economy of Colonial Rule

Colonialism is the policy or practice of acquiring full or partial political control over another country, occupying it with

---

[4] Interview 29 /09/2013 with Fo Angwafo III S.A.N one of the Southern Cameroonians who fought for the reunification of Cameroon and who also participated actively at the Foumban Conference.

[5] See Eckert, M. Andreas (1999)' Slavery in colonial Cameroon, 1880s to 1930s'in Miers et al (eds) *Slavery and colonial rule in Africa,* Frank CASS, London-Portland, OR PP133-148. Also see Le Vine 1963, pp

settlers and exploiting it economically.[6]Perhaps it may be important to outline some basic differences that existed between the French and British colonial policies, as these were to determine and affect the policy orientation of the independent state of Cameroon. Firstly, it should be understood that although they were colonialists, they operated on fundamentally different policies. While the French emphasised on a policy of assimilating the colony, the British operated on a system of loose association with the colonies (Ngoh: 2004: 1). While the British prepared Cameroon for eventual independence, the French were interested in creating an overseas colony -France *d'Outre Mer* (Ngum 2013: 2). However, both the French and the British relied on the same basic tenets of colonialism which rested on economic exploitation using different tactics such as forced labour for the establishment of cash crop plantations and the construction of colonial structures. The major differences between the British and the French have been juxtaposed below for clarity. Egbo et al. (2010: 6) have this to say about British colonial policy in Nigeria:

> of colonization, and force, its method. The government was not based on a social contract; it did not receive power from the people. Rather, it took power by force. As such, it had no loyalty, no responsibility to the people. Without the restraints that such loyalty provides, the British enjoyed absolute, unrestricted power. They could do as they pleased. And they did in many instances. In all of their actions as colonial rulers of Nigeria, the British looked after their own interest first and foremost. These interests were mostly economic-the transfer of wealth from the colony to the homeland. Thus the

---

[6] Also see Imperialism in Oxford English Dictionary for definition http://www.oxforddictionaries.com/definition/english/colonialism accessed 2/7/2014.

5

government did not exist to serve the needs of the Nigerian people. It existed to control the Nigerian people and to serve the interest of the ruling elites and their mother country.

On the other hand Asiwaju (2001: 86) also comments on the French policy as follows:

...it is generally accepted that French rule in West Africa was far less liberal than British rule. In French West Africa, the mercantilist approach to economic policy contrasted with the relatively laissez-faire attitude of the British, and placed much greater strain on the subject peoples.

Joseph (1976: 4) goes further to show how the French have continued to dominate their post independent colonies especially in the economic and cultural domains. He summarises it as follows:

France has maintained an economic and cultural stranglehold on its former colonies, backed by a significant military presence. Far from being

Colonialism, therefore, created a pattern of uneven development characterised by isolated nodes of modern economic activity, but with a universal requirement to participate in the cash economy. The major economic change of the colonial period was the development and expansion of the production of agricultural produce for sale in world markets (DeLancey 1988: 2). The Germans introduced the cultivation of cocoa, banana and rubber as early as 1903. It was the export crop, Arabica coffee, which finally took off in the Western Grassfields. It is said to have been introduced to the Bamenda plateau by a returned Bali migrant worker from a

French plantation in 1923 and by the 1930s, coffee became quite popular around Santa, very close to the border of French Cameroon, and at Bali (Chilver 1988: 6; Kah 2012: 289). Coffee, therefore, provided an opportunity for the people to generate income. In the case of Cameroon, both the French and the British turned to the African farmer as the main producer of the export crop (DeLancey 1988: 3).

Labour migrants were therefore attracted to areas with developed cash economies, each of which had its own neglected periphery from which labour was drawn (Stock 2004: 181; Asiwaju 2001: 88-96). For instance, the German plantations in the Bakweri land (Fako) and individual plantations that were already flourishing in Douala attracted seasonal workers to these export crop zones and labour was conscripted through indirect forms of coercion as a means of mobilising labour (DeLancey1988: 2). In most cases migration involved hundreds of kilometres of travel, which often had to be undertaken on foot owing to the poor development of transportation (Stock 2004: 181). There was also the use of slave labourers supplied by the kings of the grassfields. For instance, Kom became the main provider of slaves from the Grassfields and their traders exchanged kola and slaves for Jukun blue stencilled cloth (*Ndob*), salt and beads with Bum, kola for oil with Aghem, slaves, iron goods, and livestock for oil, guns, and gunpowder with Mankon, who, in its turn, obtained oil from Meta chiefdoms to the west and made a middleman's profit (Forde and Kaberry 1971: 134). The impact of migrant labour on the economies of most societies was enormously destructive as the absence of the majority of male population from many areas brought about not only the collapse of indigenous institutions but an imbalance in demographic and sex distributions (Chanock 1985: 15; Konings 1995: 4-5).

The introduction of cash crops also introduced money as a new medium of exchange but again, seriously affected the production of local crops as the men went for cash crops and the women stayed behind to cultivate local crops. In fact, colonial policy demanded that men must pay taxes and so it was the men who migrated to the cash crop zones to work for money in order to pay taxes. As Epko (1979: 195) notes, wage-earning employment was not immediately attractive to Africans because they were low and Africans were not familiar with the new money being introduced by colonial governments. They had not yet acquired the desire for the consumer goods that the new money could purchase. But because they could not escape from the demands of the colonial governments, this forced most men to abandon their wives at home to go and make money in the plantations since that was the major source of currency in the territory (DeLancey 1988: 5).In East Africa, these measures let to the export of men to work as wage labour on the Uganda railway or on the estates that were further afield (Fiona and Mackenzie 2000: 700).This led to the disintegration of family life, and also to a disorientation and redistribution of power in social life. It also brought about a change in relationships between generations and between sexes (Chanock 1985: 15). While there was an abundance of women at 'home,' a shortage of women were experienced in the cash crop zones so men sought for wives back home. Labour migration also meant that in areas where there was a shortage of labour, young women had to follow the men to the towns (*ibid:* 15).

I continue to argue that colonialism was counter-productive for Africans and Cameroon in particular and instead helped towards the underdevelopment of the continent. As mentioned earlier, African coasts were areas of early contacts with Europeans and so these centres were considered centres of modernity and civilisation by Africans themselves. Anyone who came from the 'coast' or who had been to the coast was perceived differently- a civilised and modern person. This perception has also been expressed by Schler (2005: 102) about the colonial encounter in Douala as follows:

Consumption played a crucial role, and the acquisition of material goods aided individuals in securing and displaying their membership in the community of strangers [...] Status was deeply tied to a certain "look." One particularly important marker of status was footwear, as many of the newcomers had arrived in the city barefoot [...] White tennis shoes gained particular popularity. Similarly, European-style clothes were highly sought after and were often the first purchase immigrants made in the city. The meagre salaries paid to most immigrants did not grant unlimited purchasing power, but those who did succeed in obtaining fine imported clothing wore it proudly. Other luxury goods also served as an exhibition of rank in the public spaces of New Bell. In the city, owning a gun was a particularly important marker of status, even though guns were not displayed in the streets of the city; "when you had a gun," said one informant, "you made it known. It was an object for boasting"...

It was also along these coasts that Europeans established seaports and constructed railways from the ports into the hinterlands. The railways served as conduits between the seaports and colonial plantations and so facilitated the evacuation of raw materials from the hinterlands to the seaport where they were eventually shipped to Europe. This was the case with the construction of the railway in 1903 by the Germans linking Ngaoundere the main cotton and groundnut production centre to the port of Douala and the Edea, Mbanga –Kumba stretch where cocoa; rubber and palm oil plantations were established in 1905 as well. Apart from these areas that harboured cash crops with railway lines, no other area in Cameroon benefitted from the largess of the construction of railways.

It would not benefit the reader for me to discuss forced labour and the dehumanizing conditions under which the railway lines were built. Local demand for labour was high, especially for carriers of which the colonial administration was in constant need and for the public works (Warnier 1975: 475). Delancey (1988: 4) states that plantation workers died of harsh working conditions and influenza but also because of inadequate housing, poor sanitation, improper food and lack of medical care. They also suffered from malaria, dysentery, pneumonia and a variety of other ailments. Death rates for workers who migrated, forcibly, from highland, savannah areas to the low land, forest areas of the plantations were as high as fifty percent (*ibid:4*). However, there were resistance and strikes against Europeans because of the crude nature of colonial labour and the maltreatment of Africans. Research on post-colonial rule has uncovered varied ways in which local communities resisted colonial rule especially through songs of workers engaged in forced labour (Wynchank 2013; Crowder,1970). This was a job that was not paid so people in some areas of the country referred to it as *Njockmasi (unpaid work).*[7] Although the work was much resented because it was unpaid; it made an important contribution in linking rural communities to each other and to larger commercial and administrative centres (Epko 1979: 195).

The Effects of Colonialism on Indigenous African Economies

It is important to note that the very essence of colonisation was to exploit the economic potentials of Africa which had hitherto been unexplored (See Egbo et al. 2010: 6). Colonial subjugation took different forms which included wars, gross exploitation, plundering and looting the wealth of the colonies. In the Cameroonian Grassfields, as elsewhere in Cameroon and the continent, there were war raids carried out by the

---

[7] Pa Forngang Ndenge Alphonse, interviewed 12/11/2013 at Atuazire -Mankon

colonialists as a means to force the people to submission.[8] This did not only lead to the loss of human lives, casualties, war captives and African crafts but eventually craftsmanship as Africans were forced to abandon local crafts since this technology was highly discouraged. Colonial rule also banned the consumption of alcohol and indigenous products such as the local liquor *Afofo or Aki*. The most devastating was the looting of African treasures (works of arts) to Europe. Stock (2004: 37) notes that many of the finest works of African arts were seized and shipped to Europe and are today found in museums and private collections outside of Africa. Many of these works, he contends, were seized as war booty during the colonisation of Africa and others were stolen and continued to be stolen from religious shrines[9] or from Palaces eventually finding their way into western art markets. For instance, in 1967 the Mankon Kingdom lost some of the nicest pieces of art from the Palace of Mankon and all efforts to get these antiquities back proved abortive, as Fo Angwafo (2009: 68) notes:

> In the early1960s during the Independence celebrations of Cameroon, the Minister of Education and Culture at the time and his cultural adviser Reverend Englebert Mveng, took along with them for display in America some of our antiquities. This was done rather clandestinely, as it later dawned on me. While there, they did not treat the dancers well and the dancers came back abandoning the instruments. The Mankon Traditional Council and the dancers complained about the matter to the United Nations Visiting Mission but all attempts to have these

---

[8] See Warnier (1975) on the battles of Mankon and the German of 1891 and 1901 pp92

[9] Afo Akom statue is the famous work of art that was stolen from the Kom Palace. Many stories surround the eventual return of Afo Akom but it was discovered that the statue originated from the Kom Kingdom and so it was repatriated back to Kom.

artefacts returned have generally been rebuffed. We learnt that the Cameroon Ambassador in the USA did not know about the Minister's plan of cultural display. The Mankon Traditional Council tried to hold the government responsible but the government said it was a private arrangement between the two, Le Gunsu and Reverend Englebert Mveng, and they died without paying for the antiquities

The above narrative confirms a scenario that most communities in Africa have suffered at the hands of colonialists, but more regrettably because this was done with the connivance and complicity of their own citizens or governments. The case mentioned above was masterminded by Reverend Mveng (a man of God) and even with the implication of the government of Cameroon. They facilitated the pillage and plundering of the artefacts, and one wonders how a troop of dancers could have travelled abroad without the knowledge of their government as purported. Perhaps these objects were not returned largely because of the fear that a repatriation of antiquities long held by western museums would set a precedence leading to an eventual decimation of their collections.[10]

The French system, at the same time, was sustained by the natives as they were compelled to pay the cost of the administration through a tight-fisted fiscal policy and also to supply free labour for the construction and maintenance of the necessary infrastructure (op cit: 86). On the contrary, forced labour in the British colony lasted for a shorter period of time and the emphasis was on indirect rule. Indirect rule was facilitated through the co-optation of local Chiefs to serve as auxiliaries in charge of tax collection and also for the

---

[10] Chanock (1985:37) Law, Custom and Social Order: The colonial Experience in Malawi and Zambia and Angwafo, Fo (2009:68) *Politics and Royalty: the Story of my Life* Langaa PCIG, Mankon-Bamenda

maintenance of order; a duty which necessitated wide and often arbitrary powers (Epko 1979: 195). The power of the chiefs included the recruitment of communal labour for work on local projects deemed of public benefit. For not filling their required quotas, chiefs were often threatened, fined and in some instances imprisoned for not making available sufficient labourers (DeLancey 1988: 4). Forced labour was used in the construction of local buildings and sanitation schemes, and the making and maintenance of roads and footpaths (Epko 1979: 195). To date these chiefs are still considered the 'auxiliaries' of the state though they do not collect taxes any longer (Che 2011: 6-11; Fisiy 1995: 53). Their role in the present Cameroon administration is not well defined but they are simply reduced and used as agents in disseminating information or in mobilising the population without powers. They have become an irrelevant necessity for the state and often used only as footnotes by the government.[11] For the convenience of tax collection and general control through government appointed chiefs and headmen, colonial administration required and created compact villages (Geschiere 1993: 154). The villages created by the colonial process forced people to learn how to live in them, not living traditionally.[12] Such invented villages and Chiefs did not only create tensions among the villages but led to the disintegration and dislocation of ethnic groups, usually through wars. This led to the creation of new boundaries that, even now, have remained the source of ethnic conflicts (Mbah 2009: 16; Nkwi 2011: 1). The creation of Native Authority (N.A) courts did not make things better as these courts were to enforce colonial values and not indigenous customs. Consequently, there were often misinterpretations of colonial laws. This generated conflicts and tensions amongst

---

[11] They are often used by the administration as objects of ridicule as their powers have been eroded with some only receiving small allowances from the state.

[12] Such warrant Chiefs were not recognised by the people who culturally had their own Chiefs

the natives. The revival of authority under indirect rule was both resented and resisted by many because this brought confusion between what was customarily done and what the native courts applied as customary law (Chanock 1985: 23).

One of the main logics of colonialism was that the coloniser operated from a position of superiority and considered the colonies as inferior. As it has been documented by Crowder (1970) elsewhere, the European saw himself as bringing civilisation to a primitive people always living in fear, without a culture and without clothes. The adoption of Western clothing for instance, was seen as a sign of civilisation and the change from unclothed to clothed was equated with a transition from savagery to civilisation (*ibid*: 33).To the Westerner, other societies were not only seen as inferior, but were considered, by many, as subhuman and this European domination of other societies was seen as natural and inevitable (Stock 2004: 32). This discourse typically portrayed the colonised subject as exotic, mysterious, deviant and often dangerous. Indeed, the colonised world was objectified as essentially a thing for study, display and control (*ibid*: 28).

They saw Africans as uncivilised, primitive and a people without a culture. Europeans and Americans were conditioned to think about Africans in Western terms and, of course, in terms of European interests. Crowder (1970) notes that 'during the colonial era, the European colonial powers, despite the efforts of their explorers, sincerely believed that Africa was a dark continent and that Europeans were bringing the first light of civilisation to a benighted people lost in primitivism barbarity'. He further states that the portrait of Africa painted by the colonial powers was one of a people who, on the eve of occupation, were politically decentralized, living in small villages and tree tops, often naked, dominated by witchcraft, living in terror of their neighbours. To them, Europe's progress was seen as God-given; by implication other societies following other religions were inferior and European expansion and conquest provided access to new religions and peoples who could be converted to Christianity (Stock 2004: 32). Christian missionaries assisted in the colonial enterprise by encouraging converts to accept their earthly fate and to look instead toward a heavenly reward (*ibid*).

In this book, I pay close attention to the colonial situation because most of what is experienced in the country today has a direct or indirect relationship and semblance with the scenario that I have described above or are mere manifestations, or in some instances the (re)inventions of the colonial rule.

The March towards Reunification

After German Kamerun was divided between the French and the British, Southern Cameroon, which became a British mandated territory, was ruled indirectly through Nigeria. Nigeria had three regions[13] and Southern Cameroon was attached to the Eastern region. They were treated unfairly, and this led to the clamour for reunification with French Cameroon. This ill-treatment has been captured by Fo Angwafo in the following excerpt:

> The British had very little consideration for Southern Cameroons; they simply abandoned the development of their subjects. There were no infrastructures such as schools, hospitals, and roads as developed by the French, in French Cameroon; and most of those who administered Southern Cameroon territory came from Nigeria. The Nigerians looked at us as lower class because they were our administrators. The important positions of responsibility were held by them. We were traders and it was clear even at the market place that they were positioned as masters as

---

[13] The three regions were the Northern region with the capital in Kaduna, the Eastern region with its head quarters in Enugu, and the western region ruled from Lagos.

15

sellers were forced to carry articles they bought to their residences. This treatment was tantamount to slavery and was difficult to accept. It thus set the stage and nostalgia for a return to the days of German Kamerun!

By 1961 the French and British Cameroons[14] reunified to form the Federal Republic of Cameroon with Ahmadou Ahidjo as the first President and John Ngu Foncha who was the leader of the British Cameroons became the Vice President of the new federation.[15] Preceding this reunification was the plebiscite that took place that same year. Initially, British Cameroons extended from the Gulf of Guinea into the then Adamawa province of Nigeria, but following the plebiscite results for the entire territory that were announced on the 14th of February 1961, 233,571 Southern Cameroonians voted in favour of joining the *Republique du Cameroun* and only 97,741 for joining Nigeria (Percival 2008: 102; Njeuma 2004: V, Ebune 2004: 60).[16] In what most people saw at the time as the result of manipulation of votes by Britain (Nyamnjoh and Awasom 2008: 3), the people of the northern strip of the mountainous land bordering Nigeria that also formed part of the British Trustee territory voted the other way. 'Although the conditions under which the Cameroons were to join Nigeria were clear, the implications of joining the Republique du Cameroun on the other hand were not at all clear' (Nyamnjoh and Awasom 2008: 7). Percival (2008: 103) notes perhaps with regret that for the

---

[14] The name Southern or British Cameroons are used interchangeably here to mean the same thing, referring to the territory handed to the British as a mandated territory

[15] Ahidjo was the President of the *Union Cameronaise* (UC) based in French Cameroun while J.N Foncha was the leader of the Kamerun National Democratic Party (KNDP) See more on political parties and their role towards independence and reunification in Ngoh, Victor (2004) (Eds) *Cameroon: from a Federation to a unitary State 1961-1972* Design House, Limbe pp.13-47

[16] See Ebune (2004:62) for the detailed results of the plebiscite for the entire Southern Cameroons

past 54 years it has not been an altogether happy marriage and wondered whether it would have been happier if the Anglophone Cameroonians had elected to join Nigeria as this remains an open question. 'There were great differences between the life and culture of the two colonial masters and by opting for reunification we were not only mixing two Western cultures but also many African customs and ways. This has made Cameroon a special multicultural and cosmopolitan country, a melting pot of myriad identities'![17] Here is the personal experience of Fo Angwafo III S.A.N who represented the Fons of the Ngemba area at the Foumban Conference.[18]

After the First World War, there was a general outcry for independence in Africa and our boys who fought side by side with the colonial soldiers felt that they were equals or better on the battle fields and found it unacceptable to be treated as second class citizens. The desire to be treated equally as British soldiers after the war led to legitimate aspirations for independence by returning war veterans of British Cameroon. Nigerians who returned from studies abroad established political parties and newspapers which enlightened us on our marginalisation compared to Nigerians, the British and of course Americans. We became agitated for equal status and first we wanted to have an autonomous Cameroon region detached from the eastern Region of Nigeria. By the early fifties we started searching for independence. This phenomenon was also happening in French Cameroon. We also formed political parties and we fought to link our parties to those in French Cameroon and to campaign for reunification and independence.

In 1955 when the Kamerun National Democratic Party (KNDP) was formed by Dr. John Ngu Foncha, I did not

---

[17] Interview with Fo Angwafo III 16/11/2013
[18] In that capacity he attended the Mamfe, Mankon, and Foumban Conferences

belong to any political party. Dr. Endeley was the leader of the Kamerun National Congress (KNC). However, I worked as a Returning Officer for the parties during elections of 1959. By the time the colonialists sought our opinions on independence, I had become Fon of Mankon in April 1959. Here in the then Bamenda province the prevailing parties; the KNDP and One Kamerun (OK) of Nde Ntumazah were speaking one language and that was immediate independence and reunification. I supported the platform of these two parties and the move for independence and reunification along with the Fon's conference. There were intense political activities spearheaded by the Chiefs as far back as the first elections of 1951.

Hitherto in 1948, the Union des Populations du Cameroun (UPC) was formed in French Cameroun. It later came under the leadership of charismatic Ruben Um Nyobe and Felix Moumie. This political party was anti-French and called for immediate independence. The French government banned the party and its activities.[19] 'What worried us much was the aggressive nature of the UPC. Some of them, after the UPC was banned in East Cameroon sought refuge in Mankon'. When the UPC was banned one of the prominent Southern Cameroonian politicians Nde Ntumazah who was a former militant of the UPC founded his own party- One Kamerun which had the same political doctrine as the UPC. That is, they all stood for immediate independence and reunification. One of the supporters of the UPC was actually killed in Mankon

---

[19] Um Nyobe, the leader of the UPC was armed bushed in Nkongsamba while other leaders such as Felix Moumie and Abel Kingue were poisoned and killed respectively while in exile. Also see Ndi Anthony (2013) *Southern West Cameroon Revisited 1950-1972: unveiling Inescapable Traps* Vol 1 Paul's Press Bamenda. Most of its leaders were arrested; some were killed and maimed while others were sent to jail. Some escaped into the British Cameroons

and that frightened so many people and so they pondered whether they should join the Republic of Cameroon or the Federal Republic of Nigeria. But public opinion was for reunification with the Republic of Cameroon. The colonial administration sought the Fons' opinion on independence and reunification. Their resolutions were taken to the United Nations and there it was agreed that a plebiscite should be conducted to decide whether to join the Federal Republic of Nigeria or to unite with the independent Republic of Cameroun. It should be recalled that on January 1st 1960, La Republique du Cameroun became an independent country. 'We decided and campaigned to vote in favour of reunification with La Republic of Cameroun during the 1961 Plebiscite'.[20] The most intriguing thing about the United Nations (UN) organized plebiscite which has been raising a lot of dust is the fact that the UN had prepared questions and needed only answers from Southern Cameroonians. The Southern Cameroon leadership was never given an opportunity to reflect on the questions or propose other possible alternative questions. The two questions were as follows:

- Do you wish to achieve independence by joining the independent federation of Nigeria OR
- Do you wish to achieve independence by joining the independent Republic of Cameroon?[21]

It was on the basis of the results of this plebiscite that Southern Cameroonians joined an already independent La Republique du Cameroon and they became two federated states. In the 1961 plebiscite, we lost Northern Cameroon to Nigeria. That part was administered as part of the Northern region of Nigeria and in a trail election in 1959 we went to campaign there notwithstanding our cultural differences. They

---

[20] Interview Fo Angwafo III S.A.N 20th November 2013
[21] See details of the alternatives and constitutional arrangements for the implementation of the decision at the plebiscite in (Percival 2008:113-125;Ngoh2004:3-4)

chose to join French Cameroon all the same. Unfortunately, this election was disallowed and in the second plebiscite in 1961 the Sadauna, a very influential Traditional Ruler of Northern Nigeria, swayed the people of Northern Cameroon to vote to join Nigeria. Dr Endeley's party sought our destiny with Nigeria while Foncha and Ntumazahs' parties stood for reunification with the Republic of Cameroon.[22]

Later that same year a constitutional conference took place in Foumban to present a federal constitution. The objective was also to determine the form of government for the federation. The conclusions at the Foumban Constitutional Conference in 1961 officially formalised the federal system and Southern Cameroon ceased to exist, and took on a new identity as West Cameroon. It should, however, be noted that the clamour for reunification was precipitated by the growth of nationalism throughout the African continent and formation of political parties. In Southern Cameroon the most prominent was the Kamerun National Congress led by Dr E.M.L Endeley. The ideological basis of the party was the clamour for an autonomous Southern Cameroon region, which should have equal status to all the other regions in Nigeria (Ngoh 2004: 5). On the other hand, Foncha preferred outright reunification with the French Cameroon. Others still wanted Southern Cameroon to achieve independence as a separate and autonomous state and they were led by P.M Kale (Ngum 2013: 11). Because of ideological differences between J.N Foncha who was one of the founding members of KNC, he broke away from the party and together with Augustine Ngom Jua formed the Kamerun National Democratic Party (KNDP). As I said earlier, the party stood for secession of the Southern Cameroons from Nigeria and its ultimate reunification with the Cameroons under French Administration (Ngoh 2004: 5). From 1961 to 1984, the country underwent several name changes (see Anyangwe 2009: 8 for more on the name changes.

---

[22] Interview with Fo Angwafo III S.A.N 20th November 2013

It came to pass that the federal State of Cameroon was born and so the country now became an entity and, a sovereign state; a social reality and also exists in geographical terms.

The Birth of the Federal Republic of Cameroon and its Colonial Legacies

Although almost all African states were colonised by Europeans, Cameroon's situation stands out. This is because Cameroon was colonised by more than one European country, Germany, France and Britain; what Nyamnjoh and Awasom (2008: 1) refer to as a 'triple colonial heritage'. As I mentioned earlier, before colonial divisions, ethnic groups comprised nations in their own right, having been independent kingdoms, with varied political and cultural structures. Indigenous polities were fully developed and functional (Ngoh 2004: 1; Njeuma, 1988). Most still exist even though many of their local systems of organisation have been eroded and transformed through colonialism. In many instances these groupings were larger than some European nations.

It should be recalled that, Cameroon and other African nations inherited colonial values which most often were in conflict with local ones. Because the system of colonial rule did not succeed in completely changing or replacing local values, there has been a blend of values which has produced a system and a way of life that has not solved most of the crucial problems of the new state. For instance, the new state of Cameroon has over 250 ethnic groups that have survived and still retain and maintain their ethnic identities and affiliations. Colonial rule brought along elements of French and English cultures that have also survived. For example, the political system of administration and jurisprudence existing in Cameroon today have been copied almost verbatim and transplanted in Cameroon. Also, two educational sub systems inherited from the British and the French have become very strong in the country bringing to light the notion of Anglophone and francophone segments. This has influenced the perceptions of Cameroonians and even national life greatly.

It appears that the transition from colonial rule to independence was not well conceived and so power was handed to new political elite that was not prepared or relied heavily on the dictates and policies of their colonial masters. The new state that was still in its embryonic stage of state formation inherited many problems created by the colonialists. They therefore had to grapple with the problems they inherited and some that they crafted including corruption and the mismanagement of the resources of the new state. Communities that hitherto co-existed without any form of distinction or discrimination were separated along linguistic lines with Eurocentric undertones. English and French that were part of the colonial relics that Cameroonians internalised became the dominant languages of communication. Consequently, French and English did not only provide a cultural autonomy for each sphere of Cameroon to articulate its interest but equally became identity markers. To date, in Cameroon one is first of all seen as a Francophone or an Anglophone depending on where ones parents or the person was born before independence. The definition of one's linguistic identity in terms of the region colonised by the French or the English does not seem to show clearly who is an Anglophone or a Francophone in the present day dispensation in Cameroon. This is because a person born and resident in a Francophone region of Anglophone parents is not considered a Francophone but still regarded as an Anglophone and vice versa.

The Anglophone –Francophone divide has been a subject of worry in the country when the federal system was abolished in 1972.[23] While not refusing the fact that Anglophones and

---

[23] See J.N Foncha's resignation letter of 9th June 1990 addressed to Paul Biya the National Chairman of the CPDM. One of the reasons for his

22

francophones really exist, for over 50 years now, it is increasingly becoming difficult to identify who is a Francophone or who is an Anglophone. If there is any cry of marginalisation by Anglophones it is largely ·because of the social construct imposed on them by their Francophone counterparts as second class citizens (Gros 2003: xviii). The political arrangement and the manner in which the wealth of the nation is being controlled and managed have rendered the Anglophones marginalised. See details on this issue in chapter seven of this book. Secondly, one is seen and identified by his ethnic belonging and this has been one of the major causes and tensions in the country. The country is therefore divided along ethnicised political lines and a Francophone Anglophone dichotomy.

Again, corruption and the mismanagement of public funds and office have been identified as some of the major problems that were also inherited. For several years now Cameroon has received several 'medals' as the most corrupt country in the world.[24] Despite these negative vices, Cameroonians have been able to hold tight in fragments. This unity in fragments can be seen at all levels of national life -be it economic, social, cultural, political and even religious. Although Cameroon is reputed for being an island of peace in a turbulent Central African sub region, there are dissenting voices throughout the country who feel that things are not moving.[25]

---

resignation from his position as the Vice national Chairman of the CPDM was the fact that the constitution which he considered as the supreme law of the land was in many respects ignored and manipulated by the Francophone leadership. It should be noted that Foncha was the Anglophone leader who championed the reunification of Southern Cameroons with French Cameroon (La Republique du Cameroun)

[24] See Transparency International report on Cameroon 2004

[25] Vakunta, P. Cameroon: unravelling the leadership conundrum in Cameroon   http://allafrica.com/stories/201211021100.html?viewall=1 accessed 02/11/2012

Assessing Cameroon's Human and Economic Potentials

There is nothing wrong with Cameroon. Not even with the land or climate of the country. Cameroon, in terms of its land-size, population, diversified agriculture, reserves in natural power and forestry and level of educational development (especially in the South), is one of the most strongly placed middle-level African states (Joseph 1976: 5).

The country is endowed with natural and human resources and strategically located. According to the Food and Agricultural Organisation (FAO), Cameroon has over 6 million cattle.[26] Coffee, tea, rubber, cocoa, and palm oil are cash crops that constitute the main source of government revenue. Cotton is produced by the Cotton Development Company (SODECOTON) based in Garoua and has 1.527 workers, operating eight factories that produce 152,815 tons of cotton, 62,808 tons of fibre, 76,340 tons of triturated grains and 11,345 million litres of oil on average per year.[27] Cameroon Sugar Company (SOSUCAM) produces more than 60,000 tons of sugar per annum and employs 4000 people. Cameroon Oil Palm Company (SOCAPALM) produces more than 50.000 tons of palm oil and more than 9,000 tons of palm nuts per annum. Other agro industrial plants of importance include Palm Oil Plantation (PAMOL) based in Lobe Southwest region, SEMRY in the north and Upper Noun Development Authority (UNVDA) in the northwest region involved in rice production. Beef and hides are predominantly produced in the northern regions of Cameroon where most of the cattle are also reared (See Business in Cameroon, 2012).

Forest covers a total area of 20 million hectares which is about 40% of the total surface area of the country, and by the year 2000 it was the highest exporter of timber from Africa

---

[26] Tedonkeng, E Country pasture/Forage resources profile Cameroon www.fao.org accessed 1/10/2012

[27] Special issue on projects: infrastructure, mining, energy and agriculture 'Business in Cameroon' issue 01 2012

(Stock 2004: 353). Today, Cameroon possesses Africa's greatest hydroelectric potential after the Democratic Republic of Congo (DRC) and its potential is 55.2 gigawatts, of which only 3% has been harnessed. The country also has the largest natural gas deposits in Africa. According to the Ministry of Economy, Planning and Regional Development known by its French acronym as MINEPAT, a uranium deposit of more than 1.300 tons was discovered at Poli. There are five targets of graphite at Lom around Betare-Oya, Yingui to the North-East of Douala and Mayo Boula in the Far North with 65 targets of titanium also identified. According to the CAPAM,[28] at least 140 gold deposits have been identified in Cameroon. Data published by the Australian company, Sundance Resources on June 20th 2012, shows that there are 775.4 million tons of hematite deposits in Mbalam with 57.2% iron. According to the Ministry of Mines, iron deposits of Mbalam mine are estimated at 200 million tons of rich iron and 1.2 billion tons of enriched iron. There are 2.5 million tons of marble, and limestone is estimated at 600.000 tons of reserves. Large deposits of Pozzolana exist in volcanic areas of the Southwest, West and Northwest regions.

According to the Cameroonian government, the bauxite potential of Cameroon ranks fifth in the world and the reserves are found at Minim Martap near Ngaoundal. Based on the exploration results, the bauxite reserves are estimated at 554 million tons and mineable reserves are valued at 458 million tons of ore. There are 100 million tons of ore deposits with 0.2% cobalt, 0.72 nickel and 3.71% manganese. The annual production could reach: 4. 160 tons of cobalt, 3,280 tons of nickel, 450,000 tons of manganese and 4,000tons of scandium.[29] Despite these mineral potentials, Cameroon is still

---

[28] CAPAM is a private mining company in Cameroon which deals with the extraction of mineral deposit and Gemstone .For details see: http://capam-cam-ltd.imexbb.com/ accessed 3/7/2014.

[29] Statistics culled from Business in Cameroon 2012 edition

underdeveloped and has resorted to the importation of basic necessities as I have presented below in the vignette.

Cameroon spent CFAF 96.7 billion on rice importation last year

(Business in Cameroon) – It is the sum authorities paid to import 366,600 tons of rice in the first half of 2012. Since 2004, the demand for rice has kept rising and supply of locally produced rice dwindling.

In the local markets instead of finding Ndop, SEMRY rice or rice from Santchou on the stands, Pakistani, Thailand's or Vietnamese rice occupy the shelves. Although projects have been initiated to boost production, some of them even coming from experienced nations including Japan, South Korea, and China, even though researchers keep working to introduce high yielding species into farms, the results remain discouraging in the field.

But as this is happening, demand continues to skyrocket leading the authorities to continue accepting more foreign rice into the country. Statistics indicate that Cameroon shipped in 545,000 metric tons of rice in 2011 at an amount estimated at CFAF 145 billion up from 350,000 metric tons bought a year earlier.

What is more disturbing is the fact that the country has enormous arable land fertile enough for rice cultivation. The country possesses 240,000 hectares of cultivable land. Unfortunately, barely 25,000 hectares have been developed, 13,000 of which are for the Yagoua Rice Production agro industry (SEMRY), 3,000 for the Noun Valley Development Authority (UNVDA) and the rest shared between Santchou, Nanga Eboko, and Kousseri among others.

Experts say, if just 50 per cent of the available rice land were put to use depending on the quality of production, the country could feed the rest of the countries and the Central African sub region.

Rice in effect has become a staple food for most Cameroonian with annual demand estimated at between 600,000 and 650,000 metric tons. But local production remains staggering at only 40 per cent of this amount.

Culled from www.cameroononline.org accessed 22/01/2013

The summary presentation of the natural resources of Cameroon indicates that the country is abundantly rich and ought not to have gone into huge debts until being declared as poorly indebted. It is also unbelievable that Cameroon is one of the highest importers of cereals in the sub region as the Vignette above has indicated. The following analysis from the United Nations Economic Commission for Africa (ECA) on the progress that Africa is making towards the Millennium Development Goals (MDGs) further gives startling revelations.[30] In spite of the wealth of the nation, the per capita income of Cameroon is as low as 1.202 Frs. CFA, yet over 50.8% of the population cannot afford the World Bank's minimum of 1.25 US Dollar a day. The life expectancy for women is 57 years while that for men is 54 years. The annual mortality rate is 83.7 persons per 1000, far above the African mortality rate of 78.6/1000 persons (UNDP, 2008). In Cameroon, only 74.0% of the population has access to improved water source and there is frequent breakdown of existing water schemes. Consequently, most people are forced to resort to natural water sources such as shallow wells, rivers, ponds of doubtful quality and that constitute sources of water borne diseases (Mung'ong'o 2012: 88). Water scarcity during the dry season also means an increased workload for women and children who have to trek long distances to fetch water for various household chores (*ibid*).

The country's access to sanitation is 47% and this is also higher than Africa's 41% (UNDP, 2008). The comparative enrolment level between girls and boys is 86.2% to 90.9% which is one of the highest in the continent. The only sector where the country has performed ahead of most African countries is also in universal education, moving from 76.3% in the 1990s to 82.8 % school attendance rate for both boys and

---

[30] UN/ECOSOC/Commission for Africa (2013),'Report on the progress in achieving the Millennium Development Goals in Africa'. Also see the UNDP Human Development Report for 2012

girls in 2009. The literacy rate for women stands at 76% and 87% for men (UNDP, 2008-9). This puts the country at a comfortable level in the continent. Apart from the enrolment figures that are acceptable, the rest of the figures are quite disturbing for a country that is endowed with such rich natural and human resources. With such a high literacy rate, one could conclude that Cameroon has some of the most intelligent people in the African continent. Education plays a crucial role in economic development, and progress towards this goal has positive spill over effects on other Millennium Development Goals (MDGs). Unfortunately, there are no corresponding available jobs for this educated population as most of the highly educated Cameroonians now live and work abroad or are indulged in criminal activities of all sorts. Driven by poverty, lack of job opportunities and an unhealthy economic policy, there has been an exodus of brain drain to lucrative areas. Official statistics reveal that over 137.000 Cameroonians presently live in Europe alone and about 880.000 in the United States of America.[31]More on this had been discussed in chapter four.

This begs the question: what then is wrong with Cameroon? This question appears simplistic yet the answers are difficult to come by at a glance. However, most people think that there is bad leadership and that the resources of the country are also being mismanaged. It is also believed that the economy is controlled by the West and that the country's policies do not favour a majority of Cameroonians. For instance, the prices of petroleum products are determined by the West and forced on to Cameroonians. In Cameroon the prices of petroleum products are geometrically increased every month. Surprisingly, although most Cameroonians claim to be

---

[31] Njila, Hinsley and Chia Innocent [Eds]a guide to understanding Cameroonian-Immigrants in the USA « Cameroonian-American Filmmaker Shoots compelling film on Spousal Abuse | Main | How much I miss my mother! » accessed 13/12/2013

against the monthly increases, they remain mute. This was one of the immediate causes of the February 2008 riots in the country. In conformity with our argument the then Minister of the Economy and Finance Polycarp Abah Abah (now in prison), on several occasions intimated that the price hike was due to the fact that Cameroon exports crude oil only. The refined oil is in turn sold to Cameroon at pre-fixed prices by the West. There are different sheds of opinions about the way things are moving in Cameroon but most people are not satisfied with the system. The various narratives and discourses in this text may help identify the problem with Cameroon.

To conclude, in this chapter I have presented the motives and circumstances that led to the partition of Africa and the emergence of Cameroon as a sovereign state. I have also tried to show the various exploitative strategies that the colonialists adopted to subjugate Africans and to satisfy their economic interests, and how these generated internal contradictions between African values and those imposed by the Europeans. Firstly, Africans did not participate in the Berlin Conference that took place in Germany in 1884-5 and like elsewhere in Africa; the partitioning of the continent was done without the consent of Africans.

The impact of colonial rule in Africa cannot be over emphasised because it did not only divide the people but it transformed the economic and social fabrics of Africa. For instance, subsistence economies that were largely self-sufficient were altered into mixed subsistence and export economies tied to the international economic system as inferior partners in a division of labour. In this way, Cameroon was largely defined as a producer of mainly agricultural raw materials, while Germany, France and Britain became the suppliers of finished products (DeLancey 1988: 2). To achieve this, both direct and indirect means of coercion were used to extract labour and produce from the Cameroonian to pay the costs of colonialism and to provide the goods desired by the European industries and consumers. Force continued to be relevant until such time as new habits, new customs, and new attitudes had developed within the African population so that force was no longer necessary (*Ibid*). Colonialism also created structural and institutional problems which resulted in the reconceptualization and redefinition of ethnic identities and the politics of belonging in the country. This has become a serious national question still in search of answers.

Despite its rich natural and material resources, Cameroon is still suffocating from economic stagnation which has been blamed on too much dependence on the West and for serving their interest at the expense of the local people. As DeLancey (1988: 1) notes, under the influence of colonial policies, new elites were formed to assist colonial rule, but these elites in turn sought to replace the colonial rulers. The elites that inherited the colonial structures either did not understand the colonial policies or simply used them for self-aggrandizement.

At this juncture there is no turning back, but how can Cameroon forge ahead with these problems that were inherited and created by the elite? I try to provide answers by examining the issue of leadership in the next chapter.

Chapter 2

Leadership: Where the Problem Lies

In most of African countries, [...] there was neither a return to pre-colonial institutional forms of sovereignty, nor an attempt by colonisers to remain at the levers of power in the new states. New domestic elites, trained in the colonisers' schools, speaking the coloniser's language and often wearing the coloniser's clothes, took over the coloniser's state and made it theirs. In a word they appropriated the imported state. In doing so they did not build on their institutional past and often tried to repress it, forging ahead instead with strategies of nation – building'(Englebert 2000: 1823).

One of the fundamental problems facing African states since they were handed independence by the colonialists is the crisis of leadership. Africans who took over as leaders were either hand-picked by the colonial masters or rose to prominence as freedom fighters and so ruled their countries in most cases without any program or ideology. Consequently, they were (and still are) more interested in the spoils of power and maintaining themselves in office than working for the socio-economic and political development of their countries. To date, most of them preach democracy but practice dictatorship. Some have even become Emperors or Kings in their own rights. A good example was the self –styled Emperor Jean Bedel Bokassa of the Central African Republic. Van Beek (2012: 33) notes that 'People spoke of him with great admiration and he was seen as a hero of decolonisation, which was ironic considering his dependence on French symbolism (as *empereur*), his emotional attachment to de Gaulle (who he called *Papa*) and his reliance on France under Giscard

31

d'Estaing'. Other examples include, Mobutu of the then Congo (1965-1997), F.M Nguema in Equatorial Guinea (1968-present), and Idi Amin in Uganda (1971-1979). Their reigns never lasted until they died though some enjoyed an *exil doré*. Bokassa was deposed by France and ended up as Christ's self-proclaimed thirteenth apostle (van Beek 2012: 33). Idi Amin went into self-exile and died at the banks of the Moroccan coast of Fez. The African scenario has been summarised by van Beek (2012) as follows:

> One does not share power, one eats it all… So the one who has power is an all consumer and, inversely, whoever eats a lot surely has power. The president – who is often 'president for life' – is the 'eat-all', the great digester. In practice, he is the accumulator of wealth, for himself mainly, and he is also ruthless against adversaries, disposing of justice as he sees fit. In the worst-case scenario, his exertion of power is capricious and also very visible as ruthlessness and cruelty are not hidden. Parties are either non-existent or there is one nominal party.

Joseph (1976: 12), observes that the French Secret Services always acted in co-ordination with their local counterparts to neutralize potential challengers to existing (favoured regimes), and in Paris, Faucart and his agents assisted the effective exile or liquidation of African dissidents. For over fifty years most African states acquired quasi political independence, and are still searching for the most appropriate system of leadership and governance. In some of these countries the new elite and the military resorted to coup d'états as a means to get to power.[32] While not claiming that it has all been gloomy for Africa, I plead to state that despite the fact that African

---

[32] Nigeria has a good history of leadership successions through coup d'états largely organized by the military. Since 1960 that the country had independence, leadership has been dominated by the military

countries rank very high on the list of failed states and have shown some of the worst abominations of power in human history, the continent has also produced statesmen with unsurpassed charisma (see Abbink and de Bruijn 2011: 26) and leadership qualities. This chapter examines the perennial problem of leadership and governance in Africa but with particular reference to Cameroon. I argue that Cameroon's underdevelopment and economic crisis is caused by bad leadership. It is a leadership that is not capable of inspiring a team to realize its full potentials. Following Englebert (2000: 1823), I continue to argue that the leadership, or ruling class, inherited the state rather than shaping it as an instrument of its existing or developing hegemony. I try to show how Cameroonians feel and react to the situation in their daily lives, reflections and thinking and how this has developed into a culture of laisser faire and complaining.

In his New Year's Eve address to the nation on the 31st of December 2013, President Paul Biya raised a series of issues which took many Cameroonians by surprise. He said

> Definitely, there is still room for improvement in the effectiveness of our economic policies. We have a growth and employment strategy which guides us towards achieving our goals. But, how come then that in some sectors of our economy, State action often seems to lack consistency and clarity? Why is it that in many cases, decision-making delays still constitute a bottleneck in project implementation? Why can't any region of our country achieve a public investment budget execution rate of over 50%? Lastly, one can rightfully question the usefulness of certain project monitoring committees which are unable to take any decisions.[33]

---

[33] See Paul Biya's end of year address to the nation on 31st December 2013

I try to use the complaints made by the President to his compatriots on the eve of the New Year as a mirror through which I hope to evaluate the crisis of leadership in Africa and especially in Cameroon and I emphasise that this needs to be taken seriously, especially when such pronouncements are made by the President who ought to provide solutions to complaints coming from other Cameroonians. The complaints from the Head of state however evoke fundamental questions. By complaining, was the President simply reminding Cameroonians that he is aware or unaware of these problems? Was he in essence surprised that the state machinery has failed to grind efficiently? Thirdly, was the President admitting that he has not been able to provide solutions to the problems that he raised? Since it is difficult for me to provide answers to these questions in the place of Paul Biya we can only do that in conjecture.

Nevertheless, following President Paul Biya, whenever two or more Cameroonians meet; they seem to be unhappy with the state of affairs in their country. When you meet a fellow Cameroonian and ask a simple question like this one; 'how is it'? The response is usually- 'things are not moving' or 'things are hard' or simply *'Didong, yi no di muv!! .Fo Cameroon somting di waka? All na management!!'* If you insist, he or she starts pouring a litany of problems that are never ending. In the same light, with Patricia's complaints that we saw in the introductory part of this book and those articulated by the President Biya, complaining has become a culture; a way of life. From the responses that one gets, it is evident that something is wrong somewhere in the country. The data in this chapter was derived from random interviews that I conducted in Mankon and Buea involving people from different age groups. The use of respondents from different age strata was particularly important because the responses cover the colonial era and those of the post colony from which we could draw conclusions.

34

I use the social life of a taxi which also constitutes a public space as the entry point. My inspiration to include a note on the question of leadership was triggered by a conversation I had when I boarded a taxi from Ntsuabuh Junction to Ntambeng Mankon. The distance between my point of departure and destination is about three kilometres, but for the short time that I was in the taxi, many issues were raised by my co-passengers. The discussions were provoked by one lady who could not hide her anger directed towards the driver for overloading the vehicle. In a heated exchange between this lady and the driver, the rest of the passengers intervened. Contrary to the expectations of the passengers, the driver insisted that he was right to overload the car. He insisted that taxi drivers are simply obeying the 'rules of the game' and that if any passenger felt cheated such a person could alight from his car or should pay the official fare of 200 Frs. for a drop in town. Since it appeared that most of the passengers did not pay the official fare, we gave up as we were squeezed and crammed into the car. In the following paragraphs, I present some of the issues raised by the passengers.

I noticed that, while in most countries passengers tend to increase or propose higher taxi fares or hire taxis in order to get to their destinations with ease and on time, in Cameroon it is the reverse. Whenever a Cameroonian stops a taxi, he/she is quick to inform the driver sometimes impolitely that, 'driver I have only 100 Frs' whereas the official fare for a taxi drop is 200 Frs in most towns in the country. When you want to find out why passengers prefer begging taxi drivers instead of paying the normal fare, the response is simple- times are hard or are not moving. Although the fares are fixed by the state, in Cameroon, taxi fares are determined by passengers and not the driver. If the taxi driver refuses to accept the 100 Frs., the passengers prefer to trek and most do trek.

'In this country taxi drivers are looked upon as fools, we toil all day and night and get nothing, we are only trying to make ends meet and we only hope that one day things will change'. Eric[34] (the driver) was not happy with his passengers and questioned if the passengers would also challenge the policeman who extorts money from them on the highway. Why do you people only complain about the taxi driver? He continued. As if he was recounting the ordeal of taxi drivers, Eric had this to say:

> The taxi driver has only two options- carries the passenger or park down his taxi. The second option is the one we will not afford to do because taking this option means going without food. In order to survive and keep life going, we prefer only to break even by carrying the passenger for the one hundred Francs.

Drivers do not respect the official carrying capacities of their vehicles. People are lumped together like sardines and despite complaints from some passengers, most still board the taxis under uncomfortable conditions. It therefore means that a taxi in Cameroon only gets full when it has reached its destination. The prices of petroleum products are increased each month and the surplus value of Cameroonians falls inversely. This deepens their misery and sometimes they contemplate going on strike. But with uncommitted workers' union leaders, these strikes hardly take place. So often, the people grumble and stay in their poverty and frustrations. Frustration, depression, and misery manifest themselves in a myriad of ways in Cameroon.

My encounters with Cameroonians in cafes, restaurants and even in taxis and meeting houses show that people always have something to discuss about the poor state of affairs in the

---

[34] After this encounter, Eric and I became very good friends and through this friendship I discovered that he was a holder of the General Certificate of Education (GCE) Advance Level but could not further his education because both parents died in a motor accident the same year he left the high school.

country. Most of their stories raise nostalgic feelings of the regime of the late President Ahidjo. In fact, the comparison between the first and second Republics is a serious point of argument among generations in Cameroon. Indeed, most Cameroonians who lived through the era of Ahidjo would always like to narrate stories of the past. For instance in the taxi, one of the passengers Tabufor[35] recalled that 'during the days of Ahidjo, a bag of cement was ... francs, petrol was ... per litre and there was money. Our problem at that time was not money but how to spend it'. He even dragged the argument further to the colonial era. He kept on insisting and showing his admiration for the British rule and to a lesser extent that of the Germans. When asked about his impressions about the French, he like most Anglophone Cameroonians expressed indignation and hatred about their exploitative tendencies but had a preference for the British, which suggests that he seemed to prefer the British rule and even re-colonisation.

Being an admirer of the British colonial rule, Tabufor held that the corrugated iron sheets (Zinc) "five stars" imported from Britain were better than the Aluminium sheets produced by the Cameroon Aluminium Company (ALUCAM) nowadays. He also insisted that British manufactured textiles at the time were of a superior quality than those produced today by CICAM. He was also quick to note that the money being used today is of poor quality and value compared to Pounds and Shillings that the British introduced. And so it was the same comparison with every other thing that you can imagine. Other passengers joined and supported him as they have not forgotten that even children born during the colonial era were better in all aspects of life than their neo-colonial counterparts. To them, the pre-colonial and children delivered during the

---

[35] Tabufor is a retired Police Constable who has worked in most parts of Cameroon during the era of Ahidjo and Paul Biya and is therefore, very knowledgeable about the first and second republics

colonial period were physically stronger, more respectful, more intelligent, and more responsible than their post-colonial counterparts that are weak, disrespectful, insolent, arrogant and irresponsible. The list was long and endless. Although this is true to some extent, it also implies that Cameroonians are deeply dissatisfied with the state of affairs in the country. Whatever the case, this is an indication that things are not actually moving in the right direction, so people are disgruntled with the system of governance and management.

There was also the general belief even to those who do not know Ahidjo that he had a better vision and philosophy about the country than Paul Biya. Not to say that Biya has no vision at all but to them, there seemed to have been prosperity in the country in the days of Ahidjo as he also tried to reconcile a divided nation.[36] It must also be clear that there are major differences in the way that Ahidjo ruled and of the way Paul Biya rules. For instance, before Cameroon got independence in 1960, there were nationalists and even anti-French sentiments calling for immediate unification and when Ahidjo took over, he tried to reconcile with Cameroonians who thought that he was a stooge of the French. Neba (1987: 8) also affirms that 'Ahidjo's program at independence was to seek internal autonomy of Cameroon…, to seek national reconciliation, and to seek cooperation with France in a reciprocal manner'. In 1972 Ahidjo made the country a United Republic as he thought that it was uneconomical for a small country like Cameroon to be running three governments.[37]

---

[36] See Joseph, Richard (1975) 'National politics in post war Cameroon: the difficult birth of the UPC', *Journal of African Studies* 2:2.Members of the UPC party and especially the leader Um Nyobe were killed and militants of the party were chased into exile by Ahidjo supported by the French. Also see Bayart (1973: 128)'one –party government and political development in Cameroun, African Affairs, Volume 72:287pp128

[37] Before the abrogation of the federal structure, there were three assemblies, west Cameroon House of Assembly, East Cameroon House of Assembly and a Federal Parliament. A House of Chiefs also existed in West Cameroon. The Unitary state marked the demise of these structures.

President Ahidjo developed a 'five year development plan' geared towards directing, stimulating and controlling the economy but giving room for free enterprise and initiatives by individuals. He laid emphasis on agriculture which was the main economic activity of the population. After independence, the Cameroon government continued to show a lot of concern to the development of agriculture in its five-year development plans (Fonjong 2004: 14). As earlier mentioned, the Germans introduced cocoa, rubber in 1905 and coffee in the 1920s and also established a banana plantation in the southwest region and by 1947 the Cameroon Development Corporation (CDC) took over the German plantations.[38] Most of the state revenue came from cash crops and the money was redistributed through the provision of services, acquisition of raw materials and for feeding the nation. The government also encouraged livestock production. Ahidjo's philosophy was to encourage both man and woman to engage in farming. Most of the women were and still are involved in subsistence farming but a good percentage are also employed by the agro-industrial companies. Two tea plantations were established by the Germans- one at Tole in the southwest region and another at Ndu in the northwest region. Women in particular were considered more suitable for tea plucking because they had nimble fingers and were also thought to be cheaper labourers (Konings 1998: 151). From 1967 till 1977 there was an agricultural boom in Cameroon and thereafter there was a sharp decline because prices fell drastically. This decline continued steadily until the 1980s when acute economic crisis took centre stage, coinciding with the ascension to the power of President Paul Biya following Ahidjo's resignation in 1982.

---

[38] The CDC is a state parastatal with over 100.000 hectares of estate lands which the British trusteeship authority confiscated from German planters at the outbreak of World War two see Konings, P.J.J (1998) *Women plantation workers and Economic Crisis in Cameroon*, Berg, Oxford PP151 also see DeLancey 1988, pp6-12

In 1984, Biya went ahead to scrap the 'United Republic' and the country simply became the 'Republic of Cameroon'. This change of name has been protested by the English speaking (Anglophones) who think that the abrogation of the federal system has given room for their marginalisation by the Francophnes (Konings and Nyamnjoh 2003: 197, Njeuma 1995: 30-34). It has also been argued by Nkwi and Nyamnjoh (1997: 99) that the national integration which originally was designed in the 1980s to give Cameroonians a feeling of belonging has in practice, been replaced by ethnicisation of politics. In terms of their personalities, there is however a sharp contrast between Ahidjo and Biya; the former identified himself with African values especially in his dressing habits while the later differs in so many ways.

During the nationwide strike called up by the transporter's Syndicates from February 25-28, 2008, it was noticed that most of the people expressed total annoyance with the powers that be. A young man could not hide his feelings when he told me 'I am not proud to be a Cameroonian, there is nothing that interests me in this hellish country of ours any more'. 'Why do you say so?' I asked him. He simply told me 'do not ask me why, I hope I had another country to go to'. As he moved away, he murmured 'the first line of the refrain of the National Anthem describes Cameroon as a 'Land of promise and land of Glory, but to me Cameroon is land of misery, suffering and I bet you this is hell'. He went on. In fact, he told me that each time he sings the National Anthem it is like he is singing to a Beti deity. I stood silent for a while but praised the young man for his ingenuity and dexterity.

When I triggered a discussion on the well-being of Cameroonians, a majority of respondents intimated that Cameroonians live in fear, uncertainty, misery and abject poverty. To them, many die every day from starvation, hunger and the inability to receive medical care. The problems they raised were many. This, to us, indicated that there is total confusion and chaos. They hold that there are a lot of people who are only existing or surviving in the country; and that they are Cameroonians just because they do not have another country to go to. Some even cursed God for making them Cameroonians. Very few felt Cameroonian and these were those they identified as power brokers who hang and suck the state treasury just as the blood sucking tick drains its host (cow) dry; but they insisted that the parasite is even better because it makes sure its host is alive. These people, according to them, suck their host (country) to the point of death. As a result, most of them indicated that they have lost confidence in their leaders and state institutions.

Following the analogies presented above, if you ask what the problem with Cameroon is, the answer would simply be that the country is suffering from poor leadership and bad governance. As Tumi (2006: 71) notes, in Cameroon there is no leader that can inspire the people to work for the country. To him, 'those ruling the country do not love their country and they lack the spirit of patriotism. They are ready to sell their country for a dime, if they think that would serve their selfish interests'. From our discussions above it would seem that Cameroon has a leadership fatigue. A leadership that appears to be insensitive to the plight and yearnings of its people .The insensitivity of the leadership which tends to react than acting on national issues makes most Cameroonians lose confidence in state institutions. Consequently, most Cameroonians have simply become unenthusiastic in regards to the current leadership, and instead of looking into the future with hope and optimism they have tended to admire the regime of late the Ahidjo with nostalgia.

At the level of partisan politics, the system has conditioned and forced all the active forces of the country to belong to the ruling junta. A survey of the Central Committee members of the CPDM who campaigned during the last Municipal and Parliamentary elections of September 30th 2013 showed that most of them were professors who constituted the intelligentsia.[39] By militating and romancing with the ruling party, the CPDM, they abandoned lecture theatres to become Central Committee Members, Resource Persons, and Campaign Managers. Evidence in the past has shown that once appointed into government any minister can take the title of a Professor. By implication, the title of Professor has been ridiculed by the powers that be; as Professors' spring up like mushrooms every day. This also suggests that an easy way to become a Professor in Cameroon is by occupying an influential position within the CPDM or through a ministerial appointment. Each Minister arrogates to himself or herself the title of Professor. In Cameroon, a Professor has more political and religious value than academic value. The system has conditioned and compelled academics to become subservient to the executive since appointments in the universities are the prerogative of the President.[40] Experience has shown that when you blend academics and politics what emerges is sycophancy. Because of the anticipated rewards that these 'Professors' expect from the government, they give undue praises to the Head of State and his cohorts which are usually manifested in the form of *Motions of support*.[41]

Motions of support constitute a form of lobbying. This is a process whereby influence is purchased to ensure an appointment to office. Certain offices are considered 'plums' or 'good seats' defined in terms of quality of contract awards,

---

[39] See the list of CPDM Central Committee members and campaign teams sent to the various regions of Cameroon for the twin elections of September 2013. Also see *L'Action* Newspaper September 2013

[40] In Cameroon it is the President of the Republic who appoints University administration - from the Vice Chancellors (Rectors) right down to the Head of Departments. See last appointments of February 2014

[41] Motions of support are public declarations or communiqués in praise of the Head of state and usually drafted singlehandedly by the so-called Professors then sent to the public or radio to be read on behalf of the militants of the particular organ of the CPDM who very often have no idea about them or their contents. Also see Nyamnjoh 2013pp,8

opportunities for smuggling, extortion, bribery or blackmail. Of particular importance are those offices that deal with external commercial centres such as finance, commerce, foreign affairs, customs and immigration and those that define and punish crime such as security, police and the judiciary. From my personal observations in Cameroon, academics and partisan politics are not good bed mates. While not depriving these Professors of their civic rights of belonging to political parties of their choices, we must frown at the excesses and loyalty some show in the practice of politics. Before the Head of state even utters a word, our Professors are set with ready-made motions of support which are often appointment driven. In their minds they have the imaginative thinking of being appointed or maintained as ministers or directors in an anticipated government reshuffle.

Cameroon Democracy: Governance without Ideology or Political Program

Cameroonians are systematically divided into two political groups. One group is the civil servants while non-civil servants form the other. Because they are paid by the government and are in search of 'juicy' posts and appointments, civil servants are unnecessarily loyal to President Paul Biya and the CPDM party. They see everything good in the CPDM government and anything preached or practiced by the opposition is considered bad. I consider this sycophancy. On the other hand, the opposition is largely dominated by those who are not civil servants. These are usually the unemployed, self-employed and those who have retired from the public service. This category of people tends to be those who feel cheated or have not had the opportunity to work with the public service. They appear to be those frustrated by the regime or who do not gain anything from the regime. A quick look at the genre of opposition Members of Parliament (MPs) and Mayors of municipal councils show that most of them are those who have been retired from the public service.[42] Being retired also means being tired. This means that their capacity and ability to think, reflect and sustain an argument also diminishes as they get older. Not surprisingly, most of them spend much of their time snoring during parliamentary sessions. Another distinct feature with the group is that each time someone leaves the public service, he or she suddenly sees everything in the CPDM as bad. What I consider as demagogy.

To borrow from the Americans, during the Presidential campaigns in that country in 2008 and 2012, political maturity was highly displayed by the Republican and Democratic parties and their candidates. During campaigns, whenever a candidate said something that was good, the other did not hesitate to admit it, and that showed that although they belonged to different parties they were not enemies, they have one common interest. It also indicates that politics should not breed hatred as the American people have often shown. In the USA, what matters is the ideology or program presented by a party. Irrespective of party leaning, Americans are ready to vote for a candidate that will solve the issues of the day. Therefore, Americans are, first of all, interested in the program of a party followed by the candidate who is promoting the program. That is why a Democrat can decide to vote for a Republican President during an election. It is because of this thinking that President Obama was able to win over the Republican 'Red' states of Florida and Ohio amongst others.[43] In Cameroon, party loyalty thrives on enmity and falsehood. Most Cameroonians are always ready to refuse everything that a militant of another party says or has not said so long as he/she is not 'one of us'. They are even ready to vote for anybody or

---

[42] For example, see the list of municipal councillors and parliamentarians of the opposition parties for the northwest

[43]'United States Presidential elections 2012' http://en.wikipedia.org/wiki/United_States_presidential_election accessed 3/7/2014

anything so far as he or she is standing on the platform of 'our party'.

One day, someone made an expensive joke with regards to the voting patterns and behaviours of Cameroonians. He told me that in Cameroon, people can vote a tree or stone so long as these objects represent his or her party but will refuse to vote for a human being in the other party even if he or she is very competent for a post. This appears accurate because if we look at the calibre of some of the municipal councillors and parliamentarians that were voted for, one begins to wonder whether we actually know why we vote. These types of people finish their mandate without knowing exactly what has taken place. In this way, they have no accounts to render to the electorate but interestingly they continue to win at future elections. The question that lingers in my mind is whether it is just enough to vote a member of your party? Yet both the ruling and opposition parties do not have any clear cut political programs or ideologies. Drawing from a study carried out in Ghana, Ayee (2011: 372) revealed similar findings:

> The parties have the same ideological line both in terms of manifestos and policies neo-liberal economics and liberal democracy with a huge dose of populism. In fact, they hardly articulate any identifiable ideology on their policy platforms, other than a vague 'developmental ideology' aimed at improving the lot of the people. Moreover, the parties rarely mobilise electoral support on ideological platforms. Their manifestos and campaign messages do not reflect any clear ideological stance. Rhetorical shifts in ideological positions have been largely driven by changes in domestic politics and the contingencies of outmanoeuvring political competitors and dislodging the incumbent.

Those in the CPDM see everything right in whatever the Head of State does, says or has not even said. The opposition spends its time condemning or criticizing the actions of the CPDM. They only react to any action or step taken by the CPDM regime. In truth, all Cameroonians have as a point of reference is Paul Biya! The responses that we got from militants of different political parties were at variance but here are some of the opinions:

The CPDM zealots make us to know that Cameroon cannot exist without Paul Biya. They see Paul Biya as the only one who can bring peace, development and social stability to the country. In short, to them, there can be no Cameroon without Paul Biya. Those of the opposition also saw Paul Biya as the obstacle to change or progress in the country. To them, Paul Biya is the source and epitomises misery, frustration and depression. Paul Biya therefore, is seen as the prime mover, or destroyer depending on which side you belong. He is even seen as the Alpha and the Omega.

In both camps nobody is being groomed to take over whenever President Paul Biya leaves power. In South Africa it was no secret that Jacob Zuma was being prepared to take over the leadership of the African National Congress (ANC) and the Presidency of the country. Following this arrangement, he won the April 2009 Presidential elections. South Africans knew before the elections that he would be the presidential candidate. Fidel Castrol handed over the presidency of Cuba to Raul Castrol; Eyadema took over from the father and same with Joseph Kabila who took over from Laurent Kabila -his father.[44] While not preaching that power should be handed from father to son like in a monarchy, we must acknowledge

---

[44]'Joseph Kabila', http://en.wikipedia.org/wiki/Joseph_Kabila accessed 3/7/2014

46

that these leaders were at least thinking of their successors. Cameroonians live in suspense and in the unknown. Nobody knows what will happen when Paul Biya's presidency ends.

Cameroon is a complex and complicated country in the way it is governed. It has a system where its leaders have only one ambition – to become the Head of state and occupy the Presidency (Unity Palace). This ambition has been expressed by both members of the ruling CPDM oligarchy and the opposition parties. It is true that the ultimate aim of any political party is to take over power and execute its own program. The irony is that these leaders strive to govern without clearly outlined programs or ideology as we indicated earlier. Taking the cue from Kenya, Mwangi (2008: 269) opines that most parties espouse no coherent or sound ideology or doctrine on which to articulate interests, mobilize supporters and shape or structure public opinion. Another example from Mali has also been described by van Beek (2012: 37) as follows:

A host of political parties turn around the same thing, all with names that juggle the same terms: Democracy, people, *rassemblement*, development, association, progress and liberty. It has become quite difficult for a new party to find a name to distinguish itself from the others. The root cause of all these political parties is that each has a patron, an important, rich man who is seeking political fortune in the national arena with the help of his clients in order to become the *primus inter pares*. And the few parties with a more ethnic slant have exactly the same general principles and use similar names.

Each time the leader of the Social Democratic Front (SDF), Ni John Fru Ndi, is called upon to make a public pronouncement, the usual outcry is that of stolen victory by the CPDM that has frustrated and deprived him from occupying the Unity Palace. All his attention is focused on election rigging and fraud and has never distinguished his party's ideology from that of the CPDM. Because everybody is so ambitious to get to the state house, the coalition of opposition parties has never yielded any fruits. Each time they meet to come out with a single candidate to confront Paul Biya; they disagree and come out much weaker than they went in.[45] On the other hand, the ruling CPDM uses all tactics and strategies to remain in power even if it has out lived its usefulness. The CPDM regime believes that the presidency is their private property and no other political party in the country has the right to its occupancy.

The Politics of Gift-giving and Empty Promises

Political elections in Cameroon are characterised by the distribution of gifts and money in exchange for votes. In most instances, there is a positive correlationship between the gifts that are offered by politicians and the votes that they get in return. Yet in other cases as I have demonstrated below, the voters receive the gifts but do not reciprocate with the votes. In Uganda, the same scenario was recorded during the 2011 Presidential elections where the National Resistance Movement (NRM) of President Museveni and the opposition parties exhibited wealth and power of varying degrees at campaign rallies. This has been aptly captured by Medard and Golaz (2013: 551). They describe the scenarios as such:

The electoral moment brings out crucial times of gift-giving and thanksgiving in politics which might be seen as public displays of wealth and power. Before the elections,

---

[45] See the meeting of the coalition of opposition parties that met in Yaounde before the 2007 Presidential elections, where Ndam Njoya of the Cameroon Democratic Union (CDU) was picked as the main leader to confront Paul Biya the CPDM candidate. After the meeting there was a roar and suspicion and the parties came out split into more factions than was the case before the meeting.

in rallies, and after, in 'thanksgiving' events, all politicians threw parties with music, food and dance. Yet inequalities between the National Resistance Movement (NRM) and the opposition, in terms of means, resources and presence all over the country, were striking during the campaign. The NRM benefited from state infrastructure, and its campaign was often facilitated by local government and administration. They distributed gifts and tokens, in addition to promises of new laws, closer administration and development.

It should be noted that giving or promising to give, created a moral obligation towards political leaders with an unwritten interest in maintaining this system of dependency. It is only by accepting the offer for protection that one might access certain resources (*ibid*). Following the Ugandan example, during the 2013 Municipal and Parliamentary elections in Cameroon, there was an overwhelming display of wealth and power by the different candidates. Opposition candidates also held parties with music and dance. More importantly, some of the musicians played out of political conviction, while others played for money. While some musicians sang in support of President Biya and his program of *Grand ambitions* or Greater achievements[46], those of the opposition parties sent out counter messages intended to dissuade the electorate not to be convinced by the promises of the CPDM regime but also as a strategy to mobilise support. 'If the CPDM gives money, sugar, rice, it is our money that they are sharing but on the Election

---

[46] Political campaigns are lucrative businesses for local musicians who in most cases are griots and participate at different political parties' rallies in search for money and changing the messages in their music to suit each political rally and event. They do so concealing the real parties to which they belong.

Day you know what to do, vote out of your consciences and not because of Savon or sugar'[47]

In sum, both the ruling and opposing parties have not been able to redress the burning problems of unemployment, misery and poverty. They seem to be more interested in filling their pockets and bank accounts than alleviating the sufferings of the masses. In Cameroon, the practice is the politics of promises. During the municipal and Parliamentary elections campaigns; we noticed that politicians made declarations without commitments.[48] During election campaigns, people made all sorts of promises some that are impossible and unattainable. It was normal for a politician to promise the construction of a sea port in Nkambe and for a railway to be built in Njikwa-Momo or to tar the Mundemba road in Akwaya without shame. This was common among the politicians of all the parties. From my observations I concluded that they are the same players in different uniforms.

In Cameroon, politics and government are businesses and only those who are capable of bargaining also reap the fruits. When multiparty returned to Cameroon in the early 90s the impression that most Cameroonians had was that it was the CPDM that dishes and uses money to buy votes. In truth, the CPDM brought about the idea of corrupting minds to get votes through the distribution of money and gifts to potential voters. Initially, this was seen and condemned by the opposition parties as bad but gradually, they have fallen in the same soup and even do it efficiently and better than the CPDM. Those who contested elections in 1991 on the platform of the opposition parties can attest that they won

---

[47] Message recorded at SDF rallies in 2013 elections in Cameroon by Mayor Balick Fidelis of Bamenda II Council in the northwest region considered the strong hold of the opposition SDF party.
[48] The elections took place on September 30, 2013 and we attended political rallies in Mankon and Wum for both the CPDM and SDF. This coincided with the period that I was also carrying out field research in Cameroon.

50

their tickets without spending a franc but today the scenario has changed. In fact, most of them were booted out in subsequent elections because they could not adjust or adapt to the new policy of offering money and gifts. Most of the people argue (rightly though) that 'once in office, the elected officials do not know them any longer so the only time they can get something out of the vote seekers is during the period of election campaigns'.[49] I observed that during the elections of September 2013, both parliamentary and municipal potential candidates of the various parties exhibited ostentatious displays of wealth in terms of gifts-giving and the distribution of money as a means to gain votes.[50]

Again the compositions of the various lists were configured along ethnic lines which enhanced out right political ethnicisation. The tendency for individuals in the public sphere has always been to identify themselves or to be identified with a specific ethnic group and this has resulted in the atomisation of the public sphere along ethnic lines (Orji 2010: 168). In Cameroon, political leaders form political parties and mobilise supporters by appealing to ethnocentric feelings, thereby reducing parties to ethnic- based outfits. Intra-party and inter-party competition for political power is therefore, in most instances, based on inter-ethnic competition, as different ethnic groups compete for or retain political power in a bid to have access to resources for political patronage (Mwangi 2008: 269).

Those who use political corruption to acquire finances are in turn elected to Parliament, some directors and others appointed to cabinet positions ensure that they protect the wealth acquired through corruption. This is further

---

[49] Fru Wilfred Interviewed 12th September 2013

[50] The official lunching of the elections campaigns for the CPDM by the Prime Minister ,Yang Philemon, where over 5 million francs was given to the each of the seven divisions in order to assist or what the PM called 'facilitate' their work in the field. Some of the candidates in Bamenda II CPDM municipal list were quoted as having spent a colossal sum of over 10 million francs used in buying and distributing gifts.

complicated by the strong ethnic bias characterised by illegal distribution of public wealth (Jerome 2010: 124). Often the resource curse, i.e. easy access to and a monopoly over plentiful mineral or other natural resource wealth, is in operation here, which implies that the power holder does not need the support of his people. Through oil, diamond, or coltan money he gains substantial wealth and can pay his military or police force as well as his cronies and family, leaving the general population to struggle (van Beek 2012: 87).

Most of the ministers (Mebara, Olangena, Inoni, Siyam Siwe, Marafat and Forjindam) now languishing in jail are the same ministers and directors who led the CPDM campaign delegations to their respective areas. During the 2007 Presidential Campaigns, Forjindam Zacheus distributed 500.000 Frs. to each of the 20 Parliamentary candidates for the northwest region which gave a total of 20 million Francs. Not surprisingly, he was arrested for embezzling 980 Million Francs at the Cameroon ship yard. The misuse of public enterprises in the form of political patronage and employment of incompetent persons to manage such enterprises are rampant in Africa and in Cameroon (Mwangi 2008: 269).

Just as Mwangi (2008: 272) has found out in Kenya, those who are not interested in party politics but have economic interests to be protected also contribute to the parties' campaign funds directly or indirectly. This is one of the means through which the CPDM mobilises support and sustains itself in power. For the financial support that they make to the party, most of them are often appointed into the Central Committee of the CPDM.[51] Politicians therefore practice belly politics (Bayart, 2009) and so long as the belly is full everything is alright. The politics of the belly is the dominant mode of government and the logic that guides the behaviour of

---

[51] See the comprehensive list of the CPDM central committee with the names of the economic elites in the country who own all the huge companies and industries

individual bureaucrats and politicians in Africa and Cameroon (Moritz 2006: 107). As one of our informants opines, 'in Cameroon, politicians are unnecessarily generous and polite as they dish out money and goods with ease during election campaigns but once elections are over they choose and pick who to help. Indeed, they show a lot of indifference and become very selective with the people they treat or deal with' (Ngang Christopher interviewed 15th September 2013).

Early in January 2009, the President of the republic appointed members of an 'independent election body'- Elections Cameroon (ELECAM), to replace the moribund organ of National Election Observatory (NEO). Despite the fact that the Prime Minister held consultative meetings with opinion leaders throughout the country to discuss how to set up the new organ, Cameroonians were surprised to receive the news when most of the twelve members appointed were staunch members of the ruling CPDM. For example, the Chairperson, Dr. Fonkam Azuh,[52] of ELECAM has been a leading member of the Central Committee since the inception of the CPDM; while Dr Dorothy Limunga Njeuma was a member of the Political Bureau of the same party for years. Because of their over bearing influence and public pronouncements about the CPDM, most Cameroonians did not seem to see how independent these people could be. It is true that as individuals they are people of integrity and respect. However; the issue of elections in Cameroon is a thorny one and very different from the academic prowess that some display.

Knowing very well the headache that Cameroonians have been having with the organization of elections by the Ministry of Territorial Administration and Decentralization, and the largesse that the CPDM has been enjoying from them, most Cameroonians never took the Head of state's appointments

---

[52] Dr Fonkam Azuh, holds a PhD in law and until his appointment was the assistant Secretary General of the National Assembly in Yaounde

seriously. As the chairperson Fonkam Samuel insisted, Cameroonians should wait and they have been waiting.

Vignette: *The SDF Dilemma and Regional Politics*

...The Ngwa Man, I know our electoral process is a sham, from registration to the pronouncement of the results. That is not to say from these tainted results you can't gauge how influential a political party is or the amount of support it has. Now I grew up in the South West Region and actually voted in some elections before I left Cameroon. Now let's go back to the 90s, Kupe Manunguba went to the UNDP, they will never vote SDF. They abandoned the UNDP and are now firmly behind the CPDM. The SDF has never made inroads there and hasn't even tried. The few grassland people living in Tombel can't change the outcome of the elections. Hold as free and fair an election as you possible can today, they will vote CPDM or some other party but never the SDF as it stands today. Let's go to Meme Division, apart from Kumba central, the rest of Meme used to go to the UNDP and CPDM, now with the demise of UNDP, the other parts are firmly behind CPDM. Now let's turn to Kumba Central, with decentralization, Biya death (sic) another blow to the SDF in Kumba, the town now has three councils. Kumba 1 and 11 are firmly in the hands of CPDM while Kumba 3 is SDF. Now this is the genius about this arrangement, Kumba 3 is made up of Meta Quarters, Fiango, Kosalla 1, 2, 3.If you know anything about these neighbourhoods then you will realise they're abundantly made up of people of North West extraction. Hold free and fair elections in Kumba central today and the CPDM will win the majority of the councils. The SDF has lost its foothold on Meme. Now let me take you to Ndian. It was all UNDP in the 90s. Ekondo Titi in the 90s leaned on the SDF because of the labourers in Pamol. That's as far as the SDF got. The rest of Ndian is like Kupe Manunguba, they see the SDF as a 'graffi' party and would rather vote another party if they don't want to vote for the CPDM than to vote for the SDF. For 20 years now SDF has made no inroads. Hold free and fair elections, and SDF loses badly.

I could go on with Manyu, Lebialem, and Fako but its Friday and Tuburg calls out my name. It is the same story. Where you find a huge percentage of people of North West extraction, the SDF holds sway but that's as far as it goes.

Now this is the South West Region, former partner in Southern Cameroons, Anglophone brethren, Anglo-Saxon heritage and all what not, the SDF hasn't succeeded in making any inroads in 20 years, and you expect it to do so in Central or East or Grand North? Please, don't hide behind unfair elections.

Sources: www.cameroononline.org accessed 16/11/2012

This vignette shows exactly the political configurations in Cameroon as most of the parties do not have national representation. The Cameroon Democratic Union of Dr Ndam Njoya is prominent only in the Noun Division while the National Union for Democracy and Progress (NUDP) of Bouba Bello is only spotted in some areas of the North region. Political representation in the National Assembly shows an overview of the strength of the various parties nationally. Following the September 2013 Parliamentary and Municipal elections, of the 180 parliamentarians, the CPDM party won 153 seats, the SDF: 16, the CDU: 1, the NUDP: 6, and the MP: 1 Member of Parliament. With the exception of the CPDM that seems to have national coverage on the basis of their arbitrary use of state resource, the other MPs are drawn from the fiefs of the various parties[53].

These elections are usually flawed with many irregularities but we must also agree that the CPDM has implanted itself throughout the country more than the other parties. While some of these parties contested against the results of the 2011 Presidential elections, the Mission Chief of the African Union's Observer Mission to Cameroon-Ibrahim Boubacar Keita

---

[53] As the party in power, the CPDM has been accused of fraudulence and rigging of results to their favour.

acknowledged that the African Union Judges found the elections to be 'free and fair'. This was the same affirmative observations that came from La Francophonie and Commonwealth observers.[54] Also, the impressions of Cameroonians in the vignette confirm, the southwest region as the stronghold of the CPDM. But this raises other concerns. It portrays the divisions and differences that exist between the northwest and the southwest, supposedly the only Anglophone regions. This constitutes a potential source of tension and conflict among Anglophones.

There has been the gradual return of many Cameroonians to the ruling CDPM party as most supporters of the opposition parties are in a stalemate and confused, because the SDF has not been able to fulfil their dreams.[55] In 2007, the CPDM made serious in routes and won over 18 councils of the 34 municipal councils in the Northwest. During the 2013 Municipal and Parliamentary elections, the CPDM won 16 down from 18 councils. Although the CPDM lost 2 councils that it won in the past elections, the party however defeated the SDF in the Bamenda I and Santa Councils hitherto considered the bastions of the opposition. The first time that Ni John admitted that elections were free and fair in Cameroon, his party was defeated in his home town of Santa. Haven shared some of the strategic councils with the opposition in the region, it is evident that the CPDM party has made serious in routes that threaten the survival of the SDF in the region and country as a whole. It would appear that the SDF is blind or pretend not to see the strong comeback of the CPDM in its stronghold.

Sometimes the Chairman of the SDF unwittingly threatens to boycott elections organised by ELECAM but he has never been committed to such pronouncements. No sooner than elections are announced do you find him struggling to have his

---

[54] See the commonwealth mission report headed by the foreign minister of the Bahamas in Nkwi, forthcoming

[55] To bring about reforms and to ensure political and economic change

own share of campaign money that the state dishes out to participating political parties. The first time that Senatorial elections were organised in Cameroon, Ni John headed the SDF list for the northwest region and his list was defeated by the list of the CPDM led by his long time arch political rival now Senator Achidi Achu. In the 2011 Presidential elections that took place Ni John was a candidate for his party as well. The Chairman behaves more like a chameleon probably because there is nothing more to think about than the quest to get to the Presidency. The good about SDF militants is that they never ask or use the campaign money given to their party, rather they go hunting for what they consider CPDM money and the SDF militants are not always happy with their victory at elections. They are most happy when the CPDM loses in a constituency. They also consider elections rigging as the reserve of the CPDM and only see their own victory as genuine.[56]

As van Beek (2012: 39) observes, most African leaders are extremely reluctant to retire and, if need be, change the constitution or the voting rules. Their political support is based on close well-remunerated cronies; a system that then turns to using violence against internal opponents while denying responsibility for it. Based on the results of past elections since the reintroduction of multipartism, each political party in Cameroon out manoeuvres each other in order to rig elections whenever and wherever the opportunity arises. Since all of them succeed through rigging, it is possible to find saints, angels and Satans in all the Parties.

Party Discipline and Cameroon Democracy

Since Cameroon returned to multiparty politics in the 90s, the leaders of the various parties have never been replaced. None has ever contemplated handing over to another party

---

[56] See petitions made by the SDF to the Supreme Court against the CPDM in the 30th September elections Of 2013

stalwart. Being the main opposition party that ought to lead by example, Krieger (2008: 86) notes that even Fru Ndi's long tenure as chairman is now itself a contentious fact of SDF life. Within the CPDM, nobody can afford to challenge the incumbent-Paul Biya. Each time presidential elections are organised, followers and militants of the party throughout the country start calling on their party leader (Natural candidate) to contest the elections. In the end the President who ordinarily will not step down or who refuses to yield to such calls comes out to accept the request from his party militants. Since the President gives the impression that it is the militants who want him to be there, it is probable that the President shall not leave office on his own so long as the people want him to remain as Head of state. Given such circumstances, the militants of the CPDM have become much stronger than the constitution of the country. It is they who can also manipulate the constitution so that the presidential mandate can be extended to allow their President to stand for elections several times. As usual the Head of state uses such excuses to force the CPDM dominated National Assembly to pass bills that allow an extension of the presidential mandate without limits.[57]

Talking about the National Assembly, section 2 of Law No 91-020 of 16 December 1991 stipulates that the Assembly shall be constituted of 180 Parliamentarians elected through universal suffrage for a mandate of five years. On the other hand, Law no 92/013 of 15 January 1992 gives the President the prerogative to allocate the number of seats per division.[58] It is expected that for effective planning and budgetary

---

[57] See interview with Fon Mbambi of Wum (Aghem) on the role he played to change the presidential mandate from five years to seven years renewable.

[58] Agendia, Aloysius: Cameroon 2005 census results: smack of diabolic geo-political planning. http://agendia.jigsy.com/entries/blog/cameroon-2005-census-results-smack-of-diabolic-geo-political-planning accessed 19/01/2013 also see Tande, D (2010) Cameroon:2005 census results finally published http://www.dibussi.com/2010/04/cameroon-2005-census-result-published.html

allocations, the distribution should follow the population size of each division but this is done arbitrarily.[59] There are instances where some subdivisions are more populated than some divisions and regions but have few MPs, yet very unpopulated regions have more MPs. For instance, the Mezam division alone in the northwest region has a population of over 770.000 inhabitants (Tanyi 2010: 4), but has been allocated only three MPs while the South region with 818.440 inhabitants has eleven Parliamentary seats. The highly contested 2005 population Census result clearly shows this discrepancies and manipulations.[60] To make it clearer to Cameroonians, the distribution of parliamentary seats ought to have a threshold (Minimum) population size per seat. In such a situation anybody can, without waiting on the Head of state, come out with an authentic and acceptable distribution of seats in Parliament. It would seem that those regions that are opposing the regime and the 'winnings' of the CPDM government have been 'punished' with less seats (Agendia, 2005).

It is the same scenario with the distribution of seats to the various municipal councils. It is hard to believe that Bamenda II subdivision with a population of 358.000 inhabitants has 31 Councillors and Bamenda I with a population of less than 15.000 inhabitants also has 31 Councillors. Yet the Bafoussam I Council with the same population size as that of Bamenda II has 61 Councillors. This trend is the same throughout the national territory and it is important to note that there should have been a yard stick to measure equitable and proportionate distribution of seats. In a complicated and sophisticated

---

[59] In Cameroon a Division constitutes a parliamentary constituency

[60] The 2005 population results were highly contested because, in certain regions there was a significant decline in the population whereas there was an unusual increase in other regions. Considering that the national population growth rate of 2.8% was not interrupted in any region by any calamity or epidemic, it became suspicious why there was a drop only in areas considered to be opposition strongholds.

structure where an appointed Government Delegate[61] lords it over the councils, financial allocations and development do not also follow the logic of equitable distribution of resources.

Within the SDF, any militant who contests elections with the Chairman is out rightly sacked from the party. Cases are bound, as was the case with Tabessi and Barrister Ben Muna. The Chairman has even been quick to note that the SDF is his party. Ni John Fru Ndi is considered a god within his party. Article 8.2 of the party constitution[62] forbids most militants from competing against the Chairman of the party and this has made Fru Ndi become a monarch. Ni John has become the natural Chairman of the SDF. He is the Chairman of the party, Chair at all party conventions; Chair of the Investiture Committee and also Chair of all 'Other purposes committees'. It was the same practice adopted by leaders of other parties such as the Union des Populations du Cameroon (UPC). Until his death in 2009, Nde Ntumazah was at the helm of the party (since 1991) despite his poor health and age while Kodock was the Secretary of the party until he also died. Ntumazah was more of a ceremonial head while Kodock played the role of an ombudsman. The National Union for Democracy and Progress (UNDP) threw out the party Chair-Samuel Ebuoa and he was replaced by Bouba Bello Maigari who has been using the same tactics to stay in power.

The SDF is notorious for their hide and seek game of boycotting. They boycott elections and national events each

---

[61] Government Delegate is one appointed by the President to control resources in most of the cities where the opposition parties have been very dominant. In this way, the government is able to frustrate the opposition councils by not permitting them control of their own resources. The Government Delegate is therefore not answerable to the population but to the SDO is also appointed by the President.

[62] Article 8.2 of the basic text of the SDF dismisses any militant who goes against party rules outrightly from the party and this has been criticized by lots of militants who see it as a means to keep away potential challengers to Ni John considering that even Ni John has also made mistakes but has not been excluded from the party.

time that they feel dissatisfied or manipulated by the CPDM but they never boycott receiving their parliamentary grants and privileges. Boycotting as a political strategy often used by the SDF, has proved to be ineffective and has been stretched to its limits and cannot work anymore. Seemingly, the SDF has no other alternative strategy as their thinking appears exhausted.

In Cameroon adherence to a political party depends on how much gains one can make from the party and not based on any contributions, or any achievements of the party. That is why it is common place to see people jumping like prostitutes from one party to another. In fact, militants resign and 'cross carpets' from one party to another with a lot of pride and give the impression that the former party was the wrong choice. Cases are bound and not restricted to any particular party. A suitable example is that of Honourable Rose Abunaw Makia who resigned or as it is often said, 'decamped' from the UNDP to join the CPDM and eventually became not only the Section President for Manyu but the Vice President of the National Assembly. Nkemngu Martin, who for close to fifteen years was the Deputy Chair of the SDF Communication Unit, also decamped from that party to the CPDM. Honourable Charlie Gabriel Mbock left the SDF to join the Union des Populations du Cameroun (UPC) and was eventually elected into parliament while Suleiman Mahamat and Maidadi Saidou resigned from the SDF to form the Alliance of Progressive Forces (APF) party with Lawyer Ben Muna. Barrister Muna was previously the Communication Manager of the SDF until he was thrown out.

Most of these people seem not to have consciences and it is difficult to explain the fact that a party stalwart who has been condemning the actions of another party suddenly turns around to accept all that he or she has been against. The answer probably lies in the empty stomach and when he or she is sure that another party can fill it, they jump to that party. This phenomenon is common among Cameroonians irrespective of one's position in the party. The argument that some people put across is that such militants are bribed to cross over to another party. But how come militants of the so-called opposition parties in particular that have been quick to condemn the CPDM for corruption are vulnerable to bribery and corruption?

The various political parties perhaps with the exception of the SDF have youth wings. Unfortunately, the youth wing of a party is meant only to support the main organ of the party and the youth are not allowed to aspire for any post in the party. Within the party, the youth are only to be seen and not heard. They only become relevant as vote donors. In this light, the majority of the youth have the sufficient ability to choose their leaders but not sufficient ability to be chosen as leaders; to call others to account for their administration but not to conduct the administration themselves. In Cameroon, executive power is at the service of the ruling class (Tumi 2006: 130) and the public service is not separated from politics and political parties.

Conclusion

This chapter has examined the different power hierarchies that exist in Cameroon. I contend that Cameroon's leadership style is based on political clientalism than on any ideology or democratic principles. The system is structured on social exchanges between patrons and clients seen in terms of allowances in kind or rights to state offices and resources in return for services, where these allowances or rights are not granted on hereditary principles (Joseph 1983: 27-29). At the state level these social networks provide the link between ethnic groups and villages, what Joseph (1983) calls "ethno-clientelism. Central to these relationships is the exchange of various kinds of patronage for assistance, support, and loyalty. As Joseph (1983) demonstrates in a similar situation in Nigeria, clientilistic relations have served in Africa to reinforce and even promote ethnic clustering as individuals provide the conduit for the transmission of resources from their own patrons downwards while ensuring in exchange the support of a reliable constituency. This is often done through ethnic competition and the politics of competition is the means through which part of state resources, 'a share of the national cake', are attracted to one's community. Ethnic competition or the ethnicisation of politics creates factions within parties and the militants of the party compete against each other to gain control over public resources and this is often transcended and articulated through the language of ethnic and sometimes religious identities (Szeftel 2000: 437; Mwangi 2008: 269). Intra-party and inter-party competition for political power is therefore, in most instances, based on inter-ethnic competition, as different ethnic groups compete for or retain political power in a bid to have access to resources for political patronage. In such a system, political corruption has become the dominant mode of governance in the country as political parties operate without defined rules, ideology and mechanisms for the alternation of power.

The inability of these leaders to manage the human and natural resources of the country sufficiently and effectively have created openings and closures for Cameroonians at different levels and are used for selfish reasons. Those who cannot have access to these resources in the first place have therefore adopted the culture of complaining as a coping mechanism. The envisioned democracy that most Cameroonians dream to have as a leadership style has, for the most part, been erased and only aspects of it are put in practice. I therefore admit that there is a leadership crisis in Cameroon and this can be seen at all levels be it the local councils, partisan, Parliamentary, judicial, ministerial and at the presidential levels. It therefore implies that concentrating on Paul Biya as the problem of Cameroon precludes our understanding of the issues the country is suffering from. The problems of the country have been caused by Cameroonians in different positions of leadership and I therefore need to examine the leadership crisis at different levels involving different actors in a holistic manner.

Chapter 3

Unemployment and the Cameroon Public Service Quagmire

Unemployment is one of the major problems that African countries are facing, especially with the rapid population growth that most countries in the continent are witnessing. Within the backdrop of an ailing economy and bad governance, most countries are unable to contain the huge youthful population that is in need of jobs. I cannot overemphasise the importance of work as it is the most focal point of our lives. In fact, we spend most of our lives working. Given the fact that the state plays an important role in job creation and the provision of social services, most people largely depend on the state for employment. Unfortunately, the state is unable to provide jobs or the enabling environment for private initiatives. The issue is further compounded by a highly centralised bureaucratic system that generates its own weaknesses, internal dynamics and contradictions that gives a lot of privileges and advantages to the few public servants to exploit and compel job seekers to appear desperate, helpless and hopeless. This chapter seeks to analyse the nature of these contradictions and weaknesses of the Cameroon public service. I try to show how the public service in Cameroon has more political considerations than economic which has led to nepotism, corruption, inertia, poverty, patronage politics and lack of efficiency and productivity.

Work is a necessity for all human beings and this is because it is the life wire on which people depend and also provides social status. For instance, it is through work that one gains skills and becomes a professional such as a doctor, a nurse, or a Teacher. Work also provides self-esteem and respect. It leads to the fulfilment of goals and self-satisfaction. Also, it is through work that one has the opportunity to create friendships, and social relations and networks. Therefore, without work ones social environment could be affected negatively. Once there is a problem at the workplace it affects the whole life cycle of a person. In Cameroon the public service labour force stretches from 18-65 years. Startling and disturbing revelations from Cameroon's Minister of Labour and Social Security show that the rate of unemployment has moved from 13% in 2013 to 15% by the beginning of 2014.[63]

The idea of work depends on our cultural view about it. In pre-industrial societies, the Asian and Greeks despised work. In fact, work was considered a curse and that is why only slaves had to work. This attitude might have been influenced by the lack of practical technology although they had a lot of ideas about society. The Romans on the other hand, felt that work was a necessity and they needed to work to pay for their sins. Begging was preferred to work; begging was seen as some form of purification.

In the African context, there is a different idea about work. To us, a person is first seen as a worker. In order to be a leader, one must either be a farmer or a hunter. In Cameroon most of the festivals that we have are celebrations of work. In Nigeria there is the Yam Festival and in Cameroon we have the Fishing Festivals.[64] In Africa, it is only through work that you can survive and create civilisation. While the notion of work is not a recent creation, it has always constituted part of human history. In fact, the first punishment that God gave to Adam and Eve was that they must work before they can eat.[65] Unfortunately, there are so many people in Cameroon who are

---

[63] See Press Conference of Minister Robert Nkili of January 2014

[64] For instance, the Ngondo Festival among the Bassa people of the Littoral region of Cameroon

[65] See *Holy Bible: New Revised Standard Version* Genesis 3,16-20, Thomas Nelson Publishers, Nashville

unemployed. The 2012 UN Human Development Report puts the unemployment rate at 30% of the labour force.[66]

With the situation in Cameroon, there are two main problems associated to work. The first is that of unemployment and the second is that of underemployment. In most instances, it is even difficult to define who a worker is. It is common place to hear someone say that he/she is not working or that 'I am only a tapper and do not have a job'. These types of statements bring to question what constitutes work in the first place. I understand this to simply mean that he/she is not being paid by the government. Many rich businessmen give the same impressions. But it should be noted that the farmer, though not paid by the state, is actually working and contributes more to the development of the country than the majority of the civil servants. The farmer probably argues that he/she is not working because they do not receive a salary at the end of the month; but considers those in the public service as workers because perception dictates that they receive a salary at the end of the month. Unfortunately, the state is unable to provide jobs to most of the job seekers as there are around eight million young Cameroonians that are jobless- not being employed by the state and unable or unwilling to create their own jobs (UNDP, 2008-9).

Cameroon started experiencing the problem of unemployment in the mid-80s when the economic crisis set in; and by the end of the 80s it reached a very high degree. Since then, the trend has been on the increase. Every year, about 30.000 graduates join the job market but unfortunately less that 5000 of them find employment.[67] This problem has resulted

---

[66] Country comparison: unemployment rate: This is the percentage of those at the age of 18years and above who ought to be employed but are jobless. The figures may be higher if we consider those who are underemployed or in the informal sector http://www.indexmundi.com/g/r.aspx?c=cm&v=74 accessed 18/01/2013

[67] See Cameroon Strategic and Poverty Reduction Paper 2011

into actual joblessness. Some people that are employed are under paid leading to underemployment. Their pay packages are not commensurate with their qualifications or skills. One of the causes of unemployment is the lack of an enabling and conducive economic environment in the private sector.[68] Setting up a private company or initiative in Cameroon is not easy. The taxation system and corrupt practices stifle such initiatives that are also not business friendly. Unemployment is also a result of poor orientation and an educational system that is not adapted to local realities of the job market.

The issue of unemployment is also linked to underemployment as the two are interrelated. In Cameroon, about 40% of the potential work force is underemployed or unemployed. This is highly manifested in the urban centres and usually in the informal sector. It is an economy of desperation where the informal sector is only considered an alternative to joblessness and an escape from starvation.[69] There is a lot of child labour as children that ought to be in school go out to fend for themselves and families. They are either engaged in selling peanuts or roam the streets as beggars. Most of these street children come from a home where there is a lack of parental care or support.

The labour force in Cameroon shows that in both urban and rural areas unemployment stands at 40 % amounting to eight million youths between the ages of 18 and 35 years who are jobless.[70] Cameroon's labour force is rather described but in terms of the unemployed. Given an annual population growth rate of about 2.8 %,[71] it is estimated that the unemployment rate will triple within the next decade. According to the recent

---

[68] Simply refers to conditions that are favourable for job creation, such low taxes and moratorium, business financing by the state

[69] See UN statistics on urban unemployment in Cameroon

[70] Not having a formal employment with the state or in the private sector. They are mostly engaged in subsistence farming, petit trading or artisanal activities

[71] See 2005 Cameroon population and housing census

survey carried out in 2006 by Cameroon's Ministry of Employment and Vocational Training, about 70% of all unemployed persons were between the ages of 15-24 while 28% were between the ages of 25-44 years. The majority of those in the first category are primary and secondary school leavers, whereas the second group consists of university graduates. So far, there has not been an in-depth study on the occupational structure of Cameroon labour force. It would have been important to know how many are in the primary, secondary and tertiary sectors and the various professions. Unfortunately, little data exists for selected professions. Furthermore, the figures above however, do not take into account the quality of jobs available to the labour force. In the absence of functional social protection systems in most of African Countries including Cameroon, most workers have no choice but to work in the informal sector, and in conditions where minimum occupational safety and health standards are often not met (UNDP,2008)

As I mentioned, earlier having a job in Cameroon is much more difficult than the proverbial saying of passing through the eye of a needle to enter the kingdom of Heaven. Concours[72] have become the only safety valves through which people circumscribe and navigate their way to occupy public service spaces. Cameroonians have come to know, through the type of the educational training that they acquire, that jobs are offered by the government. The greatest ambition, then, of any Cameroonian is to seek employment into the public service. The only way to go about this is to write what is referred to as a competitive entrance examination. In February 2008, the government launched a *Concours* to recruit forty police superintendents for which 2824 candidates applied. In the same way 1028 students were vying for fifteen places at the

---

[72] "Concours" is a French word which refers to competitive entrance examinations and that is used in Cameroon interchangeably to mean an entrance examination organized for the recruitment of civil servants

International Relations Institute of Cameroon (IRIC).[73] And so it is the same trend with all the public recruitment exams. From the figures presented above, one begins to wonder what sort of magic the recruiting officers used to select the best candidates on merit. Following the government's policy of regional balance, it is still puzzling how these candidates were selected genuinely on merit. Going by the Cameroon tradition, in these recruitments, 'the Presidency has its quota, the President of the Senate, National Assembly and the Prime Minister and then Ministers; Directors in that descending order have theirs'.[74] One's success here is more associated with social affiliations and relationships than intelligence.

The preferred and surest means to gain access into the public service in Cameroon is through bribery and corruption. Every year or periodically the government, through the Ministry of Public Service and Administrative Reforms, advertises vacancies into the public service. Before registering for *Concours* in Cameroon, one has to be sure of how much money is needed for bribery and the person to whom the money will be given. Once this network (commonly known as *reseaux*) is established, the next thing is to look for money. It should be clear that once the network is assured, money will always be available even if it means selling plots or other property to get into the public service. Those without money go hunting for 'god fathers' who will enable them have the job (Albert, 2005). This god father syndrome is applicable to those who parade the corridors of power; especially politicians and businessmen. Most poor female students or applicants will always use sex to negotiate for these positions if the opportunity comes their way. It should be noted, however, that not all the professional schools in Cameroon have the same entry requirements nor are rated or perceived in the same manner. The bribe amount given each time corresponds to the

---

[73] *Cameroon Tribune* No 9090/5289 of April 30th 2008
[74] Anye Francis, interviewed 12/11/2013 in Yaounde

weight given to a school. Those that are not considered very important or 'juicy' receive less amounts of bribery whereas those placed at the highest echelon take more money. 'There are some schools that are considered more prestigious than others, such as the School of Administration and Magistracy (hence, ENAM), International Relations Institute of Cameroon (IRIC) and Higher Military Academy (EMIA)'.[75] Apart from the prestige and privileges that graduates from these schools enjoy, they also serve as lever for the perpetuation of corruption in Cameroon. For instance, access to the occupation of the military is one of the oldest and well rooted networks of corruption in Cameroon. Potential applicants are required to pay bribes of 800.000 Frs.-CFA (about $1500.00) or more to be admitted to the military Inter-Arms School (EMIA).[76]

In order to curb unemployment, the government created several structures and ministries such as the Ministry of Employment and Vocational Training, and the National Employment Fund, (NEF). They were expected to assist job seekers in finding jobs or to create an enabling environment for them to become self-employed. Unfortunately, both the Ministry and NEF have continued to fail woefully to meet this objective. Instead, most job seekers have been frustrated by these institutions. The NEF for example, has turned out to be a veritable arena and a favourable place for corrupt practices, favouritism and embezzlement. While the rate of unemployment continues to rise disproportionately, the bank accounts of the officials of NEF swell in the same proportion

---

[75] Ngang Martin is a graduate who has made several abortive attempts to gain admission into any of these 'prestigious' schools for years and was unable to provide the amount of money requested as bribes. He finally gave up and decided to write the Teachers' Grade One exams. He is now a Primary school teacher in Bafoussam

[76] 'The Biya Military Regime, a tradition of corruption' *African Independent* http://www.africanindependent.com/cam_military_regime_corruption0128 06.html accessed 06/3/2014

in local and foreign banks. NEF has been politicised and ethnicised.[77] Projects submitted by unfamiliar graduates are never funded and money that would have been used to assist young university graduates is used to buy the most expensive and luxurious cars.[78]

One of the key issues often raised by the President of the Republic in his speeches is *inertia*. This literally means that things are at a standstill- not moving. In order words, there is no progress as everything is on hold. When the Head of state talks about inertia he is in essence referring to the public service and civil servants. This *inertia* is manifested in the public service to the fullest and is orchestrated by a system of hierarchical organisation that is full of routine ordering. In principle, the public service is meant to serve the citizens of the country free of charge. This idea has been re-echoed on notice boards in public offices and even at entrances. Unfortunately, you cannot have your documents treated in these offices free of charge. The workers always look for a means to get money from people who seek assistance from these offices. At times, one may be required to give money for a realm of papers even if he or she does not use up to two sheets; or for the typing of documents or depending on the office, they always know what story to tell so that they can get money.

The Cameroon public service is plagued with much inefficiency including inertia, nepotism, disrespect, nonchalance, and a lack of duty consciousness, amongst other things. For those Cameroonians who have never had anything to do with the public service, they would find the analysis below strange and embarrassing. I am, however, convinced

---

[77] See clerical staff at the Yaounde head office of the National Employment Fund, most come from 3 ethnic groups and from one region.- Beti-Fang-Ewondo Trio

[78] For more on that see the type of cars used by the personnel of the National Employment Fund (NEF) at the national office in Yaounde and at the regional offices. NEF is not an isolated case, generally in Cameroon, the state spends more on luxurious vehicles than even on roads.

that a reasonable number of Cameroonians understand what I am saying. I sought to learn the general perceptions of Cameroonians on the conduct of recruitments in the country and this is what Ali had to say:

Jobs are offered to people depending on the relationship that they have with those at the corridors of power. Having a job in Cameroon is considered a favour but not a right and people do their work as if they are being forced- twisting their faces, not even putting up a smile.

In the USA and the Netherlands for instance where I have interacted with people, workers are trained how to receive and smile at costumers. On the contrary, Cameroon civil servants tend to complain even more than those who are unemployed. Here, there is institutionalised and structured injustice in the selection of candidates for employment as this is often given political considerations, particularly those who romance with the CPDM or who come from the grand south or northern Regions.[79] Most of the clerical staff in the ministries are handpicked from the Beti and Ewondo ethnic groups because a majority of the ministers and directors come from the centre and south regions.[80] Once recruited into the public service, one can then be sure of a successful life and start setting priorities and vying for positions.

---

[79] These are the regions with the highest number of ministers who use their positions to recruit jobseekers from their regions. Recruitment is based on clientalism and patronage as the ministers expect favours in terms of votes when elections are called. His maintenance or re-appointment is based on how many votes he produces from his area. If the votes do not come then he will be replaced. Areas that do not vote for the CPDM will never have ministerial appointments. Most of the CPDM votes come from these areas.

[80] See the list of the 69 Ministers and 58 Senior Divisional Officers, the majority of which come from the South, the birth place of the President of the Republic.

First, Cameroonians enjoy occupying posts of (ir) responsibilities no matter how small or inferior such positions may be. The dream of civil servants is to be appointed a prestigious position. Their preferences for duty posts are understandable in a system where civil servants only struggle to gain access to state resources. In a group discussion with students at the National School of Youth and Sports (CENAJES Bamenda) I wanted to know how they would feel if they were appointed to duty positions and what benefits they may derive from such positions. Nine of the twelve students that participated in the discussion wished and hoped to be appointed into positions in the public service. This is what one student had to say:

Being a Director, Inspector, Minister, and Regional delegate, Government Delegate, Principal, or simply Chief of Bureau entails a lot of advantages and privileges. In such positions, one commands self-esteem and respect from subordinates. Again, it is the surest way to have a running budget or *credits*. It is also an avenue to loot and plunder or milk the public treasury dry. It simply means one may have a service car that is chauffeur driven or live in government rented apartments.

Cameroonians know how these service heads (mis) use and (mis) direct public funds into their bank accounts to establish businesses or to construct huge mansions. An honest civil servant who depends solely on the salary will not be able to build the type of house that one finds in some of the big cities.[81] The only justification that one can give for building and owning such houses is that money must have been embezzled.

---

[81] The minimum monthly wage in Cameroon is just 28.216 Frs and the Maximum for those in the highest Echelon 'category A' is 250.000Frs which makes it difficult for civil servants to invest and save enough money for themselves. See details in Cameroon Labour Code on the different categories for wages.

As the next statements show every time someone is appointed into any of the desired positions a lavish party is offered in honour of the appointment. This also explains why the first visit of any Minister upon appointment by the Head of state is usually to his 'home village' to show to his people that he now has a power base of some sort (Nyamnjoh 2013a). This visit is also meant to 'thank' the Head of state for thinking about them. It is also to let his kinsmen/folk understand that failure to support the Head of state is tantamount to losing the appointment at the expense of another ethnic group or region. To ensure that this appointment should not slip out of their hands, the people must 'pay back' by voting for the President or the CPDM party. This type of politicking is what Hon Senator Achidi Achu[82] refers to as 'scratch my back I scratch your own' (Nyamnjoh: 2013). He sees politics as a thrift and loan scheme where each person saves and expects to benefit following pre-made rules. He contends that politics is a form of social capital (*Njangi*) with rules, obligations, expectations and rewards which the electorate must abide by in order to achieve maximum benefits. Following this logic, it therefore implies that it is needless for people to cast their votes for someone or a party that will not be able to 'pay back' in the form of providing social services. Following Senator Achidi Achu, Prime Minister Philemon Yang castigated the opposition parties during the 2013 Municipal and Parliamentary elections as barren mango trees that cannot bear fruits.[83] According to Philemon Yang, the CPDM remains the only mango tree that bears good fruit and in order to eat the fat and juicy mangoes

---

[82] Achidi Achu joined the government in 1972 as a Justice Minister and was appointed Prime Minister in 1991 when multi-party politics was re-introduced in Cameroon. He was later dropped from that post in 1997. In 2013, he was appointed as one of the pioneer Senators from the northwest region. He has held several positions within the CPDM party for decades.

[83] Prime Minister Philemon Yang was the campaign manager of the CPDM party during the 2013 elections and insisted that his party is the only party that has the financial and human resources that can solve the problems of Cameroonians because it is the party in power.

the people should vote for the CPDM. In fact, he suggests that the barren mango trees (opposition) should be cut down and destroyed. To these individuals and others, there are benefits accruing for voting the CPDM and for being appointed into positions of responsibilities; not only to relatives but to friends as well. Once people are appointed to positions of responsibilities, they know that the time has come for them to enjoy the spoils of the 'national cake'. They use money from the public treasury to buy luxurious cars and mansions. It is also an opportunity for them to swell their foreign accounts and open new ones for their numerous girlfriends and relations. This scenario has resulted in the massive arrests of Ministers and former ministers for misappropriating public funds and abuse of the public service.[84] I asked several civil servants their experiences when they go to the ministries to do something and they told me that several things happen when you approach a Private Secretary in an office and request to see the boss.

If she (because they are usually women) is exceptionally polite, she will listen to you and respond to you. War betides if you speak in English. Of course, she will never respond in English even if she is a typical Anglophone or should I say "Anglofool". Most often the response is; *Je ne comprends pas votre anglais, parle en français.* Or: *Nous ne sommes pas ici à Bamenda;* translated to mean, 'I don't understand your English, speak in French.' And, 'We are not here in Bamenda.' *Le directeur n'est pas la or le directeur est en mission, or yet Il est en reunion or Il est voyager* and so on and so forth. In their usual arrogance she or he will simply say *Je n'est sais pas*, meaning 'I do not know'. If you can have the courage to insist, and you are fortunate to have a response; these are some of the answers you may still get. *Il faut repasser dans*

[84] See operation 'Sparrow Hawk' where over 20 members of government have been arrested for embezzling public funds.

l'apres midi –'come back in the afternoon', or *Il faut repasser la sermiane prochaine* .

This has been well captured by the Cameroonian Musician Beko Sadey in her music album entitled *function publique*. These responses came from people who are being paid by the state. These people are polite because a majority of them will just ignore your presence. They consider people coming to their offices as a bore or nuisance. For example, I had a personal experience when I went to one of the ministries to inquire about scholarships in 2003. When I entered the office, the lady who was in charge simply gazed at me and continued reading a newspaper and kept me waiting for over 45 minutes before attending to me. Asked about their perceptions of the workers they usually meet in the ministries, one respondent who was generally disappointed with his encounters in the ministries commented that:

> If you are unfortunate to meet a lady; you should be ready to fight or hold your breath. The ladies who are generally not educated and have no work etiquettes are very insolent, disrespectful and uncouth in their behaviour. Usually, they turn the offices into kitchens. They may be busy preparing spices and vegetables, cleaning their finger nails or simply playing computer games, or spend all the time wasting the tax payers' money making telephone calls to friends and relatives just to keep you waiting or be annoyed. If you follow their conversations over the phone, you may then know how much the state is losing through these types of people. Sometimes these conversations range from long hours of greetings to simply making rendezvous. One cannot prefer to work in a country with government bureaucrats who are so impolite and shower insults to the very people they are supposed to serve.

The above statement shows that bureaucracy is not an instrument of development but of subjugation and intimidation in Cameroon. My informant also observed that 'some of them are very happy receiving "visitors", especially those who come from the regions to "chase" files'.[85] When I inquired to know what chasing files was all about, he said chasing files in Cameroon is tantamount to bribery and corruption since money must change hands before files are treated. 'In order to attract money from people they hide these files. Once money changes hands, these dossiers reappear without any further delay. They feed fat on people who come to "follow up" documents in the ministries'. Implicitly, I conclude from this statements that one of the logics of the public service is that files do not move from one office to another unless accompanied by money or gifts. According to Forsah Delphine[86] 'when you submit a document in any of the ministries and you fail to make the "usual follow up" or put enough 'weight', just know that the document will remain on the spot for years or will even go missing'. Missing documents in Cameroon may mean several things .That one has not toed the line or spoken (*il faut parler*), and secondly, the file could be missing because nobody was 'assigned to take care of them'.

Because of the over centralised nature of the public service, chasing dossiers in Yaoundé, particularly for those coming from the different Regions, is a profitable business and it also means risking one's life. File chasing is not only a pretext to stay away from the job sites but has become a way of life for civil servants. I tried to find out how they cope in the midst of all these intrigues, Ade who was just recruited as a Grade One teacher observed that:

---

[85] The files usually are reclassification, integration, retirement and change of grade documents.

[86] She graduated from CENAJES Bamenda in 2008 and it took her two years to be integrated into the Public service because some of the documents she submitted were always 'missing'

Apart from spending huge sums of money in the process, one is forced to move to Yaoundé. We are definitely familiar with a lot of people who have lost their lives or have their arms amputated through road accidents on their way to or from chasing files. File chasing may take several months or years but never days!! The inconveniences are multifold. Apart from the risk of traveling, people abandon their workplaces for months. This is even worse with new recruits into the service who go through the baptismal fire of staying for years without salaries.

In early July of 2007, a strike by 2,500 health workers recruited in 2005 exposed the real and deplorable state of government employees in the public sector: the workers were demanding payment for two years of unpaid wages and their integration into the civil service.[87] If not for the syndrome of chasing files, there are so many Cameroonians who ordinarily wouldn't have had anything to do with Yaoundé. Some do not even have relatives or friends who live in Yaoundé where they can squat for some time. But because the system compels all civil servants to move over to Yaoundé, they are obliged to negotiate accommodations or live in hotels. The most important thing with chasing dossiers is that corruption and bribery must take place before anything can happen. In truth, it is money that is being chased and not even the dossiers. If the money finishes it is important to go into debt and the spiral continues. Within the ministries there are intermediaries who serve as liaison officers between the Minister, Delegate, Director and/or Inspectors. Their bosses do not touch money but the money gets to them through intermediaries or into their negotiated local bank accounts.

---

[87] See Fanny, Pigeaud, (2011) *Africa Yearbook* Volume 8, Brill Publishers Leiden. Some statistics on Cameroon presented at Cameroon country meeting at African Studies Centre Leiden on 25/01/2013

The public service is also about attending workshops, seminars and conferences. To talk about workshops and conferences, they go along with allowances or call it *per diem*. Once there is no assurance that per diem will be available no one, not even the minister is interested in such events. It also means having a mission order which carries a financial weight. It may also provide an opportunity for the big man to have access to government hotels. The public service is a lucrative business for the squandering and plundering of the resources of the state.

Everything in the public service is taxed; even the signature of the Civil Administrator has a price tag of 1000 Frs. For a document to be certified, a fiscal stamp must be affixed on it. Normally, fiscal stamps are sold at the taxation and treasury offices but it is 'normal' to find workers at a Divisional Officer's office selling stamps with one hundred francs added to the official price. They argue that the one hundred francs is compensation for their transport and for making the stamp available at the DO's, where it is used. If we think that these stamps can also be sold by the staff of the Senior Divisional Officers, it would be better for these offices to be legalised as sales points and not allow unscrupulous workers to feed fat on the people. What is most annoying is the fact that when you get to this office with a stamp bought elsewhere, they refuse to use it; instead they force you to buy from them.

A document is only authentic if it has a government stamp affixed on it by the designated state bureaucrat. The paradox is that certificates of academicians and even Professors are authenticated or legalised by the so-called Civil Administrators who in most cases are not scholars and do not have authentic certificates themselves. Some do not have academic certificates or have barely obtained the lower certificates such as the first school leaving certificates, GCE O/A Levels. How can someone who cannot interpret or appreciate a certificate give approval or disapproval to it? It is not surprising that these administrators legalise fake and fraudulent certificates.

As mentioned earlier, each service head has an assistant and both head and assistant have their private secretaries. The irony is that when the head is not there, the presence of the assistant is irrelevant. He cannot make any decisions nor can he act or sign a document. Everything is on hold until the *Oga* himself comes back. This brings to mind the raison d'etre of all these assistants. One thing is clear, Cameroonians enjoy having titles no matter how small or inferior a title may be. In most conversations and introductions, you often hear them say, I am the Director of… or I am the personal representative of… or simply *Je suis chef de cellule de… aux Ministère du…* The question that I may ask is; what is in these titles? The answer to this question can be given when one juxtaposes the Dutch experience and that of Cameroon as discussed below.

While pursuing postgraduate studies at the African Studies Centre in Leiden –The Netherlands, I learned that while Cameroonians glorify titles, the Dutch do not. One of my greatest shocks was when I was rebuked by my lecturer for addressing her as a Doctor. I felt embarrassed and guilty. In what was already a tense relationship, she told me, to call her Rebecca and never to call her Doctor. I retorted that I thought I was simply being polite and respectful. She insisted NO!!! NEVER ADDRESS ME AS Doctor.[88] Indeed, she was not even a Doctor but a Professor of Cultural Anthropology at the best Dutch University-Leiden and was one of the best Professors I have ever known. Before long I realised that she is not the only one, the Dutch generally abhor to be addressed by their titles. This was very strange to me especially coming from a country where people glorify titles and honours. Just look at the complimentary cards of Cameroonians and their titles and you may be saddened by the fact that the entire card is full of

---

[88] Rebecca is a pseudonym that is used in this book because I do not want to use that of the said Professor

81

titles. According to the 2012/2013 World University rankings,[89] The Netherlands ranked third in the production of Knowledge capital after the USA and the United Kingdom. In that same report, *Leiden Universitiet* was the best Dutch University occupying the 64th position in the world and the 13th position in Europe. The best of Cameroon's University in 2012 was the University of Buea occupying the 8701 position followed by the University of Yaounde 1 at the 9552 position.[90] Every other thing being constant, knowledge capital is produced by these Professors and in such a production chain where would you place the Cameroon Professor? Your guess is mine. We can conclude that those who have something to offer do not want to be known by their titles, rather they prefer to be known by their achievements and those who have nothing to offer want to conceal their emptiness with their titles. This has been well captured by Nyamnjoh (2012: 34) when he says that:

> They crave external recognition and environments over internal relevance. They internalise and reproduce irrelevance through an unjustifiable sense of superiority and priorities. They 'boast in the market place showing off to people' instead of proving the merits of their education through real achievements. It is an education for keeping up appearances for self –dilution and self-belittlement and for talking without listening.

The Dutch are known for what they are while titles in Cameroon reflect what people are not and so the scenario goes on in every aspect of life in Cameroon. This has even trickled

[89] The World University Rankings http://www.timeshighereducation.co.uk/world-university-rankings/2012-13/world-ranking/region/europe accessed 18/01/2013
[90] Also see World University rankings http://www.webometrics.info/en/Africa/Cameroon%20 Accessed 18/01/2013

down to the villages where traditional decorations and titles are conferred on the new elite who most often does not hold any hereditary titles but buys the titles with money. The quest for such decorations and titles have become a source of power and can be seen as a way of allowing the traditional notables and institutions to tap into new sources of wealth without becoming involved directly in the market place (Goheen 1996: 153).

Back in the big man's office his coat is usually hung over his seat to give the impression that he has just stepped in or stepped out. Behold that is not true!! The coat can be in that position for days, weeks or even months whereas the said big man is elsewhere or even overseas. There is much pretence and deceit within the public service in the country. Yet nobody cares! Promotions in Cameroon do not go with merit but are determined by one's position or associations with those in power .They are based on mediocrity and not meritocracy. Output is never measured and efficiency is not the hallmark of the public service. It could be embarrassing if you tried to find out how much contribution a civil servant has made to the growth of the country. Generally, they are only present at the job site, waiting for time to come when they can go home.

By way of conclusion, in this chapter I started by defining work and the various parameters that explain the concept of work. With the current situation, Cameroon has a very high rate of youth unemployment and underemployment in sub Saharan Africa. Presently, the most lucrative jobs are offered by the state and the private sector is not fully developed, and there are no state incentives to encourage private initiatives. Whereas a strong economy is dependent on a well-developed private sector, in Cameroon this sector is very weak. This is exacerbated by a complicated tax and fiscal policy that discourages private initiatives. Consequently, the public service has become the only escape route for job seekers and as a result, people are recruited not for the skills they have and what they can offer but just to have access to what Cameroonians call the 'maticule number'.[91] The public service is therefore considered, by Cameroonians, as a means to gain access to state resources and to escape from poverty and misery.

The bureaucratic nature of the public service and the low salaries that civil servants receive have pushed them to use unorthodox means to generate and accumulate state resources, especially through bribery and embezzlement of state resources. Unlike Weber's *ideal type* of bureaucracy[92] that is impersonal and based on rules, routines and meritocracy, the Cameroon public service is rather based on personal relations and networks that often do not lead to efficiency and maximum output. Here, one's political belonging and loyalty determines his or her position in the public service. In Cameroon once you are against the way the regime in power carries out its business, your family, relatives, friends and close collaborators equally become the regime's enemy. They will not be promoted on the job, no guaranteed employment, and they will be subjected to forceful transfers that are usually punitive (Tumi 2006: 130). Finally, the Cameroon public service is highly centralised and this provides the leverage for those in these offices to request favours before doing their work. Until the public service is decentralised, the public service will remain, for long time, an avenue for nepotism and corrupt practices. The public service in Cameroon has become the nursery for corruption and bribery. Since the direction of justice or job offer is determined by money, only the rich can occupy the few jobs. In the next chapter, I shall examine the phenomena of corruption and bribery and to see how they are related to each other.

---

[91] The 'maticule number syndrome' is the passport that provides access to employment into the public service and ensures that one receives a monthly salary irrespective of work done or services rendered.

[92] See Roth and Wittich (1978)[eds] 'economy and society: an outline of interpretative sociology' *in Max Weber and idea bureaucracy* California University Press, California

Chapter 4

Poverty, Corruption and Bribery

This chapter examines the fundamental social problems of poverty, corruption and bribery and how they manifest in Cameroonian society. I try to show that there is a strong positive correlation between poverty, unemployment and corruption. As I said earlier, when a person is jobless, he/she is bound to be poor. I argue that corruption is a white collar crime which is orchestrated by the mismanagement of public funds. This is done mostly by civil servants who have access to state resources to the detriment of the poor. Despite the efforts being made by the state to fight corruption, the number of people arrested for embezzling public funds is on the rise. Following the arguments presented in this chapter, I conclude that unless there is the political will to ensure that there is a vibrant private economic sector and appropriate sanctions that can deter corruption, the current measures being undertaken by the state will only be cosmetic solutions.

Poverty can be defined as a state of being poor. To consider someone as poor means the person is not having and is not able to afford the basic necessities of life. Life necessities here include access to food, shelter, clothing, good education and good health. A person or a society that cannot afford these necessities of life is regarded and seen as poor. That is, not having access or opportunity to the productive forces of land, capital, labour and technology for a good well-being. Poverty is a relative term; relative in the sense that what may be considered as poverty in one society may not be poverty in another. Poverty is a concept with multiple and contested definitions that sometimes overlap and at times contradict each other. However poverty remains a visible social problem that can be felt practically in every society. Although it varies from one country, region, and continent to another, I however admit that there is a yardstick through which we can measure the degree of poverty.[93]

According to the World Bank, one is said to be poor if he/she does not consume up to 1.25 US Dollar a day.[94] Poverty in Cameroon is experienced in rural and urban centres. It is therefore common to the entire country. There are millions of people in the country that do not consume even half a Dollar a week. According to the United Nation Development Program-UNDP (2011: 5) report, 30% of Cameroonians live in severe poverty while 19.3% are vulnerable to poverty. This therefore implies that over 50% of Cameroonians fall below the poverty bracket or are highly threatened by poverty.[95] A majority of Cameroonians live in abject poverty and misery while the minorities who control the resources of the country flow in affluence. If one were to go by the World Bank definition, then we would agree that poverty is largely caused by growing inequalities influenced by a huge international debt burden, the mismanagement of resources and the embezzlement of state funds. This has made it difficult for the state to service its debts. Consequently, because of poverty, the country was declared as a heavily indebted poor country. Most developing countries are considered poor because they share the common problem of huge debts and mismanagement. How then can we come out of poverty? It has been suggested that the only way to eliminate poverty is to industrialise the economy, yet industrial development in Cameroon is problematic as potential investors are scared by a heavy tax system. This is one of the major social problems that

---

[93] There is both relative and absolute poverty, yet to be poor simply means lacking basic necessities of life

[94] See UNDP 2008 MDGs and the indices of poverty

[95] See UNDP (2011) Explanatory note on Human Development Report, sustainability and Equity: a better future for all http://hdrstats.undp.org/images/explanations/CMR.pdf Accessed 28/01/2013

have eaten too deep into the social fabrics of national life in Cameroon.

Corruption and bribery are some of the oldest forms of social problems.[96] They are thought to be two sides of the same coin. It appears that I cannot understand one without the other, and the practice of corruption presupposes that bribery has also taken place. It would appear that these social vices are found in all known human society; yet what matters is the degree of its existence and practice. This assertion seems to be supported by the reports published annually by local newspapers and International Non-Governmental organisation -Transparency International. All societies have and give different names, conceptions and interpretations to corruption. In some Cameroonian societies, it is known as *kola,* and others call it *appreciation,* while it is also known to others as *Gumbo, Soya* or *Awuf.* Following Epko (1979:163) bribery has several linguistic hints. For instance, 'to an American, a tip is a legitimate token of appreciation for services rendered, or about to be rendered... a bribe, on the other hand is payment for non-legitimate services rendered' (*ibid:* 171). In Cameroon and Nigeria, the word 'dash' is commonly used to refer to money, goods or services that change hands in many contexts. There are different ways of giving 'dash' to someone in these societies. For instance, money, goods or services which are offered to someone or to other people in excess for no work done are simply referred to as 'dash'. Better put, money that one gives in many situations to keep the machinery oiled is simply 'dash'. On the other hand, a commonly used synonym for dash is the term 'drink'. To paraphrase Epko (1979:171), if a Cameroonian says that he has bought someone drink, the symbolic interpretation of this is that he has paid him 'dash' where the 'dash' may refer to money, other goods or services.

---

[96] Even in the Bible Zachaeus the Tax Collect was said to be very corrupt

87

Irrespective of the name that is given to it, what is important is the consequences it has on society as a whole.

Prior to the advent of colonisation, Africa had cultures and practices that developed out of the peculiarities of its circumstances which at the time were not seen as corrupt. This was at least in part because chiefs and Kings received no salaries and relied on gifts, booty, tributes and levies for their upkeep and there was practically no distinction between private and public purse.[97] In traditional and pre-colonial African societies, the giving of gifts was an integral part of the social structure. Gift giving was, however, obligatory but was embedded in a complex network of social alliances and status differentiation. Persons who held positions of leadership (e.g. chiefs, Fons or Kings) were often obliged, as patrons to make gifts to their power clientele or to their community as a whole (Epko 1979: 174). In return, the poorer clientele were expected to make token offerings to their patrons or leaders as a demonstration of their support (Fisiy 1992). In pre-colonial Africa, although these practices were given different connotation, they remained until they were 'infiltrated' by the introduction of colonialism, and corruption and bribery took a different twist.

The monetisation of the economy made Africans develop unorthodox means of grabbing money here and there. During this period, warrant chiefs, court clerks and messengers who served the colonial administration saw the Whiteman as a foolish intruder who should be outwitted at every possible opportunity. The effect of all these was to make, for instance the native courts notorious centres of *gombo*; in which everyone was out for what he could get. The natives thought they were sabotaging the Whiteman but they were in fact destroying the moral fabric of their own society. Until now, a civil service appointment or employment is still regarded by many

---

[97] Egbo, et al (2010), legitimizing corruption in government: security votes in Nigeria ASC Working Paper 91 PP.5

Cameroonians as a Whitman's job in which it is acceptable to cheat. Since then, corruption and bribery have become a way of life- a culture.

This social vice is found in every facet of life in the country but it is intense and rampant within the public service. Unfortunately, the Anti-Corruption Commissions instituted by governments in Africa to fight corruption have yielded little or no fruits. As Egbo et al (2010: 11) note, the reason is that the very people called upon to make the structural changes necessary to limit opportunities for corruption are the very actors who benefit most from the status quo. Also, corruption takes several forms and since most government bureaucrats are usually implicated, it becomes difficult to solve this problem. Corruption is arguably defined as the use of public power and resources for private purposes, but such a definition seems to distinguish between the state and its rulers and their variant economic interests; and so does not only limit but precludes our understanding of the whole corruption complex (Egbo et al. 2013: 4-5). From the foregoing, the basis of corruption must transcend the distinction between the property rights of the state and its rulers and include acts like nepotism, misappropriation, influence peddling, speed money, embezzlement, fraud, bribery, extortion and insider trading and abuse (Obuah 2010: 20).[98] Adebanwi and Obadare (2011: 203) describe corruption as 'an octopus which changes its shape and size'. As the metaphor shows, 'it contracts, expands, lowers and blows out differently'. The different forms and ways that corruption manifests include kickbacks, percentages, and over invoicing amongst others.

Corruption in Cameroon is endemic and systemic and this includes public officials accepting, soliciting, or extorting bribes, and private actors offering bribes to subvert or circumvent public policies for competitive advantage and profit. Following Egbo et al (2010: 9), on a similar situation in

---

[98] Also see Obuah 2010,p20 for UNDP definition of corruption

Nigeria, corruption has not only become what they call 'notorious' but a generalised instrument of government. Different schools of thoughts have offered different reasons as to why people become corrupt and one reason holds that corruption is orchestrated by poverty, unemployment and even low salaries. Obuah (2010: 10-20) opines that people become corrupt because their salaries are so low that they cannot make ends meet by depending solely on their meagre salaries. Furthermore, strong kinship ties characteristic of these societies place nepotistic pressure on public officials. Accordingly, they resort to corrupt activities to make ends meet and help their relatives. This argument however offers only partial answers to the corrupt practices because statistics have shown that those who are employed and rich, and enjoy high salary scales are more corrupt than the poor and unemployed and all government institutions are involved in it. It has become a way of life. Those who have access to the resources are highly corrupt. Most judges would take money before passing judgment in favour of the highest bidder. Corruption is not necessarily when money changes hands; it also involves some considerations usually through the use of public positions to gain favours (Obuah, 2010).

Writing on some of the main causes of the Nigerian military coup d'état in 1966, Major Nzeogwu put it in his first broadcast as follows

Our enemies are the political profiteers; the swindlers; the men in high and low places that seek bribes and demand 10 per cent; those that seek to keep the country divided permanently so that they can remain in office as Ministers, Permanent Secretaries, or VIPs at least, the tribalists, the nepotists; those that make the country look big for nothing before international circles; those that have corrupted our society and put the Nigerian political calendar back by their words and deeds (Epko 1979: 163).

In a question and answer session at the National Assembly, the Minister of State in charge of Justice and keeper of the Seal Amadu Ali once acknowledged that over one hundred and six (106) billion francs had been looted from the public treasury by 133 top civil servants in 2006 alone. These people committed these crimes because their superiors, to whom they pay allegiance, protect them. The law protects them from conviction. This is the case with Members of Parliament who have state immunity and can be charged or tried only after their immunity is removed. This was the case with His Royal Highness Fon Doh Gahnwayi of Balikumbat constituency who was again a Member of Parliament.[99]

Some treasury clerks routinely demand bribes from contractors before paying them money duly approved by the government for a contract properly executed. Sometimes contractors bribe the treasury clerk to pay for a contract he has executed poorly or not executed at all (Obuah 2010: 25). Time keepers demand *awuf* to make even diligent labourers present; while headmasters, principals, and directors take *gumbo* to protect workers absent from duty. Messengers receive tips from members of the public in order to trace files dealing with their affairs. Even secretaries demand *soya* before they give out supposedly free forms to members of the public. The whole public service is just like a stock exchange market- a market where there is illicit buying and selling of money. The situation is not different with the police superintendent who receives 500 Frs. from taxi drivers and the driver who feels excited and proud to have given money since he, the driver, does not possess the necessary car documents. Some drivers can ignore all traffic rules because they have 'bought' the road for the day

---

[99] This Traditional Ruler has since died. Before his death he was convicted but his immunity was never lifted and he never served a prison term nor paid any fines. There is preferential treatment in the off lifting of immunity

or week from the shameless traffic police. In the same way a complainant can become the accused at a police station.

Recruitment officers ignore qualified candidates and recommend poorly qualified ones; top civil servants inflate contract figures and arrange for the balance (30%) to be paid into their bank accounts locally or overseas; official examination questions are leaked to the public in exchange for sex or money. At the universities, admissions are sometimes made for reasons other than academics. When an unintelligent female student achieves a first in her degree examinations, her success may not be attributable to a sudden upsurge of intellect (*ibid*). Her success may rather be the result of "sexually transmitted marks" from her male lecturer. This situation is usually compounded by sexual harassment on female students by lecturers. It is however important to note that even these female students also harass these lecturers using seductive means.

Gumbo manifest itself in Cameroon at all levels. The gumbo syndrome in this great nation has debased the practice of journalism that was once considered a noble profession to that of beggars. Journalism is one of the professions reserved for those who are intelligent but that is not the case in Cameroon. Apart from being infested by quacks, it is now practiced by people as a last resort. Ordinarily, the journalist searches for news and nothing but the news. Today, they are in search of gumbo. This is not to say that they should not receive gifts or money, but when they are induced to write what is not true because they have been bribed, it is referred to as gumbo. Most of them only cover events when they are sure that the organisers will give them gumbo. When they do come, the amount of gumbo has to be negotiated first before they can cover the event. If there is no assurance that there is gumbo, they leave immediately. If a journalist has been "treated well" then the occasion will be given maximum coverage, even with some exaggeration. It is very common for journalists to report

92

on an event that has never even taken place if someone is willing to give them the "brown envelope". Journalists are considered, by most educated people, as hungry men and women, pests, parasites and nuisance to the public. 'They are often seen roaming the streets or forcing officials to grant press interviews or conferences' (Awah Ngang interviewed 23/5/2012).

The Government media organs are not different from the private press where the latter receive meagre wages or catechists allowances. The government media often demands what they term a 'coverage fee' or 'petrol money' before they go out to cover an event. The Governor or Senior Divisional Officer (SDO) who plans to carry out socio-economic and contact tours within their areas of jurisdictions, demand 'petrol money' from poor villagers before these tours take place. These villagers are often forced to stage a reception for the 'big man' whenever a visit is undertaken. Interestingly, after the people have presented their grievances or problems, which often range from lack of electricity, bad or no roads, lack of schools and health services, amongst others, to land disputes, the big man's response is that 'I have heard all your problems and I will channel them to the right quarters or to the hierarchy'. One begins to wonder whether the Governor, DO or SDO are not mere messengers. Or was it not possible to send the list of problems to the hierarchy without the big man paying a visit?

Another thing that is worthy to note with these officials is their attributions to land issues and to solving land disputes between communities and between people. Most of them have been noted for creating and fanning these land disputes for financial gains (Moritz 2006: 118) more than providing lasting solutions. Often, they are transferred without solving the problems they have contributed to create. In this manner, the conflicts become complicated with the arrival of another administrator. These conflicts are perennial because most of those in charge of land disputes are often strangers and know nothing about the customary laws of the groups they work with. To the best of my knowledge very few DOs or SDOs have ever succeeded in solving land disputes in any community.

Back to the men and women of the press, while those of the private press are seen as frustrated and hungry, or say angry men and women, their counterparts of the government or official press are known to be praise singers, boot lickers or errand boys and girls. It is common practice for journalists to also bribe their bosses in order to be assigned to cover a Minister's visit or any other official program or occasion where there is anticipated windfall. With such attitudes, most people now know that news reports are fabricated according to the amount of gumbo received and also to please those who care to give gumbo. Just like motions of support, journalists sometimes sit in their bedrooms and offices and invent news stories on certain personalities that are "heady"-that is to punish those who do not what to toe the line and give them the desired gumbo. The type of journalism that is practiced in Cameroon is junk or what some refer to as 'yellow journalism'.

When the colonialists "left" Africa, Africans found it difficult to follow the democratic principles that the Europeans introduced and imposed. The emerging elite soon fell back on their ethnic cleavages for political support. Thus ethnic politics became a mechanism used for manipulation by African leaders to stay in power for long periods of time, (sometimes for up to 40years). These leaders also received the strong support of a docile military who after all, were contented with the military 'honours' conferred on them and the huge budgetary allocations put at their disposal. For decades, the Ministry of Defence has always had the highest share of the national budget. Biya has taken great care to put loyalists in key military posts usually from the Beti clan while rotating and retiring others whose allegiance is suspect (Gros 2003: 23). This is done intentionally to distract the military from power. Most Cameroonians ask why the government spends so much on the military in times of peace.

Since Africa got political 'independence' very little has changed in the manner in which their leaders are selected or chosen. Elections are usually marred by fraud. Potential voters are bribed and promised job opportunities. During campaign periods, voters are bribed with money, drinks, meat, bags of rice, and vegetable oil. Sometimes, politicians distribute money up to the voting day. They argue that such money is to facilitate the voting process for their supporters. Using money to corrupt militants also implies spending money. Once elected into office, the next thing is for them to replenish the emptied purses and accounts. Irrespective of party leaning, the majority of these people, once voted for, do everything to loot the public treasury and/or inflate bills in their favour. There is combined corruption and conspicuous consumption; and it is business which can be considered the second factor of production after land which we cannot do much to change. Corruption thrives on clientalism and patronage in Cameroon and such corrupt practices lead to the decline of the economic and social well-being of the citizenry. It also erodes the legitimacy of the government which in turn applies all possible tactics to retain power (Egbo 2010: 4).

Corruption involves influential politicians of all sorts. I cite the case of Edouard Etondo Ekotto from Douala, whose immunity was lifted before he could be tried for embezzling 55 billion.[100] This is just one of many cases. Thousands of politicians embezzle and carry out corrupt practices, and go free because the bureaucratic nature of the public service prevents these "criminals" from facing trial. In recent years, the government arrested some well-placed state officials for embezzling state funds. Among them were the then Minister of

---

[100] He was a member of parliament from the Littoral region and was finally sentenced to 25years in prison for corruption charges.

Mines Water and Energy-Siyam, Siwe and the Director of the National Fund for Council Support, Emmanuel Gerald Odong Dong.

Here is the list of those arrested and convicted as of 31st march 2008. They include:

- Urban Olangena Awono, former Minister of Public Health;
- Polycarp Abah Abah, former Minister of Finance;
- Mouchipou Seidou, former Minister of Post and Telecommunications, the first Minister ever to be arrested. He has been in jail since 1999;
- Pierre Desire Engo, former General Manager of the National Social Insurance Fund (CNPS);
- Gilles Roger Belinga worker at CNPS
- Joseph Edou-workers at CNPS
- Zachaeus Fornjidam, General Manager of Chantier Naval;
- Atangana Mebara, former Secretary General at the Presidency of the Republic;
- Gervais Mendo Ze, former manager of the state owned Television and Radio Corporation (CRTV); looted 2.7 billion francs CFA; was charged 2 million francs for prejudice caused on CRTV.
- Ephraim Inoni, Former Prime Minister (2004-2009)

Gerald Ondo Ndong and the FEICOM Embezzlement Scandal

No	Embezzler	Initial sentence	Reduced sentence
1	Gerald Ondo Ndong	50 years	20 years
2	Jean Bessala Nsana	45 years	15 years
3	Moise mbella	45 years	15 years
4	Dieudonne Nguema Ondo	45 years	15 years
5	Charles ketchami	35 years	10 years
6	RoselyneBi Ebanga	20 years	10 years
7	Justin Zeze	30 years	20 years
8	Leonie Angue	25 years	10 years
9	Grace Ellesa Soppo	10 years	10 years
10	Laurentine Ngo	10 years	10 years
11	Edmond Medjo	10 years	10 years
12	Jeremiah Ndode	10 years	10 years
13	Marie-Gabrielle Etoga	10 years	10 years
14	Celestin Nube	10 years	10 years
15	Pierre Ndoukam	10 years	10 years
16	Venceslas Ndjomo	10 years	10 years
17	Olinga Mvogo	10 years	10 years
18	Ruben Abel Ze	10 years	10 years
19	Ngo Cho Nyamsi	10 years	10 years
20	Besthe kooh	10 years	10 years
21	Oblavie Ombella	10 years	10 years
22	Daniel Peh	40 years	10 years
23	Aaron Raymond	20 years	10 years
24	Bonaventure Ndema	25 years	10 years

Source: the Post No 0946 of Monday April 21, 2008

Some of them were discharged and acquitted, including Tchuente Namtchueng the Director of human resources who was freed from his 20 years jail term. Additionally, Eviria Bidoung, Luc Albert Ekomessa, and Janvier Onana were freed.

It should be recalled that the cases cited above are only the tip of the ice berg because those arrested so far are only the sacrificial lambs; as there are more people in similar positions who do the same thing. There is the over protection of corrupt officials by the law which makes it difficult for us to effectively research criminality and corruption in the country. As it is, there are more Cameroonians who are still walking around with billions of Francs CFA in their Swiss bank accounts. Proof of this is the demonstration carried out by, Cameroonians in Switzerland in front of the Embassy in Bern; calling on the Swiss government to investigate and block their accounts on April 19th 2008. The 2012 report of the UN Commission for Africa chaired by former South African President, Thabo Mbeki revealed that '…the illicit transfer of funds from the developing world to developed countries could amount to a staggering $1.5 trillion (about $50bn) per year. All these huge sums were stolen and kept in foreign banks with the assistance of multinationals', the report added.[101]

It is common knowledge, in Cameroon, that a top government official who has influence sometimes stops an investigation or court judgment in his favour because of the position he holds or the power he wields in society. They also use the money to buy positions and titles from their patrons. Again, the direction of justice in the country is determined and influenced by the status of an individual. Most of those convicted are usually the poor who do not have relations in positions of leadership. The problem is created by inequality and social exclusion. Once an individual does not have access to resources or the ability to influence decisions in his community, that individual becomes voiceless. As one of the informants notes 'there are people who embezzle state finances who ought to be in prison, but they are the ones holding the keys to the prison gates'[102]

Although Cameroon is arguably one of the most corrupt nations in the world, it is only of late that Biya began to make top-ranking public officers pay the penalty for official

---

[101] See UN Commission report for Africa Chaired by Mbeki "Multinationals 'steal'$50bn per year from Africa, in New African, an IC Publication http://www.newafricanmagazine.com/blogs/money-talks/multinationals-steal-$50bn-per-year-from-africa accessed 28/01/2013
[102] Anye Wilfred interviewed 12/6/2013 Buea

corruption. The imprisonments of Marafa Hamidou Yaya, Jean-Marie Atangana Mebara, Ephraim Inoni, and Yves Fostso, thanks to President Biya's Operation Sparrow Hawk, have set tongues wagging.[103] Intriguingly, Marafat, Mebara and Inoni who are now gnashing their teeth in prison today have served as Secretary Generals at the Presidency of the republic. These were the closest aides to the President of the Republic. These acts of corruption reveal that the President was working with people he did not know. In Cameroon, corruption is an obsession that has systematically legalised bribery. Unfortunately, corruption is fought over the television, radio, and newspapers without any concrete results as the persons involved hardly pay for the money they have stolen or for the acts they have committed.

Conclusion

So far, I have demonstrated in the previous chapters that corruption, bribery and the misuse of public resources have been recurrent in Cameroon. The interconnections between these vices have also been discussed. Corruption and bribery therefore, seem to be the way of life and a culture in Cameroon. Unfortunately, this has brought about the stigmatisation of the country as it has, on several occasions, been classified as the most corrupt country in the world.[104] As I have argued in this chapter, corruption, bribery and embezzlement of state funds are perpetuated by state bureaucrats who have the political and economic leverage to influence and manipulate the distribution of resources and services in the country in their favour. Despite government efforts to stop these vices more people are frequently arrested,

---

[103] Vakunta, P. Cameroon: unravelling the leadership conundrum in Cameroon http://allafrica.com/stories/201211021100.html?viewall=1 accessed 02/11/2012

[104] Corruption Perception Index-Transparency International from 2000-2010 http://www.transparency.org/country#CMR accessed 3/7/2014

indicating that the mechanisms put in place by the state to fight corruption and embezzlement are not effective. This is more importantly true as Cameroonians question why state bureaucrats are arrested without recovering the stolen money. To me and many Cameroonians, the most important thing is to recover the funds that have been stolen and not the arrests.[105]

Article 66 of the 1996 constitution stipulates that state officials shall declare their assets before they assume, and after they leave office. Since the constitution was promulgated by the president of the republic 19 years ago, this clause has never been implemented and there has been no explanation from the government. The National Anti-Corruption Unit has not been able to track down people involved in corrupt practices. Unless the government adopts a new strategy, corruption will forever continue. Corruption and embezzlement have negative impacts on the economy as the few who control the resources of the state enrich themselves and accumulate wealth at the detriment of the poor.

---

[105] Since the government started arresting ministers, only 2 billion Frs. has been recovered by the state out of a colossal sum of over 300 billion Frs. Figures revealed by Laurent Esso Minister of Justice and keeper of the Seal during a 'Question and Answer' session with Parliamentarians during the March 2014 session.

Chapter 5

Crime and Violence

Sociologists have always argued that there is no society that is void of crime but contend that what is considered a criminal offence is in the eyes of the beholder. That is, an act may be a crime to an individual or in one society but the same act may not necessarily be a crime to another person or in another society (Horton et al 1984). Furthermore, an act is considered a crime if it deviates from the social norms of that society. Yet such deviant behaviour does not in itself constitute a crime because not all deviant behaviours are considered as criminal offenses (*ibid*). Despite the difficulty in establishing what is considered a criminal offense, I must also admit that all human societies are able to distinguish between normal behaviour and deviant behaviour. Deviation from social norms also presupposes that there are socially acceptable mechanisms for social control and sanctions. An act must therefore, be seen by the other as a deviation and such an act must have consequences on the viewer. Because of the difficulty and complexity in determining what a crime is, the crime index[106] has been developed. This index is a classification of deviant acts that are severe in terms of how much it affects the society. Misdemeanours may not be accepted but will hardly attract sanctions (punishment), because they have little or no consequences on the society. On the other hand, acts that have greater consequences on society generally attract severe sanctions (*ibid*). Within the ambit of the law, the Cameroon penal code contains all crimes that are punishable with the corresponding sanctions for each crime.

---

[106] This is an attempt to provide statistical measures of the crimes committed in societies over a given period, say monthly or over a year. http://en.wikipedia.org/wiki/Crime_statistics accessed 28/01/2013

From the above points, what I am referring to in this text are those offenses that have great consequences on the society and are punishable by the law. Because I cannot handle all the criminal offenses in this issue, only a few have been selected for analysis. These are those that weigh highest in the crime index and their gravity is also enormous on society. For the purpose of this text, the following crimes have been selected: armed robbery, burglary, rape, murder, and assault, burglary and vehicle theft. Because of the peculiarities of corruption, bribery and embezzlement, I decided to focus on them in a separate chapter (see Chapter Four) as special crimes. Whatever crime I discuss affects people directly or their property indirectly. Some of them are violent and others are not but that notwithstanding Cameroon has a very high crime rate and this is a serious problem.[107] To wonder whether crimes are committed in Cameroon is a foregone conclusion as rarely a day goes by without a media report on a crime that has been committed. It should however, be noted that the rate of criminality and the type of crimes committed depicts the structural arrangements of the society and the value system.

Reports by the national television station have shown that the weapons that most robbers use are sophisticated guns and this raises the question as to where they get these guns from. This is more so as Cameroon forbids the possession of arms unless they are duly registered with the administration. The incessant use of arms by robbers is an indication of the inefficiency or leakages that exist within the system. Informed sources indicate that some of the guns that bandits use are gotten from the armed forces and the police. Some bandits pass for soldiers in military uniforms. Armed robbery is one of the crimes with the highest incidences in Cameroon. As the

[107] See USA Department of State Bureau of Diplomatic Security(2012) Cameroon OSAC Crime and Safety Report. https://www.osac.gov/Pages/ContentReportDetails.aspx?cid=12083 Accessed 28/01/2013

name depicts it is a crime committed with the aid of arms. This may include the use of guns, clubs, spears, knives, or any weapon to facilitate the execution of the act. In the same manner that the forces connive with drivers on the high way, so too are they with bandits. 'They supply guns, bullets, uniforms and even information or road maps to bandits. Not surprisingly, every time these bandits are taken to the police or gendarmes custody they are released even with firmer instructions on how to do it better the next time.' It therefore becomes difficult to distinguish between a Security Officer and a thief. 'The man in uniform sometimes is the disguised and can be a more dangerous criminal than the one being chased. Because of their involvement in criminal offenses, the security forces have lost all respect in the eyes of the public.'[108]

On the 29th of December 2012, the US State department issued a release in which Cameroon was rated as a critical crime threat country.[109] The explanations and statistics that follow are excerpts from that report. The report states that 'high unemployment and an under-equipped police force continue to fuel criminality, particularly in Yaoundé, Douala and other major towns in the country.' It notes further that persons have been robbed inside and outside their residences, on the street, in restaurants and in shops. In 2012, the report went on, numerous reports were received in increased street crime, thefts from vehicles, residential break-ins, highway banditry and armed robberies in the weeks leading up to and during the 2011 holiday season.

These crimes are known to be economically motivated and often involve violence, especially when victims attempt to resist or fight back. In all, more than 40 thefts, robberies and /or assaults against American citizens and Cameroonians were reported to the regional security office in 2011. Of particular

---

[108] Ade Christopher, Interviewed 27/7/2012 Mankon
[109] See OSAC Report of the USA Embassy Yaoundé of 29th December 2012

note was the armed robbery and shooting of a US citizen working with an American based NGO in February 2011. In March 2011, sexual assaults against an American and British National in Yaoundé resulted in the US Embassy placing the *Par Cour Vita* exercise area off limits to its American staff.

Residential crime also occurs frequently and most diplomats, expatriates and wealthy Cameroonians rely on 24 hour, private security guards to protect residences and other property. Most residential break-ins are perpetrated by small groups of armed bandits. They break into homes, their preferred method of entry being stealth techniques, especially during a rainstorm to make their movements, or sneaking past a sleeping guard. Bandits are increasingly overpowering guards to enter residences. Usually using some ruse to get the guard to open the gate (or shooting them if they do not obey instructions). Women of all ages are often sexually assaulted and some have even become pregnant from such assaults. Faced with this situation, the US Government and other foreign services in Cameroon provide 24 hour security for all of their official residences and even offices as unguarded properties are vulnerable and inviting to burglaries. Those whose lives and property are endangered are the poor who cannot afford to hire the services of security guards.[110]

Although there is a mechanism or requirement to inspect roadworthiness for vehicles, they are still poorly maintained.[111] During festive periods such as Christmas and New Year, special road safety campaigns are organized since there is often anticipated high traffic. This is often the case when school children are about to go on vacation or about to go back to school. Usually, the rate of accidents and deaths appear to fall during such periods but after the road campaigns exercise,

---

[110] Bi-Awah has suffered from armed robbery several times at her Ntarinkon residence and she argues that it is because her house is not fenced and which makes her vulnerable to frequent attacks by bandits.

[111] See vehicle testing centre at Nacho college Atuakom -Mankon

things go back to normal. One begins to wonder why drivers need to be checked all the time before they respect road signs and the Highway Code. Talking about the Highway Code, it is unfortunate that road safety rules are frequently ignored even in cities where road police exist. Generally, there are few road signs but speed limits are rarely respected and are never enforced. This is because the road police prefer bribery to people's safety. Security road blocks set up throughout the country serve mostly as collecting points of bribery for road police and the military from motorists.[112] Buses and logging trucks travel at excessive speeds and are a constant threat to other road traffic. At night, logging trucks, have, on several occasions, derailed and injured people in shops and private homes with some dying in deep sleep.

In June 2011, a spontaneous and violent riot broke out in Yaounde after a football match in which Cameroon recorded a tie against Senegal. Also in the early morning hours of September 29 2011, four men in military–style clothing brandishing firearms walked onto the Bonaberi Bridge in Douala and stopped traffic for over three hours. The men began firing their weapons into the air presumably to gain attention and to stop traffic from crossing the bridge. Units from the National Police, the Gendarmes and the Rapid Intervention Battalion known by its French acronym BIR responded to the scene and restored order after exchanging gun shots with the protestors. Reading this, several questions arise: where were our security and where did the bandits get their guns from? And most importantly: were the bandits caught?

Although the Government of Cameroon has made excellent progress in reducing instances of piracy off the coast

---

[112] 'Cameroon Police and Gendarmes, Crooks in government: in the case of the Bamenda Ring Road, they operate like toll gates' http://www.cameroonjournal.com/Cameroon%20Police%20and%20Gend armes.html accessed 14/7/2014

of Cameroon near the Bakassi Peninsula, piracy still remains a concern. Attacks against oil platforms and ships off the coast often involve armed assaults and kidnappings. In the past, these 'pirates' have claimed a political motivation for their activities, but it is believed that these are crimes perpetrated by thieves who are exploiting a weakness in Cameroon's existing law enforcement and security structure.

Armed vehicle hijackings also continue to be a major cause for concern. Some victims of vehicle hijackings are taken in the car by the bandits for several kilometres to ensure that any anti-theft device is deactivated.[113] Persons resisting theft are likely to be injured or killed by the bandits. Sometimes they carry the booty and still kill, especially if their concealed identity has been uncovered. The bandits prefer luxury four wheel drive vehicles such as Toyota land Cruisers. Most vehicle hijackings occur at night against vehicles with a single occupant. In some cases they stop the vehicle and order the owner to move to a particular direction where the contents of the car are taken or the car seized and taken away.

Coupeurs de route, (highway robbers) are gangs of armed bandits that target vehicles on the main commercial routes in the rural areas and thick forest regions of the country. These gangs are known to operate out of areas close to the borders of Chad, Central African Republic, and Nigeria. Rampant cases of assault have been recorded along the Eyumunjock- Mamfe and the Bafut forest reserves. The bandits are known to be more active on market days and in the case of Bafut on cattle market days. It has been noted that most of these bandits use their cell phones to track their culprits with ease. It is important to however acknowledge that the government has continued to register success in breaking up these gangs using rapid reaction

---

[113] The kidnapping of three French and Canadian priests is a case in point. They were kidnapped in April 2014 and only released in June of the same year through the intervention of Cameroon and French governments

forces stationed near the borders; but more could be achieved if the police were serious.[114]

There are several reasons why drivers prefer to give bribes than to have the necessary vehicle documents. This is because many times the amount of documentation requested is excessive and difficult to provide. Fru Peter who is a taxi driver describes the situation as follows: 'a driver in Cameroon does not know the exact number of vehicle documents that are required by the police. A driver will always think that he has all the documents of the vehicle until the police says that the documents are not enough or incorrect'. As it has become a common saying amongst drivers; *even if you have all the documents, the police and Gendarmes will always look for a motive*. This simply means that documents are only considered correct after the road has been 'settled' with the 500 Frs. bribes.

There are reports of numerous deadly accidents on major roads and highways throughout the country on a daily basis. A large percentage of the population has not received any formal driving training and obtaining a driver's license through corrupt and fraudulent activities is common. The competence needed to issue driver's license is with the Ministry of Transport and they are unable to check corrupt practices and are the same people who organise road safety campaigns; what a paradox! It is the same ministry that organises seminars on how to curb road accidents. Usually I am told that some of the root causes of road accidents include poor state of the vehicle, bad roads, overload, drunkenness, fatigue, and speeding among other things. My interests do not lie on the fact that we do not know the causes of these accidents; rather I am interested in what solutions are provided to the problem. Take for instance the issue of poor state of the vehicle. There are vehicles plying the highway in Cameroon that were manufactured in 1950. They have undergone all sorts of refurbishing, panel beating and

---

[114] See 'Cameroon military kill 40 militants of Boko Haram' www.cameroononline.org accessed 30/6/2014

remodelling. You do not need to test such vehicles for road worthiness but they remain fashionable so long as they move. As they say *motor na engine*. This implies that so long as the engine of the vehicle can pull, other considerations about the state of the car do not matter. Here vehicles travel without lights and even shooters and are frequently broken down by the road side or even in the road. Frequent break down gives the opportunity for the highway bandits to predict and be sure of customers at all times. Associated to poor state of vehicles is drunkenness and speeding which is also a major concern, and poses significant risk, especially after dark. This situation has also been observed by Carrier (2009: 189) among transporters in Kenya but emphasises that 'while many view such driving with distain as reckless and the cause of many accidents, others seem quite awestruck by the courage shown by such drivers, and individual drivers can become famous for their skill and exploits'

Ironically, alcohol testing devices have been provided to the road police to control drivers but this is hardly enforced because even the supposed enforcer is usually drunk. On several occasions, vehicles have been stopped by intoxicated policemen and military. The police and military drink in bars during working hours, in uniforms and even brandish pistols. They fight with civilians sometimes over prostitutes and other things.

Suspects are rarely caught and police response (if they respond at all) to an incident is often delayed. 'We do not have a vehicle. There is neither fuel nor a driver on duty'- that is the excuse they often give. But generally, they simply do not answer or respond since they often abandon the police stations at the expense of beer parlours. In some cases police forces have perpetrated criminal acts or they have been complicit with criminal elements. 'They supply guns, bullets, uniforms and even information or road maps to bandits' (Ade Christopher, interviewed 12/11/2013).

I cannot belabour the issue of bad roads in Cameroon. The high way in Cameroon constitutes a potential source of danger to people's lives. Only about 32% of existing 5.500 kilometres of national roads in Cameroon are tarred and the rest are earth roads that are never or poorly maintained. In 2011, the President of the Republic ordered the disbursement of 100 billion Frs. CFA for the rehabilitation of the Douala-Bafoussam-Bamenda highway. In 2012, the road became worse than what it was before the maintenance work started. In 2010, 5 billion Frs. CFA was alleged to have been spent in road and infrastructural development when the President was to preside over the 50th anniversary of the Cameroon armed forces in Bamenda. By 2011, all the pot holes that were filled came back to square one. The street lights in the city of Bamenda have gradually disappeared. As most inhabitants of the city hold, the roads were only maintained to please the President and his visitors. According to a report on road accidents published on 17 August 2012, there were 30.858 road accidents along highways in the country. In 2010, there were 1.741 accidents, 5292 persons were injured and 1259 deaths. From January 1st – December 31st 2011 a total of 2.607 accidents occurred on the highways. These figures exclude accidents that occurred within the cities or in villages.[115]

A few examples may suffice here; on the night of 26th October 2012, a man by the name of Richard Tabu a resident of Munyenge in the Muyuka Subdivision was attacked by bandits in his home. The bandits left him wounded with a bullet in his skull and his pregnant wife was shot dead.[116] As usual, the Divisional Officer for Muyuka visited the scene and the Muyuka Police opened investigations into the matter. Still in Tiko, the Assistant Police Commissioner shot his own boss

---

[115] Cameroon: Kumba-Mamfe road development project, African Development Fund, Project appraisal report.

[116] See Effa tambe Ncham (2012) A man's head receives bullet in Baffia http://allafrica.com/stories/201211010852.html Accessed 02/11/2012

to death and escaped with the gun and was never caught. In the same light, on the night of October 22nd 2012, two bandits armed with automatic pistols assaulted a motorbike rider at the *Camp des Officiers* in Bepanda-Douala doing away with his bike.[117] Interestingly, the two bandits-23-year old Darisse Keda and 25-year old Cedric Momo were former detainees of the Douala New Bell maximum prison. When I heard of maximum prison some years ago, I had the feeling that this was a prison with maximum security but I have come to know that maximum may after all mean minimum in Cameroon. Perhaps suffering from nemesis, they were caught a few hours later. Again, we are told 'they are helping the police with further investigations while waiting to appear before the State Council of the Military Tribunal in Bonanjo for aggravated theft and illegal detention of firearms'. Because these two gentlemen just escaped from the New Bell prison and one wonders how many times these same boys will keep appearing in front of the tribunal or go to prison.

Between August and October 2012, robbery took centre stage in four prominent secondary schools in some parts of the country. Sacred Heart College Mankon, Sasse College Buea, PNEU Yaoundé, and Star light College Nkwen were all attacked by bandits and over 100 million Francs CFA was looted and their whereabouts remained a mystery even to the police.[118] The case of the English High School Yaoundé was the most memorable because apart from taking away the safe, valuables and a vehicle, the night watchmen could not be found. But since I cannot take anything for granted in Cameroon, the night watchmen were highly suspected to be accomplices as it has happened in other instances. You can never be sure of the man you are dealing with when it comes to

---

[117]Mosima Elizabeth http://allafrica.com/stories/201211020157.html accessed 02/11/2012 Automatic pistols of mark valtro, a charger and nine bullets

[118] http://allafrica.com/stories/201211020024.html accessed 02/11/2012

criminal matters in Cameroon. You may just be sleeping or playing with a snake.

On December10th 2012, three armed bandits were arrested in Garoua after they used automatic pistols to rob one Muhamat of Chadian nationality taking away three million francs and a Toyota vehicle. The leader of the gang- Hamidou was found to be an ex-convict. In another case of robbery that took place on Tuesday 15th January 2013 in a Terminus Bonamoussadi neighbourhood in Douala, two bandits tried to rob an Off License. In a cross fire with the Rapid Intervention Unit (BIR) they were killed.[119] In most of these incidences, there is hardly any intervention by the police force. For instance, banks have been attacked by bandits in broad day light in Douala and Yaoundé under the watchful eyes of security guards and the police.

There are hundreds of such incidences that happen all over the country but the crucial thing is the manner in which the police have handled these crimes. In all the cases cited above, the Police and Gendarmes carried out investigations but the results of their investigations were shrouded with lots of suspicions. Apart from the motor bike theft in Bepanda where the two bandits were arrested, in the other cases the bandits escaped. Generally, investigations or enquiries are meant to acquire more knowledge into a phenomenon in order to provide solutions. To someone who is so familiar with the Cameroonian system, commissions of enquiries and police investigations do not have any relevance. They simply constitute some of the ways through which money can be extorted and squandered.

Another dimension of crime which is very common in the country is highway robbery (*Coupe du route*). Travelling on the highway in most parts of Cameroon has become very unsafe for passengers because of frequent attacks by robbers. The

---

[119] Luncheon date Reports from Robert Taboh and Agnes Ngwalupenja from Garoura and Douala respectively 16/01/2013

strategy of attacking and harassing passengers for money and valuables developed about a decade ago along the Ngaoundere-Maroua high way. I cannot narrate how many people have lost their lives and property to highway robbers on that road. Since Cameroonians are very good at copying what is bad, the phenomenon later on spread to other parts of the country including villages. Everyday there are news reports of people who have been killed and others maimed by armed robbers; sometimes right into their bedrooms. Evidence has shown that violent crimes have actually increased in Cameroon over the past three decades [120] It is also important to note that juvenile delinquency is not only a social problem but also a criminal issue. Delinquency is generally associated with teenagers and this has become an issue of national concern. It has also been observed that most of the juveniles are involved in property crimes. This is not to say that the youth should indulge in criminal acts, but I also note that those who occupy very high positions (offices) in government usually commit crimes that have huge consequences on the economy than teenagers.[121]

The police and the Gendarmes have not been able to curb the incessant criminal activities because they are also corrupt. The Secretary of state for the Gendarmeries, Jean Baptiste Bokam, dismissed the entire staff of the Baleng Gendarmerie Brigade in Bafoussam on the 10th of October 2011 for killing an innocent motor bike rider (*Ben skin)* for what they claim was the violation of traffic rules. In actual fact the boy's crime was the non-compliance with police orders to give the much needed 500 Frs. bribe. After investigations were carried out, it was discovered that the check point mounted by the gendarmes was, after all, illegal. It should be recalled that the

---

[120] 'Crime rates in Cameroon' http://www.numbeo.com/crime/country_result.jsp?country=Cameroon accessed 3/7/2014

[121] See Report of National Anti-Corruption Commission (CONAC) http://www.conac-cameroun.net/en/index_en.php accessed 25/6/2014 Also see list of ministers convicted of embezzlement in chapter

entire staff of the Melen Gendarmes were equally dismissed on the 20th of June 2007 for the same uncouth behaviour.

'It suffices a Gendarme or a Police Officer to wake up one morning, pick up his whistle and uniform and jump into the high way and harass law abiding citizens for money'. In most instances, these people who ought to protect lives and property rather take away lives. They have been known to be accomplices and even organise gangs of armed robbers to loot the property of people.

There is no security for people or their property in Cameroon. It is common knowledge that for any prisoner to be kept in prison, such a person must have been searched thoroughly. Following a riot carried out by the prisoners of the New Bell prison in Douala, the public was shocked to uncover harmful weapons such as pistols from the prison cells. As if this was not enough, the prisoners had communication gadgets such as mobile phones with internet facilities. The only thing that made them prisoners was the fact that their movements were restricted, otherwise they were connected to the world through these sophisticated communication apparatuses. The question that lingers is how come prisoners in a prison such as New Bell could afford to have access to such gadgets and weapons? It would appear the Prison Wardens or Guards were accomplices.

One of the things that Cameroonians in high positions have deliberately refused to learn is the culture of resigning. In societies where people have dignity and are not ashamed to admit failure, they gracefully resign from their positions. In the Western Grassfields of Cameroon, brevity and pride are social values that accord people a high social status.[122] The history of origin and migration of the people of the Grassfields is highly associated with warfare and conquest. The area also has a long history of inter-ethnic trade migration and was also an entrepot

---

[122] This could be seen when one kills a ferocious animal and is considered brave and therefore, earns a title.

for the 16th century Atlantic Slave Trade (de Bruijn, Nyamnjoh and Angwafo 2010). Early trade links and contacts with European traders and explorers allowed them to exchange ivory, kola and iron ore for guns, silk, whisky and beads. The guns became very instrumental for the subjugation and acquisition of more territories by powerful and influential kings, sometimes through raids (Chilver and Kaberry 1970: 255). Guns and gunpowder were not only important sources for the generation of wealth and for the protection of the community, but they also became status markers and were also used for hunting throughout the Western Grassfields of Cameroon (Kopytoff 1981: 377). These exchanges become incorporated into the material culture of things and made some of these kingdoms wealthy.[123] After the invention of the Cameroon state, these kingdoms continued to exist as quasi states; having inter-ethnic boundaries that were also created by the colonial administration. In most cases, inter-ethnic boundaries were influenced and determined by Cameroonians who served as clerks in the colonial offices to their own advantage (Mbah 2009). Petitions and disputes over these boundaries were usually submitted to the colonial office where decisions were made. The creation of these boundaries went along with the creation of Warrant chiefs for the purpose of tax collection. The promulgation of the Cameroon land law in 1974 made it possible for a Cameroonian to settle in any part of the country. All occupied lands before that year was declared private and any unoccupied land became state land.[124] One would have imagined that the land law would be implemented on issues raised over inter-ethnic boundaries that go back to the period before 1974. That is, each village respecting the boundaries that existed before the 1974 law. Rather, the Western Grassfields has recorded many inter-ethnic conflicts after the law was passed in 1974. Although the

---

[123] See Chem-Langhee (1995)
[124] See the Cameroon Land Ordinance No.74-1 and 74-2 of 6 July 1974

reasons are attributed to population pressure, the trigger is the administration that actually fans these flames (Dafinger, Andreas and Pelican 2006). Skirmishes over land disputes have often resulted in blood bath, arson, brutality and displacements.

Let me come back to my point now. In 2012, the Governor of the northwest region banned the use and parade of guns at all public ceremonies in the region; arguing that people used guns to settle scores embedded in land disputes. This decision was highly criticised by the Traditional authorities in the region on the grounds that the numbers of people who died in motor accidents and armed robbery annually in Cameroon far superseded the few accidents that occurred during death celebrations or even in inter-tribal disputes. Following the statistics on poverty in Cameroon, most people die of hunger, misery, and malaria than from gun shots in the region. Secondly, there was no threat to peace in the region given that there was a huge detachment of the Cameroon Army in this part of the country. Talking about peace, Cameroon is often considered a peaceful country in a turbulent sub region but the paradox is that the death rate in Cameroon is higher than those who die from war in Democratic Republic of Congo (DRC) and the Central African Republic. The death rate is so high that there are specialised programs devoted only to death announcements in all radio stations in Cameroon.[125] The Fons argued that the decision to ban the use of guns was a deliberate attempt by the regime to destroy the culture of the northwest region, insisting that it is not only in the northwest region where inter-ethnic conflicts have been recorded. For example, on the 12 of January 2013, eight people were killed and 20 others were wounded when violence broke out between neighbouring villages in Rey Bouba in the north region. There have been protracted boundary disputes between the people of Lebialem and some villages in the west region as well.

---

[125] Follow *Luncheon date, Cameroon Midi* amongst others program.

The West region that constitutes part of the Western Grassfields has similar cultural aspects with people of the northwest region and the possession and use of guns is an integral part of the culture. The Governor of the region and his cohorts who originate from the West region know too well the important role of guns in the cultures of the region. If the ban was a national policy it would have been better but to single out a region and place it under surveillance with an embargo on the use of guns was considered treacherous by traditional rulers. Gun parade constitutes a vital component at annual festivals in the Grassfields of Cameroon. The traditional festivals in Bafut, Bali and Mankon that are often celebrated annually failed to take place in 2012 because of the ban on the use of guns. This had serious repercussions on the traditions and cultures of these kingdoms. Although there are land disputes among families in these kingdoms, rarely have they used these festivals to hunt down their opponents with guns.

The Governor's decision may not be challenged but one thing is clear, the administration is the cause of the land disputes in the region; because they indulge in corrupt practices (Moritz, 2009; Kah 2009). One such case involving the people of Mankon and Nkwen can elucidate the point further. In 2012, the SDO for Mezam emerged with a new boundary map for Mankon and Nkwen intended to cede parts of their land to Mendakwe. The final boundary between Mankon and Mendakwe was established in 1967 with funds contributed by the two Fondoms.[126] This boundary was marked by the planting of pillars and there was no objection. It should be recalled that in 1967, Mendakwe was part of the Ndop Council with its headquarters in Bamunka. Mankon had its own council, the Mankon Area Council. By 1977, the Bamenda Urban Council was created and Mendakwe and Nkwen were

---

[126] See letter of Fo Angwafo addressed to the Administration of Mezam http://cameroonlatest.blogspot.nl/2012/09/bamenda-on-time-bomb-fon-angwafo-iii.html accessed 28/01/2013

transferred from Ndop to join Mankon in the Urban Council.[127] When Presidential Decree No 2007/115 and Decree No 117 of 24th April 2007 created three new councils out of the defunct Bamenda Urban Council, the boundaries of the new administrative units were confined to those of the various villages. For example, Decree Number 2007/115 of April 13 2007 defined the administrative boundaries of Bamenda I Council as follows:

Le resort territorial du dit arrondissement s'entend sur celui de la Chefferie de Bamendakwe. Pour Bamenda II le resort territorial du dit arrondissement s'entend sur celui de la chefferie du Mankon, Chomba, Mbatu et Nsongwa.

The translation in English goes thus:

The resort territorial of the said district is defined on that of the chiefdom of Bamendakwe. For Bamenda II the resort territorial of the said district is defined on that of the leadership of the Mankon, Chomba, Mbatu and Nsongwa.

It became an embarrassment to the Mankon and Nkwen people when an administrator who was supposed to implement the decree instead took upon himself to carve new boundaries contrary to the ones enshrined in the decree. The two villages cried foul and staged public protests forcing the SDO to withdraw the maps. One thing remains clear; the new maps designed by the SDO now constitute sites for land claims and political struggles in the area and source of potential conflict between these communities.[128] As Fisiy (1992) notes the recurrent skirmishes are blamed on the incessant changes of

---

[127] Decree of 1977 creating the Bamenda Urban Council
[128] See letter of 16th July 2012 by His Majesty Fo Angwafo III 'creation of an illegal boundary between Mankon and Bamendakwe' by the SDO for Mezam Joseph Mache Betrand

inter-ethnic boundaries by SDOs in defiance of all previous decisions taken by their predecessors. It therefore becomes difficult to blame people when they react violently in order to defend themselves with Guns.

To conclude, I want to emphasise that there is growing evidence that the incidences of criminality, insecurity and violence are on the rise in Cameroon. The examples that I have quoted in this chapter are drawn from the different regions and towns and people with different back grounds, indicating that they are not endemic to a particular region or ethnic group. However, I must quickly add that according to the research, most of those who commit these crimes (especially property crimes) are youths who seem to have been blocked from having access to opportunities and life chances for their well-being. While I do not support youths who indulge in criminal activities, I also note that they have been pushed to the wall by the negligence of the state that has not created a social welfare system that enable the youths to sustain their livelihoods, even while searching for jobs.

Secondly, the justice system has been blamed for the persistent criminality in the country since court judges and the police prefer to take bribes and kick-backs. Cases are bound where a criminal taken for police custody is released a few hours later. 'Because of these attitudes, the population does not have confidence in the entire justice system. Field accounts indicate that the police and the Gendarmes respond too late or never show up when homes are invaded by bandits'.[129] It is even alleged that these criminals act sometimes with the complicity of the police and Gendarmes in carrying out their criminal activities. As more and more Cameroonians feel insecure even in the hands of their own police forces, they have devised different means and options of fighting

---

[129] They often complain of lack of vehicles or fuel and even sometimes personnel. It is even a piety to note that sometimes they are not on duty, either they are in a bar drinking or simply doing some other business.

criminality. Consequently, the people have resorted to what is known in Cameroon as 'Jungle or mob justice'. By Jungle justice, 'we mean a situation where a thief is instantly brutalised or maimed to death by a mob after being arrested'.[130]

To human rights activists, and by the legal provisions of the state, such actions from the population are punishable by law. Unfortunately, it is often difficult to identify who is in the crowd let alone assigning blame to each of them. To reduce the crime wave in the country, the government must therefore provide or create job opportunities or create an environment such that people can make choices and be fully employed. There is also the need to improve on the working conditions of the security forces so that they can act promptly when people are attacked by bandits.

---

[130] Fru Awah interviewed at Ntarinkon Mankon 24/5/2011

Chapter 6

The Bush faller Syndrome

This chapter draws on inspiration from an article published by Alpes (2011: 6) about young Cameroonians in which she examines the challenges that aspiring migrants and their families face, as well as the ways in which different actors try to achieve their ambitions of mobility to European countries and the USA at all cost. I argue that the history of migration is not new but it is as old as the history of human existence (Nyamnjoh 2013b: 654) and the drivers for such movements have often been diversified and/or not limited to the search for a comfortable life. They have always been determined by the cultural, material conditions and historical experiences at different stages in the development of a people. Though the reasons for such movements may differ substantially from one epoch to another and from one society to another, they are always driven by man's desire to cope with and harness nature and culture as Nyamnjoh (2013b: 111) demonstrates in his research on the Fulani of the Western Grassfields of Cameroon. Following Appadurai (2008), I maintain that not only do people migrate but it is also true of ideas, technologies, cultures and 'things' that flow sometimes in multidirectional and disjunctive manners. However, while acknowledging the different 'flows', I am focused on Cameroonians who migrate to European and North American countries and how their perceived migrations are interpreted by their peers back in their homeland. While the Fulani migrate to ensure the well-being of their cattle and not necessarily for personal comfort (Nyamnjoh 2013b: 113), the reasons why the African youth in particular tend to migrate today are linked to what Nyamnjoh and Page (2002: 608) refer to as the 'imaginative geography' of the *Whiteman Kontri* characterized by dreams and expectations.

Economics and population studies theories of migration posit that there are often centrifugal (push) and centripetal (pull) forces that influence the possibility for people to migrate (Parkins, 2011).Following Parkins (2011: 12), I contend that 'the major factors influencing migration include but not limited to general crime and violence, an unstable economy which in turn affects an individual's social and economic opportunities and career advancement'. Admittedly, I argue that the opulent countries of the North,-(USA & Europe) offer the most attractive conditions pulling potential migrants from the South, while the difficult conditions of life in the latter are pushing these would-be migrants out of their homeland. Following these basic theoretical assumptions, the purpose of this chapter is therefore to explore some of those reasons that have increasingly forced most African youth to migrate or to engage in unsuccessful attempts trying to travel to affluent societies. I have however moved away from the simple analysis of the ambitions of aspiring migrants and their families to show how successful migrants appropriate the *bushfallerness* by trying to 'catch up' with the demands and expectations of relatives and friends even with the insecurity and difficulties they encounter in the game hunt-money (Alpes 2011, Nyamnjoh 2011).

I use the example of Binwi[131] who after several years of unsuccessful attempts to travel abroad finally got a visa and abandoned her job in Cameroon in an effort to 'realize' her dreams in Europe. I consider Binwi my sister because we grew up in the same neighbourhood in Mankon and our families have a long history of close and strong social ties. The age difference between Binwi and me is very small, so we are peers and consequently interact frequently; sharing our dreams, desires and ambitions together especially during holidays. On

---

[131] Binwi is a pseudonym and except indicated, all the names in the case studies in this chapter are pseudonyms as well. Considering the delicate and complicated regime of bushfallers, I have decided to conceal the identity of my informants from whom this data was collected.

the 23rd of December 2009, I stood in front of the popular Simplicity Bar at Ntarinkon waiting for a taxi and Binwi walked up to me to seek advice. When I inquired to know what the issue was, she told me that she was confused as to whom to get married to. She told me that she has been in a love relationship for over four years with one Tambungang David and both of them were planning marriage. When I asked what the confusion was about, she explained that she was no longer interested in this guy because she had just found someone else to marry. When I asked who this person was, she revealed that it was a medical doctor from Germany by the name Dr Ma'amuzam Simon. Binwi told me that she met Dr Ma'amuzam at a wedding not long ago. When I tried to find out from her why the switch from Tambugang and the preference for Ma'amuzam, she told me that her greatest ambition has always been to travel abroad. 'Getting married to Ma'amuzam was the opportunity I have been yearning for and I cannot allow such an opportunity to slip off my hands', she insisted. Then I cautioned her that it would be even more dangerous and slippery getting married to someone she just met and was not familiar with, and that she may be walking on egg shells. Unfortunately my advice persuading her not to marry Ma'amuzam fell on deaf ears as she considered him a gift from God and saw me as an obstacle.

Binwi was a Geography Teacher in one of the renowned Secondary Schools in Mankon. Tambugang was also a History Teacher and both of them graduated from the Advanced Teachers Training College (ENS) in Bambili. It was during their school days in Bambili that they fell in love. Binwi, however, admitted that Tambungang was a nice and caring man who would do all he could to provide for her needs. She reiterated that all she wanted was an opportunity to go to Europe at all costs.[132] When I noticed that Binwi was not

---

[132] Also see Alpes (2011) *Bushfalling :How young Cameroonians dare to migrate,* PhD Thesis Kiel

comfortable with anything that I said which was meant to dissuade or deter her from getting married to Ma'amuzam, I decided to leave. That is how we parted company. I later learned that Binwi abandoned her job and got married to the medical doctor from Germany. Binwi's dreams of becoming a 'bush faller' were realized after all!

The narrative about Binwi is just one of the many stories involving aspiring migrants not only from Cameroon but from other African countries. On 28th February 2014, the Cameroon Radio and Television Corporation (CRTV) reported that some 600 African migrants from (mostly Cameroon and Guinea) sub-Saharan Africa, broke into the Spanish North African borders of Mellila incurring injuries and cuts.[133] In 2012 and 2013, there were 6,400 and 8,300 illegal African immigrants in Europe respectively and within the last 20 years, there have been 20.000 illegal immigrants in Europe alone.[134] While the central issue is the desire to migrate to Europe and/or the USA, aspiring migrants use different routes and strategies to fulfil their dreams. In this chapter, Cameroon is used as a lens through which we can see and understand the anthropology of mobility and traveling cultures within the context of the African youth. I will come back to other examples from Cameroon later.

For over a decade now, a phenomenon has gripped Cameroon wherein most young people tend to migrate from the country to the United States of America and Europe in search of greener pastures. In local parlance this is commonly referred to as *bush falling*.[135] This metaphoric comparison considers the desire to travel and settle abroad as a bush which is a type of ecological anthropology. Normally, most people do not like to go into the bush. The reasons for such dislikes are

---

[133] See Cameroononline.org accessed 12/4/2014
[134] See 'Deadly Migration CNN' anchored by Becky Anderson @becky Anderson 12/05/2014
[135] For detail explanation on bushfalling see Nyamnjoh 2011,pp 703

many because the bush is a dirty place. A bush contains many harmful living and non-living organisms made up of plants, animals and reptiles. Some of the living harmful organisms include snakes, ants, and insects. Some plants have thorns that inflict serious injuries and to avoid being injured, one needs to be careful while moving in the bush. At the same time, the bush is also known to harbour lots of natural resources on which man depends for his livelihoods. These may include fruits, herbs, animals, fuel wood, and grass. It therefore seems that although the bush is a harmful place, human beings cannot avoid going there because of its significant importance. In this light, what matters is one's ability and skills to exploit the bush.

The 'bush' that I am talking about is the *white man kontri* (overseas) which simply refers to the Diaspora of some sort. In Cameroon, people have likened what a natural bush is to overseas. They see these places as having the characteristics of the natural bush that is described above. After all both overseas and the bush are a source of livelihood and both are places of productivity (Alpes 2012: 96). Despite the fact Europe and the USA are surrounded with a lot of uncertainties and undesirable stories, young African still dare to fall bush(Alpes,2011).These sometimes include strict and tough immigration laws, scarcity of jobs and accommodation, and even the difficulty of obtaining a visa to go overseas (Nyamnjoh and Page, 2002). Travelling abroad is therefore not a bed of roses. One's success or failure in the 'bush' depends on the skills and ability to survive or 'harvest' the desired fruits. Yet the bush is also seen by many as a haven, an El Dorado,[136]-a place flowing with milk and honey. African youths and adults (my emphasis) see Europe and USA as paradise (Nyamnjoh and Page 2002: 612)

---

[136] El Dorado is used here metaphorically to mean any place where wealth can be rapidly acquired. It also represents an ultimate prize that one might spend one's life seeking. It could represent love, heaven, happiness or success. It simply refers to something much sought after that may not even exist, or, at least, may not ever be found. http://en.wikipedia.org/wiki/El_Dorado. accessed 3/7/2014

or heaven on earth. Their commitment to the course of travelling to an unknown destination is likened to that of a Christian who must obey his or her Godly vows to ensure eventual entry into heaven. Therefore, just as heaven is to Christians, so too are Europe and the USA that epitomise the final destination on earth not withstanding what expectations there may be.

Television and newspaper accounts of hardship for African immigrants in Europe and the USA are no deterrent, as every potential migrant (bushfaller) either hopes to be luckier than those described in newspaper accounts or to embrace the hardship which, by the standards of life in the African cities, is imagined as paradise (*ibid*: 612). Despite Sergeo Polo's insistence in his musical track *C'est dur: Europe c'est difficile* -that Europe is not Paradise, most youths still want to travel abroad against all odds. The growing desire to travel has also been visualised in the form of films and especially the all-time Cameroonian film, *Paris a Tout Prix* directed by the French Comedian Reem Kherici[137] and also dramatized by the humourist Valery Ndongo but these dramas seem not to have paid off.

Irrespective of the means and ways, anybody who successfully moves out of Cameroon or any other African country to Europe, the USA and recently to Asia, is considered and referred to as a *Bush faller*. It is interesting to note that going abroad to any of the African countries with perhaps the exception of South Africa is not considered bush falling. It seems therefore that the notion of bush falling is restricted to the developed countries and continents of the world where there is affluence and opulence. When asked why travelling to

---

[137] The film portrays the risks and potential downfalls of migration, such as unwanted sex work, money swindlers, failure, and deportation. See also Alpines 2012, pp91

126

the opulent society is considered as *bush falling*. Evelyn[138] notes that:

> The main idea here is that to get to USA or to Europe the most convenient transport means is through the use of the plane and not by land (though some use road transport). The scenario entails that one boards an air craft which gets into the air bypassing all obstacles and barriers then gradually lands (falls) in the desired country. It is the landing of the plane that is liken to a person falling from the sky to the country of destination.

When I tried to find out why most young people want to fall bush in the first place George simply said: 'The economic and political conditions in most of African countries are really bad and frustrating. Most of African youth cannot afford jobs nor is there the enabling environment for them to kick start their own businesses. Most youths in Africa are unemployed and live in abject poverty and misery.'[139] Bush falling means different things to different people. To some, just falling bush is an achievement in itself. To others, it is only a measure of success. While to others, it is an escape from poverty, disease and misery. 'Having internalised that no future is possible in Cameroon, leaving the country has become a prized escape route for many frustrated young Cameroonians' (Alpes 2012: 92). Driven by hardship, abject poverty and lack of opportunities, the African youths and Cameroonians see the streets of the United States, Europe and Asia as flooded with gold and silver. The USA, Europe and to an extent Asia are considered by Cameroonians as El Dorado, sources of salvation and hope. The *Whiteman Kontri* therefore signifies

---

[138] Evelyn is a pseudonym and she lives at The Hague after having migrated from Cameroon to serve as a house help for the uncle who was a clerical staff at the Cameroon Embassy in The Hague in 2004.

[139] A Cameroonian who migrated from the northwest region of Cameroon and settled in The Netherlands

luck. It is even considered an omen. I cannot deny the fact that there are millions of Cameroonians living in misery. The Cameroon labour market is structured in such a way that only the rich and the privilege few have the opportunity to be employed as these are orchestrated by endemic corruption and bribery.

The whiteman and *whiteman Kontri* (my emphasis), are still seen very much as a solution to misery and impoverishment- the gate way to a brighter future in the West itself, where menial work brings great financial reward (Nyamnjoh and Page 2002: 628). Unfortunately, most European countries have instituted tougher conditions for the issuance of visas to potential migrants (Nyamnjoh and Page 2002). As Nyamnjoh and Page (2002: 11) note, 'the difficulty of travelling abroad is usually embedded in the bureaucratic rituals of visas, which are a means of denying potential migrants the opportunity of realizing their dreams of sharing in the good life that whiteman-driven modernisation has brought about'. Given the difficulties that people go through to fall bush, a family is generally very comfortable when one of theirs falls bush.

In an attempt to find out what possible rewards one can make by becoming a bushfaller, my informants held that having a relative or even a friend overseas also means a change in one's life style. It also makes parents start dreaming of an eventual visit to the 'bush' one day, especially as Cameroonian youths (Nyamnjoh 2011: 707) studying or working abroad are more likely to invite their mothers to assist in housekeeping, cooking and babysitting. Now-a-days, it is more fashionable to invite both parents, particularly for graduation ceremonies. 'Upon return, these parents try to adopt different life styles and dress habits as a means to show off to their kin and folk who have not had the opportunity to go abroad. They show a lot of indifference and despise what is happening around them as a mark of self-esteem, fulfilment and self-sufficiency'.[140] This is

---

[140] Mbangnu interviewed 23/5/2011 at Altsu- Mankon

usually short lived as they soon readjust and fall back to their old habits.

Bush fallers are known for their excessive and extravagant spending every time they come back home. They carry out remittances to support relatives. Evidence from West Africa suggests that remittances are often allocated towards investment in land improvement in some cases, to crucial consumption expenditure in others, and also to pay hired labour in agriculture (Sender, Cramer and Oya 2005: 46). Bush fallers constitute nodes on which family members and friends depend and revolve around. They can change the living conditions of their family members. Some have scattered shanty houses and reconstructed mansions for their parents. Others carry the burden of sponsoring relatives and siblings; and so many people depend on them for their daily bread and survival. In the same light, most socio-economic activities in their home land are largely determined and influenced by bush fallers. Those of them who have 'made it' out there have established lucrative businesses for relatives. In fact, the successes, changes and social transformations impacted on those at home by relatives coming from the Diaspora constitute what can be termed the 'bushfalling miracle':

> Migration has brought about significant increases in the life chances of these African immigrants. Their incomes have increased relative to what they earned prior to migration. Living and working in the United States enables most of the immigrants to support extended families through regular remittances. Many of the immigrants often contribute to the socio-economic and cultural development of their hometowns and villages by supporting scholarship programs for students; building roads, bridges, schools, libraries, and recreational centres; and digging wells to provide safe drinking water for poor rural and village

communities. Some buy generators to provide much-needed electricity for their hometowns (Arthur 2010: 39).

This scenario is not applicable to all bush fallers. There are some who have failed to produce the expected results (i.e. sending the much needed money home, carrying out investment projects back home or changing people's lives). Two categories of bush fallers have been identified. The first category is made up of those who despite their presence in the 'bush' do not 'make things happen'. They are either in asylum camps or are mere beggars and squatters. They therefore have nothing to offer or show off to their families and friends back home as they are barely surviving abroad. Some have raped the family fortunes to the disappointment of all. There are bush fallers who, for decades, do not even have the financial or immigration papers that would allow them to visit their families in the home land. Others have effectively lost contacts with home. For some bushfallers, the separation from home lasts a long time. Long separation from close family members and friends may affect the identities of these fallers as some of them may have to contend with a permanent settlement in the host societies. Memories of the home left behind may undergo significant transformations, sometimes beyond the recognition of the immigrants (Arthur 2010: 87). Yet some do not simply respond to calls from home any longer. In this category, every time a family member is seriously sick or dies, and the bush faller is informed, he simply says 'I have heard and I will see what I can do' and that will be the end of the story.[141] Life in the African Diaspora usually revolves around and is centred on the social and cultural happenings at home in Africa. The transnational spaces created by the African immigrants in the West are merely mechanisms and agencies for articulating and rationalizing the contents of the transnational cultural Diaspora communities (Arthur 2010: 80).

---

[141] Tanikvu A interviewed 20/10/2013 in The Hague Netherlands

Nevertheless, bush fallers highly influence the lives and actions of those back home. Although they are far away, overseas, events are determined and dictated by them. Evidence from Cameroon has shown that once a family member of a bush faller dies, the burial and funeral program is on hold, until the children or child living in the United States or Europe can be present (de Bruijn and Dijk 2012: 50); or send directives on the burial arrangements and funeral rites. It is the bush faller who determines when the burial should take place. He or she will be the one(s) to order that the corpse be put in the mortuary after all (s) he/they will be the one to settle the bills. Those at home generally shift their responsibilities to the bush faller. The bush faller is expected to incur all the funeral expenses. Each time such an occasion arises, the first question is: what has the son or daughter, sister or brother from abroad said? In sum, the rest of the family members look up to the bush faller(s). For funerals that are done in church, sometimes, eulogies and tributes are offered or fabricated on behalf of the bush faller and read during the funeral service in church. In order not to lose contact and to keep surveillance on the progress of the burial rites and also to participate live from a distance, the bush faller makes phone calls in church or in the compound to find out how the burial is proceeding.[142]

For funerals, the mobile phone has become an indispensable tool for keeping in contact with people who are at distance, either in the village or abroad (de Bruijn, Nyamnjoh and Angwafo 2010: 278). 'People are even happy and excited receiving phone calls by the grave site from relatives abroad'.[143] Speaking of mobile phones, everyone at home negotiates and expects a phone from a relative in the Diaspora. The phone eventually does not only affirm stronger long-distance family ties and relationships (de Bruijn, Nyamnjoh and Angwafo 2010: 279), but also provides access

---

[142] Tanikvu A interviewed about the father's funeral 20/10/2013
[143] Tse Michael interviewed 2/3/2013 at Ntambeng-Mankon

and opportunities to keep closer contacts for negotiations and channelling of demands. The continuous demands and pressures from families have made some migrants see Europe as a place where one can escape from the family, and seek refuge and freedom away from the demands of the family and socio-cultural engagements, which are sometimes cumbersome and hinder personal development. In fact, the excessive demands of their families inhibit people from saving and planning for the future (Nyamnjoh, 2008: 139).'The inability to fulfil these demands and expectations is contrary to the initial feeling before departure from the homeland that 'things' would be easy out there in Europe'.[144]

Nevertheless, bush falling has changed many things, not least of which, the social relations in Cameroon. It has become a means through which people negotiate social space and belonging. The example of the funeral is therefore not only an opportunity for the faller to appropriate the bushness and display wealth, but also emphasizes ones belonging and the reaffirmation of social ties (Geschiere 2005a: 47; de Bruijn, Nyamnjoh and Angwafo 2010: 280). In a sense, 'their migration serves as the rising tide that continues to lift up the spirits and lighten the burdens of hundreds of thousands of people, some of whom they know, many of whom they do not know or have no contacts with' (Arthur 2010: 39).

While most families tend to complain about the rising cost of living, the paradox is that they squander millions during funerals (*ibid*: 46). They always go for the most expensive coffins, and suits for the deceased. They hire a funeral service and conspicuous feeding is often done by a specialised catering service. The home of the deceased is often renovated, decorated and given a face lift to avoid disgracing even the

---

[144] For instance, Chinda Michael had promised to send money back to his mother immediately he gets to Holland but upon arrival, he was shocked to see that there was no job-not even the menial ones that he was sure of picking. At this juncture, I was difficult to explain to the mother why the much needed money never came as Michael had promised.

corpse of the deceased during the funeral ceremony. On their part, the family members are expected to appear in a special uniform or scarf. If the deceased is a husband, the wife must appear in an expensive white fabric and sit in the front seat of the funeral van; what Geschiere (2005a: 46) has referred to as 'the ostentatious display at funerals'. This accords her the stigma and status of a widow and she is expected to advertise her widowhood for some time before she engages in new forms of social relations. During this period she is supposed to relinquish and renounce her status as a married woman and learns to accept the status of a widow. 'Keeping corpses in the mortuary is now acceptable and getting a corpse from the mortuary is usually accompanied by huge crowds of relatives and friends. Often, the size of the crowd reflects the status of the deceased and what extravagances and lavishing one can expect at the funeral'.[145]

Attending funerals is not necessarily linked to one's social ties or belonging to the deceased's family, but the lure that there will be abundances to be consumed. 'They prefer to attend funerals that will soon become the talk of the town for weeks or months and the memories will live for long' (Geschiere, 2005a). These are memories of the calibre of people who attended the funeral to memories of conspicuous display of wealth and extravagances. Sometimes a family tries to give a false impression of its self by going into debt to give one of theirs a befitting burial even if during the life time of the person a family member never assisted paying the hospital bills. This scenario has been captured by one of Cameroon's musicians, Loh Benson. Generally, it has become a norm to hold a funeral service in the most renowned churches even if the deceased was never a convert, baptized or attended church services.

The bush faller becomes an epicentre where all relations radiate and oscillate to and fro. 'Because of the anticipated

---

[145] Akwen Quendoline interviewed 12/7/2013 at Ntambeng Mankon

social and material benefits that people could gain from bush fallers, most families and people have tended to regard bush fallers as demi- gods. Bush fallers are treated with much preference and reverence every time they get back to their communities.[146] This is sometimes transcended in the honours and awards that are conferred on them. They may be rewarded with neo traditional titles which constitute symbolic capital that is sustained by 'the conspicuous display of decorum and accompanied by public respect' (Nyamnjoh 2011: 709).

There is usually great anxiety and expectations from bush fallers. They spend lavishly on beer and also offer a lot of gifts. Most ladies prefer getting married to a suitor they have never seen so long as he is a bush faller. In fact most ladies in Cameroon claim to have their fiancées overseas. And so are ladies that have refused their potential husbands in preference for the fallers, a situation that Nyamnjoh (2011: 707) describes as 'sweeping a girl off her feet to the detriment of an established relationship'. As the case of Binwi demonstrates, people sometimes prefer to abandon well paid jobs at home in preference for less paid (menial) or inferior positions overseas. Less paid jobs may include prostitution, taking basic computer classes, and being a cleaner. But often fallers conceal the real things they do and prefer to talk of fictitious but prestigious jobs such as being a medical doctor, engineer, or even being a Professor (*ibid: 710*) as Mamuzam's case has revealed .

As I indicated before, I would like to present another encounter involving bushfalling where the fallers were victims of their bushness. This epic concerns Michael (a pseudonym), a Cameroonian who migrated to the Netherlands in 2004. During one of his frequent visits to Cameroon, Michael met Swiri at Malingo Junction in Buea. The latter had just graduated from the Department of Sociology and Anthropology at the University of Buea in 2009 and was engaged in a computer training program not only as a way of relieving herself from

---

[146] Acha Bonaventure interviewed 23/2/2014 at Mbingfibie- Mankon

unemployment and boredom, but as a means of acquiring computer skills that could improve her chances of getting a job.

It was in one of the cyber cafes at Malingo Junction that Michael was introduced to Swiri by his junior brother who was a customer to this cyber café and was very familiar with Swiri. Michael offered Swiri for a drink and she accepted. It was during their drinking extravaganza that Michael declared his intentions for marriage. Thereafter, the two kept close contact and engaged in frequent and intense communication. For the sojourn in Cameroon, Michael lived with his parents in Douala (about 45 minutes' drive from Buea). Often, he would drive his mother's vehicle to Buea on weekends to meet Swiri and eventually Michael introduced her to his parents. She sometimes spent the weekends in Douala with the would-be husband's parents. Before Michael returned to The Netherlands, the traditional marriage rites and arrangements had progressed steadily and Swiri suspended her computer lessons and moved to Douala to meet her mother-in-law. Through Michael's efforts, Swiri was admitted into a Masters programme in one of the Dutch universities. Michael incurred all the financial expenses for the 'wife 'to travel and meet him abroad'. At long last Swiri arrived at Schiphol Airport and accompanied by his friends, Michael picked up the wife that he has often advertised to his friends. For four years, Swiri hadn't a child on grounds of family planning and because of her studies. I will come back to that later.

In 2012, I was awarded a scholarship by the University of Leiden and the African Studies Centre for a postgraduate program. I went to the Cameroon Embassy at The Hague to introduce and regularise my status as a student as was customary. There I learned that under the auspices of the Ambassador, Cameroonian Diasporans shall be presenting New Year wishes to the Ambassador. On the day of the presentation of the New Year wishes, I met Swiri and her husband Michael. Michael was my acquaintance ever since I came to The Netherlands. I met him for the first time at a vigil in honour of a Cameroonian lady who lost her mother back home. After a brief introductory note, I left for the Banquet Hall. Michael appeared very happy when he introduced his wife to me.

But as it turned out, Michael was not only presenting New Year wishes to the Ambassador but also presenting his 'beloved wife' to someone that Swiri had been dating while in Cameroon. The event also provided a forum for Swiri to meet face-to face with her former boyfriend that migrated to The Netherlands in 2009. Since her arrival in Holland, Swiri had never seen her former boyfriend and the event provided an opportunity for them to exchange phone numbers and renew contacts as well. Ever since the event took place, there was a sudden change in Swiri's attitude towards Michael. She became very arrogant and never prepared meals for both of them. She started complaining about the husband about crimes he did not commit. On his return from work one day, Michael saw a letter on the dining table written by Swiri.

> Michael, I thank you very much for the assistance that you have given me for all these years but I will like to inform you that I cannot continue to live with you. I have found someone else to live with. I know this will hurt you but there is nothing I can do. I have kept the keys of the house with Vero so you can pick them from her. I wish you good luck.

After reading the letter Michael went straight to Vero (full name-Veronica) to find out what was going on. When he met Vero she told him that Swiri left for Nijmegen to meet her former boyfriend. Vero recounted how Swiri on several occasions had told her that she met Ade during the ceremony of the presentation of the New Year wishes and that this was her former lover who left for The Netherlands some time ago; and that she had no option but to go back to Ade, her ex-lover. Michael wept. This troubled him so much but that was the end of the story. It was only a few years later that Michael was able to contract a new marriage, this time with a Nigerian lady he met in Utrecht. These narratives and discourses reflect the difficulties, frustrations, ordeals and intrigues through which some bushfallers undergo in the 'bush'.

As I said earlier, the driving force for migration is largely economic. Starting a private business in Cameroon can be a nightmare because the country depends largely on collecting money from taxes as a means of raising revenue. The difficulty in establishing a business is also exacerbated by the fact that it takes several years to register a business in Cameroon. In such situations, it is not always easy for starters to contemplate going into business. No sooner has the business started than a heavy tax is imposed on the proprietor. Under this prevailing condition, the only alternative has been for most graduates and youths to turn their attention to overseas in search of a better life. 'They are attracted to what they consider 'greener pastures' in Europe at the expense of 'drought stricken pastures' in their homeland'.[147] That is how large Cameroonian communities have grown up in Europe and the USA (de Bruijn, Nyamnjoh and Angwafo 2010: 271). Statistics show that there are over 14,000 Cameroonians in Germany, about 5000 in the Netherlands 25,000 in Belgium and the largest, 40,000 are found in France. The figures for the USA have reached a souring number of over 880,000. The emigration of medical doctors who graduated from the Yaounde Medical School (CUSS) between 1995- 2005 to seek greener pastures overseas is alarming (Schmelz 2007) and the essence is well captured in the analysis below.

In the new global systems of economic and industrial production, African labour and migrants are fast becoming a

---

[147] Pa Mantobang Lawrence interviewed 3/8/2013 Mankon Palace

visible aspect of the international movement of labour and skilled workers (Arthur 2010: 36). According to the Cameroon Medical Association, 4,200 doctors, mostly specialists, are working abroad. That is 40% of Cameroonian doctors and 19% of nurses immigrated to selected countries between 1995 and 2005. Only 800, that is, 1 doctor for 10,000-20,000 inhabitants are left in the cities and in the distressed areas the ratio is 1 doctor for 40,000-50,000 inhabitants.[148] To sum it up, the most powerful, able and intelligent breeds of Cameroonians are all in the Diaspora struggling; sometimes under very harsh immigration and working conditions. Faced with these conditions they have been forced to adopt unorthodox tactics to survive.[149] As a part-time University Graduate in Cameroon, one is paid 40.000 Frs. whereas his classmates who now live and work abroad receive lucrative salaries and live comfortable lives.

It is even sad to note that some of the people trekked or swam through the Mediterranean Sea to get to Europe, and many of them have drowned in the process. Since getting a visa is not an easy task, some of the youths have resorted to consulting charlatans, totems and even witch doctors for charms so that they can obtain visas. Because of the belief that life is better overseas and not in Cameroon, people have become so xenocentric in their views and perceptions. Most Cameroonians believe that their own products, styles, culture or ideas are necessarily inferior to those, which originate elsewhere (Horton et al, 1984). It is the conviction that the exotic has a special charm that the familiar can never achieve. This is based on the glamour of the strange and faraway and the prestige of distant centres, supposedly removed from the sordid limitations of one's own community (Horton and Hunt,

---

[148] *Cameroon: Migration profile* (2009) http://www.iomdakar.org/profiles/content/migration-profiles-cameroon accessed 30th/01/2013

[149] Acquiring double nationality or getting married to partners from their host countries, for example.

1984). For example, most Cameroonians prefer and are happy to pay more for imported goods on the assumption that anything from abroad is better or 'original'. They are inclined to assume that they are superior because of the lure of the foreign label *(Ibid)*, and what applies to material products is also true of ideas and life-style. This has been captured by Nnam (2007: vii) as follows:

> It makes us appear to be ashamed of our culture, customs, and who we are. We pretend to be what we are not by trying to dress like foreigners, speak like foreigners, and even alienate our God in order to pray like foreigners. We become estranged in our motherland. We begin to see everything African as bad and inferior. African festivals, masquerades, folktales, proverbs, names, attires and even languages begin to disappear because they are diabolic, evil, backward, primitive, and uncivil.

Cameroonians adore, cherish and believe in European visitors more than Cameroonians from the Diaspora. In fact, they will stop at nothing even if it means leaving a better paying or lucrative job at home to become a sales person or a scavenger abroad. 'There is a tendency to think that all a young person needs is to make his or her way to Europe, and everything else will take care of itself' (Nyamnjoh and Page 2002). This 'bush falling' syndrome has stretched Cameroonians to the extent that millions of Francs (FCFA) is being extorted from candidates by middlemen or intermediaries who claim they can facilitate the acquisition of visas from the embassies for their compatriots. Some of these middlemen indulge in criminal acts such as crookery, trickery and what is now known as 'scamming' or '419'.[150] A report

---

[150] 'Nigeria 419 Scams' the number "419" refers to the article of the Nigerian Criminal Code dealing with fraud. The scam has been used with

from the US State Department, (Nyamnjoh 2011: 704) notes that:

> Cameroon's rank as one of the top sending countries for asylum cases is more an indication of the rampant fraud and corruption that exist in the country than of political repression or other abuses that might prompt someone to seek refuge in the United States. With every conceivable document readily available for sale (including, but not limited to affidavits, newspaper articles, membership cards and birth certificates), it is relatively easy for unscrupulous claimants to produce ample "evidence" of persecution which would appear genuine to adjudicators not familiar with country conditions.

Because of the high level of enthusiasm and possibilities of falling bush, families are willing to mobilize considerable sums of money for both their daughters and sons to go to bush (Alpes 2012: 94).

In another dimension, the mentality of Cameroonians is largely foreign. Football is the main spectator game in Cameroon, but sometimes one wonders why local football teams carry with them foreign names. In a typical inter village or quarter football tournament, there are often foreign names attached to local teams such as Manchester United, Liverpool F.C, Milano F.C, Ajax or Arab contractors amongst others. In major cities and even in the remote areas of the country, business titles take the same trend. Although in Cameroon, there are business titles such as Johannesburg, Hollywood, Denver, New Orleans, and Dallas snack bars. We also have the London Fashion Tailoring workshop, Manchester upholstery, New York Saloon, Dallas, and the San Paolo pharmacy amongst others. Young Cameroonians also take on the names

---

fax and traditional mail and is now used with the internet
http://en.wikipedia.org/wiki/419_scams Accessed 8/7/2014

of European footballers such as Zidane, Pele, Beckamp, Ronaldo and Maradona.

Although all the ten Regions of Cameroon have state owned radio stations and a television centre in Yaoundé, people in Cameroon believe fervently in news reports from foreign stations such as the British Broadcasting Corporation (BBC) and the Voice of America (VOA) as authentic and reliable. They also prefer to watch foreign television channels and consider news reports from the local media as lies or half-truths. Summarily, the average African young person is generally better informed about the West than about their own country (Nyamnjoh and Page 2002: 628).

Conclusion

Following Appadurai's (2008) *theoryscapes,* it is difficult not to be connected in the global flow of people, technologies, cultures, finance and ideas. As the saying goes, the world has become a global village where people, cultures, technology and ideas flow in a disjunctive manner. It is important to note are the reasons why Africans prefer to travel abroad. I have identified some of the factors that are compelling African youths to migrate. The argument here is not that Africans migrate to other countries and continents but the price they pay for engaging in such migrations, whether in their country of departure or host country. Presently, Europe is facing an economic crisis and even the menial jobs that were abandoned to African immigrants are being taken over by Europeans themselves.[151] This makes it difficult for African immigrants to raise money and to meet the demands coming from their homeland. What most African migrants had in mind about

---

[151] The Eurozone crisis in 2012 had adverse economic effects for the worst hit countries. For example, unemployment in Greece and Spain went up to 27% and Europe has also witnessed a lot of protests for the last three years especially in Spain, Portugal, Italy and Greece http://en.wikipedia.org/wiki/El_Dorado accessed 3/7/2014

Europe and the USA before they departed from their homelands is definitely different from what they have found in their host countries.[152] In this dilemma, they find it difficult to return to their home land considering that a lot of money was spent in the process of getting to the bush, and after acquiring the new status as bushfallers most of them prefer to remain abroad. It is even difficult for someone back home to accept that life is difficult in Europe or the USA even if the bushfaller tells the truth. In such circumstances, the bush faller either appropriates the *bushfallingness* or simply decides to avoid having contacts with family members or close friends in the home land.

I have also highlighted the social and economic impact of these migrations for the individuals, families and even to the state. Research on capital flow has shown that the volume of remittances from the Diaspora supersedes Western aid to Africa in recent years. Many bushfallers contribute towards the development of their homelands through economic investments and social schemes. Despite the successes and achievements of bushfallers, they are, in the first place, detached from their homeland and are sometimes even forgotten by their kin and kith. This social detachment also leads to the breakdown of family ties and social harmony.[153] There are instances where a son or daughter has not been physically able to participate in the burial rite of a loved one because of several reasons that may prevent him or her from going back to the homeland for the burial. The consequences of not being able to bury ones relative are multifold. It

---

[152] Marcellus is a Cameroonian living in The Hague-The Netherlands (interviewed 16/4/2014) Before leaving Cameroon in 2010, he had promised sending money to his money

[153] Samuel has been leaving in the Netherlands for fourteen years and his wife Rose joined him from Cameroon in 2009. Their three children were delivered in Holland and have never been to Cameroon. Samuel's parents only knowing these children by name, photographs and they children do not know them. They belong to the same family but the social and emotional attachment is not there because of the separation.

becomes even more burdensome when a family has to bring back the corpse of a relative from the bush. The financial and social stresses with regards to transporting corpses from abroad are enormous.

I also note that Africa and Cameroon are suffering from the brain-drain syndrome (i.e. most of Cameroon intelligentsia now live and work abroad). In the early 1970s and 80s, the government of Cameroon instituted a scholarship scheme for young and talented Cameroonians to study abroad and through this scheme, hundreds of Cameroonians were trained in some of the most prestigious European and American universities. Unfortunately, not even 15% of those who received government scholarships have returned to Cameroon because of lack of jobs or an enabling environment to create jobs. Today the government has stopped offering foreign scholarships to its citizens. In a way, the scholarship program facilitated the migration of its intellectual class to the affluent countries. In this light, the technological revolution that the government thought these awardees would bring to the country upon completion of their studies has never been realized. To encourage most of them to return to the homeland, the government should be able to provide incentives for investments to the Diaspora. Unless this strategy is adopted, most of the Cameroonians in the Diaspora will only be virtual citizens, after all many of them have acquired the nationality of their host countries.

Chapter 7

The 'Anglophone Problem' and Cameroon Bilingualism

One of the thorny issues that have been a source of trouble and menace to the social harmony of Cameroon is what has become the 'Anglophone Problem'. That the Cameroonian post-colonial state's nation building project has failed is clearly evidenced by the fact that nationalist feelings are still rife in Anglophone territory more than forty years after reunification with Francophone Cameroon (Jua and Konings 2004: 2). Ethnic/linguistic differences between the Anglophones and Francophone segments of the population as well as tribal differences continue to be a potential source of friction in the country. Furthermore, one of the reasons that Anglophone Diasporans give for their migration is the outright marginalisation and discrimination by the Francophones. This explains why a majority of the members of the Anglophone pressure group-Southern Cameroon National Council (hence-SCNC) are in the Diaspora.[154] At the beginning of this work, I explained that what is now known as Cameroon emerged from the ashes of colonial rule. The entire territory was initially annexed by the Germans and known as Kamerun. Unfortunately, during the First World War, Germany was defeated by the allied forces. Consequently, their overseas territories including Kamerun were ceded to other countries. Following the defeat of Germany by the allied forces, the German Kamerun territory became a United Nations Trust Territory. Consequently, the UN arbitrarily divided the territory between the French and the British. France administered the French Cameroun territory while Britain administered the

---

[154] SCNC groups exist in almost all European countries and use the social media to mobilise and galvanise support for the 'Anglophone course'.

Southern and northern Cameroons. (Nyamnjoh and Awasom 2008, Percival 2008; Jua and Konings (2004: 4) note that:

> ...the partitioning of the territory into French and English spheres had some significant consequences for future political developments. Importantly, it laid the historical and spatial foundation for the construction of Anglophone and Francophone identities in the territory. The populations in each sphere come to see themselves as distinct communities, defined by differences in language and inherited colonial traditions of education, law, public administration and world view.

In 1961, the UN decided to organize a plebiscite in the Northern and Southern Cameroons to enable the people to freely decide with whom they would like to attain independence. The two alternatives were proposed and the people of the Southern Cameroons voted to join La Republique du Cameroun, while Northern Cameroons decided to join the Federal Republic of Nigeria.[155] There were only two alternatives-joining the Federal Republic of Nigeria or La Republic. There was never a third option of having self-independence. The UN resolution, after the plebiscite, stated clearly that the Southern Cameroons would attain statehood and independence by uniting with La Republique Du Cameroun as equal partners. Confronted with only two alternatives, the Anglophones had no choice but to choose between what Jua and Konings (2004: 4) and Njeuma, (1995)

---

[155] See Le Vine, (1963, pp.281) the results of the plebiscite in the Southern Cameroons were received with joy in the Republic (East Cameroon) and Foncha became the hero of the hour. In contrast, the republic took the results in the Northern Cameroons with grace. It claimed at the UN that Great Britain and Nigeria had exerted undue pressure on the Northern electorate by bringing 700 armed Nigerian policemen to coerce the voters into voting for Nigeria

have qualified as the 'lesser of the two evils'-uniting with the already independent Cameroon.

The constitutional arrangement that emerged during the Foumban Conference stood for a Federal system of Government. Contrary to Anglophone expectations, federalism did not result in an equal partnership of both parties, or in the preservation of the cultural heritage and identity of the Anglophone minority (Konings 1999: 181). From 1955, politics in the Southern Cameroons was championed by two main parties the Kamerun National Democratic party of J.N Foncha and the Kamerun National Congress of E.M.L Endeley. Although a new party has been created, Dr Endeley was still very popular in the Southern Cameroons. This explains why he won in the 1957 elections organized in the territory to transform the territory from a quasi-region to a full autonomous region within the Eastern region of Nigeria. Endeley's fame was to be short lived, however, as his political opponents who were all from the Bamenda Grassfields and who understood just how close their people were to tradition decided to use this strategy to discredit the Endeley regime (Ngum 2013: 3). In the ensuing politics, Bamenda Grassfielders seeking to unite with French Cameroun gave Endeley several bad names that made him unpopular. Some said that he got money from Obafemi Awolowo.[156] The best opinions would have come from Dr. Endeley whose party had lawyers at that time but their performance was dismal. The KNDP did not take Endeley seriously and relied on the British who were not enthusiastic about an independent Southern Cameroons.[157]

---

[156] Obafemi Awolowo was a Nigerian nationalist, political writer and statesman. He was the leader of the opposition in the Federal parliament to the Tafawa Balewa government from 1952- 1963. During this period, British Southern Cameroons was represented in the Eastern House of Assembly in Nigeria, so it was thought that he was supporting Endeley's position that British Cameroons should join Nigeria.

[157] Interview with Fon Angwafo III, Fo Mankon and representative of the Ngemba Area at the Foumban Conference in 1961

Before the Foumban Conference that same year, a meeting took place in Mankon at the Mankon Community Hall under the chairmanship of the KNDP leader-Dr J.N Foncha who had been elected Prime Minister in 1959. He too had discussions with Ahidjo-the President of the independent La Republique du Cameroun on the matter of reunification. Foncha's government convened that meeting in Mankon. The prime objective of the Foumban Conference was to create a one state federation but while in Foumban the KNDP government did not emphasize the idea. The Southern Cameroon delegation was not united because the results of the plebiscite had divided them. Before moving to Foumban, there was already a division among Foncha and Endeley as Fo Angwafo notes, 'I noticed that there was a rife between Endeley and Foncha and we (Southern Cameroon Delegates) did not have confidence in ourselves and so we came back even more divided then ever'. At the end of the Foumban Conference there was an agreement for two Federated states in lieu of one federated Republic. Unfortunately for the Southern Cameroon delegates, there were no lawyers to present the nature of the federation firmly on the side of Anglophones but Ahidjo had the assistance of French legal experts (Le Vine 1962). If only the KNDP and KNC had gone to Foumban in block the results would have been different, at the very least better. [158]

Today many young Cameroonians think that the Anglophone option for reunification in 1961 was wrong but given the prevailing circumstances at the time; Fo Angwafo has a contrary view as he maintains that if the plebiscite was to be re-conducted today, he would still stand for reunification. He contends that Anglophones have benefitted immensely from the reunification such that it does not matter what opinions people have in retrospect. To him:

---

[158] Konings 1999,pp183

The situation might have changed but remember six years after the plebiscite the Nigerian civil war started. I shiver as I imagine what could have befallen us if we were part of an independent Nigeria during that war. Looking back, we had precious little. I went to school in Nigeria and I think I was one of the first to go there. There were no roads, no secondary schools in Southern Cameroon except St. Joseph College Sasse. Today we have many schools; primary schools, vocational centres; and even universities. The level of enlightenment is incomparable.

Certainly, the British did not support Southern Cameroonians the way that the French supported French Cameroon. They felt that they could not stand as an independent country. Though there was a third party, Kale's Kamerun Peoples Party, that thought that Southern Cameroons (S.C) could become an independent country (the often talked of third option), the British would not trust Anglophones with this option to run business. Fo Angwafo sees the situation as oranges and apples that cannot be compared. This was clearly the best choice they made, although there are dissenting voices about the marginalization of Anglophones.

Therefore in sharing the national cake proportionately, one third would naturally go to the Anglophones and two third to the Francophones. In the present dispensation, Anglophone's one third is not even there.

I think Anglophones deserve more and the French majority is conscious of that. If tempers had flared we would not be addressing reunification the way we are today. Yet Anglophones have been selfless and patient in spite of the shortcomings and have been steadfast on the course. This commitment to the ideal of the Cameroon union is the defining character that the Anglophone leadership brought to the foundation of a great Cameroon.[159]

The federation actually existed and operated until 1972 when this was abrogated and a unitary state was put in place (Ngum 2013: 12). 'Biya went as far as possible to legalise Ahidjo's turpitudes with his problematic and provocative change of name of the country back to "Republic of Cameroon" using law N° 84-1 of 4th February 1984' (Asonganyi 2013: xxvi). This was the beginning of an unholy alliance with La Republic du Cameroun. Since then, many people in Southern Cameroons saw this as a ploy to undermine state institutions and authority. '...the constitution which I have held and preached as the supreme law of the land is in many respects being ignored or manipulated'[160] Since 1972, things have never been the same as Anglophones have seen themselves systematically being marginalized, assimilated and exploited by the Francophone dominated state in the post-colonial state (Jua and Konings 2004: 3). To paraphrase (Enloe 1979: 13), most Anglophones relate to the larger Cameroon society not as participants who belong but as resources to be exploited and administered. Foncha has expressed his frustrations in the following excerpts. '...I had become an irrelevant nuisance that had to be ignored and ridiculed. I was to be used now only as window dressing and not listened to. I am most of the time summoned to meetings by radio without any courtesy of my consultation on the agenda.' Thus, a nation state which leaves certain sectors of the populace on the peripheries of irrelevancies to be discarded or mere resources to be exploited are in fact only states masquerading as nation states (*ibid*: 5). This has been shown through appointments and the distribution of the national wealth. Some have blamed the

---

[159] Fo AngwafoIII interviewed November 2013
[160] See Foncha's resignation letter of 9th June 1990 addressed to Paul Biya

leaders of Anglophones, especially J.N Foncha and S.T Muna, for betraying the Anglophones in exchange for sinecures from the Francophone. Others have argued that the late President Ahidjo was very dishonest and outwitted his Anglophone counter parts.

Anglophones have continued to think that they were co-opted to be used as mere objects or appendices for references. The gradual co-optation of the Anglophone political elite into what Konings (1999: 183) refers to as the 'hegemonic alliance' and the autocratic nature of the Ahidjo regime largely explain why they did not resist the abolition of the federation in 1972. In truth, Anglophone leaders also contributed to the unmaking of the federal system in Cameroon. In support of the views of Jua and Konings (2004: 4), I maintain that this was caused by greed and the quest for power which brought about internal divisions among the Anglophone political elite. While Foncha's complaints are legitimate, he too has been blamed for not having consultations with his own people-Anglophones on the way things were moving for all the time that he was in the system. Apart from erasing the federation, the unitary state succeeded in removing all those who mattered in West Cameroon politics. The wave of dismissals started with Augustine Ngom Jua who, with the complicity of S.T Muna, was dismissed and replaced with S.T Muna by Ahidjo (Ngum 2013: 5). Again, after the federal system was abolished, J.N Foncha was co-opted as the Vice President of the United Republic and by 1966; he was the Vice President of Ahidjo's Cameroon National Union Party - CNU.[161] A few years later, it was the turn of J.N Foncha as he was overthrown and Muna became the Vice President. Under Ahidjo, S.T Muna served as the Speaker of the National Assembly for over 18 years. Until they retired from these positions, none of them raised a finger

---

[161] See Konings (1999:183). In fact rivalry among West Cameroonian leaders provided an excellent opportunity for Ahidjo to dissolve West Cameroonian parties and to create a single party in 1966.

about the marginalisation and ill-treatment of Anglophones. Foncha and Muna lived their lives and educated their children in Yaoundé amongst Francophones. Their children attended some of the best schools in the world. So many people have argued that at the time of the plebiscite that there were no educated people or legal minds in Southern Cameroons. I differ here; I argue that Endeley was already a medical doctor at the time and Z.M Abendong was a political scientist.[162] Rather, I feel that the Anglophones went to the Foumban conference divided and so gave undue advantage to the Francophone. Competition for power, personal interest and aggrandizement between competing Anglophone elite especially Foncha, versus Muna and the Jua/Muna imbroglio gave the leeway for Ahidjo to manipulate (Ettahgondop 2004; 118-127). On the other hand, it was the inability of Foncha and Endeley to come to an agreement on the future of Southern Cameroons fanned by tribal affinities, especially between the Bamenda Grassfields politicians and the coastal inhabitants (Ngum 2013: 19). The internal rankling, selfish interest and personality clashes among Anglophone politicians played to the advantage of the Francophones, particularly Ahidjo to step in and create a semblance of order (Ettagondop 2004: 130;Ngum 2013: 19).

I do not have the space here to belabour the Anglophone problem. The truth is that the structural arrangements in Cameroon seem not to favour certain people because of their belonging to the Anglophone sub group. The situation in Cameroon is rather different and unfortunate. The partitioning of the territory into an English and a French sphere had some consequences because it brought about the construction of Anglophone and Francophone identities- the Anglophone minority and a Francophone majority that would affect the structure and distribution of power resources and

---

[162] He was the Secretary General of KNDP and was shot in an ambush in the West region during the UPC insurgence

opportunities between the two communities in the post colony (Konings and Nyamnjoh 2003; Jua and Konings 2004: 6). An Anglophone identity is experienced in everyday space in Cameroon. This has been captured by Jua and Konings (2004: 14) who note that:

> Anglophones are daily reminded of their identity and homeland in language, in individual and collective experiences, and in stereotyping. They tend to perceive themselves as different from Francophones and are equally categorized and treated as 'others' by Francophones, manifest already in the constant use of 'we' and 'they' in everyday speech for designating or delineating each other's homeland.

For instance, despite the fact that Cameroon has over 250 ethnic groups, the English speaking Regions of the northwest and southwest have often been intentionally lumped together and identified as an ethnic group. This discriminatory practice is transcended into reality in the way ministerial appointments and senior officials of the state are appointed. While the Beti, Ewondo and Fang ethnic groups of the Centre and South Regions have over 20 strategic ministerial offices, the English speaking; seen here in terms of Regions (northwest and south west), with over 100 ethnic groups are usually 'given' only a few sine curial ministries as they often play second class fiddle to national issues. In order of importance, Anglophones are continuously being excluded within the power structures of the country as evidence shows that the President of the republic, President of the Senate, President of the Supreme Court, the Speaker of the National Assembly, Paul Biya, Niat Njipenji Marcel, Alexi Dipanda Mouelle and Cavaye Jibril are all Francophones respectively. It should be noted that the Prime Ministry is just an office under the executive arm of government (Presidency of the Republic).

153

It would seem that there are certain administrative responsibilities that cannot be assigned to a Cameroonian from the northwest and southwest regions of the country. I think of positions such as the Secretary General at the Presidency, Minister of Territorial Administration and Decentralization, Foreign Affairs, Armed Forces, and National Education. No Anglophone has ever been in charge of the National Police Force. No Anglophone has ever been Ambassador to France, let alone to Nigeria or South Africa which are English speaking.[163] No Anglophone has ever been at the helm of National Oil Refinery (SONARA) although it is located in the heart of Limbe which is an English speaking region. Anglophones seem to be only good as assistants since all the posts mentioned above are considered no -go areas to them.

I think the Foumban constitutional talks did not address the nature of the Federation adequately and that is why some feeling of unfinished business lingers. Two cultures, two official languages, two systems of government led to two federated states. Unfortunately, no mechanisms to streamline and emphasise equity as a solid constitutional foundation at that defining moment were agreed upon (Fo Angwafo interviewed November 2013).

The system has conditioned Cameroonians to think in French and act in French. French is used in Cameroon as a language for Anglophone domination, subjugation and marginalisation. It is even seen by many Anglophones as a language of corruption, greed, favouritism, division, bribery and deception. It is not a language for development as even the children of French power brokers in Cameroon attend English-speaking schools since they have been compelled by the forces of globalisation to accept English as the language of

---

[163] The marginalisation of Anglophones See www.cameroononline.org accessed 23/5/2014

international commerce and diplomacy. Yet in Cameroon, they use French mainly to suppress Anglophones and make political and economic fortunes out of the system. This has been summarized by Foncha in his resignation letter[164] as follows:

> All progress of employment, appointments, etc. meant to promote adequate regional representation in government and its services have been revised or changed at the expense of those who stood for truth and justice. They are identified as 'Foncha-man' and put aside.

In the Netherlands, English is a compulsory second language and the Dutch switch from English to their own language with ease. Nobody complains or sees the complexities of learning the two languages. In Cameroon it is the reverse; French and English are found on the educational curriculum and also claimed as the two official languages of the Republic but rarely do pupils or students speak the two languages with the proficiency that their Dutch counter–parts would .You may ask why? The answer is simple; Francophone children, in particular, have been conditioned by their parents and the system to know that they are superior to their inferior Anglophone compatriots, and that French is the administrative language in the country so it is not necessary to learn English.

Similarly, Anglophones have been forced by the system to learn that they are an inferior minority and that English only comes second regardless of whether or not they learn French. So any Francophone who condenses from his superior

---

[164] See Foncha's resignation letter of 9th June 1990 addressed to Paul Biya, Head of State and National Chairman of the CPDM where Fon was his Vice. In this letter Foncha complained about the marginalisation of Anglophones, and also that all demands that he made for audience with his chairman to discuss issues were systematically turned down. Also, that memos that he submitted in writing on several important national issues were constantly ignored and he saw himself as an irrelevant nuisance that was being used only as a window dressing and not listened to.

position to learn English only does so if he or she expects favours from the inferior Anglophone or to continuously occupy the social space nationally or internationally that Anglophones would have occupied. In their daily lives, Francophones are very proud and boastful of their Francophoneness. This binary opposition is generating tensions and suspicions among the people. As Ngwa Martin[165] opines 'some Anglophones learn French because they want to uplift themselves from their inferior positions in order to get closer to their superior masters; and not necessarily because it is an official language.

The Anglophone problem in Cameroon is really complex with outright misrepresentations and contradictions. Of late, it is even difficult to distinguish who an Anglophone really is. There are a few questions that we need to ask. Is an Anglophone someone born in the southwest and northwest regions or one who speaks the English language? This raises ethnographic problems because those who migrated from French Cameroons during the era of the *Marquise* rebellions and settled in Southern Cameroons are neither seen as Anglophones nor are they considered as Francophones. Often, they are looked upon as what Nyamnjoh and Awasom (2008: 2) refer to as 'the 11th Province'.[166] Even Anglophones who speak impeccable French and have lived in Francophone Cameroon for years are constantly reminded of the fact that they are different (Jua and Konings 2004: 15). In Cameroon Anglophones constantly make reference to an Anglo Saxon

---

[165] He is a strong supporter of the Southern Cameroon National Council, a pressure group that is advocating for secession from the Present day Cameroon.

[166] Cameroon is divided into ten administrative regions (formerly known as provinces), 'the 11th province' refers to Cameroonians whose roots are in French Cameroon but grew up in English speaking regions of Cameroon and vice versa. These are Cameroonians who are not accepted as Anglophones and not also considered as Francophones and so face the double jeopardy of marginalisation within the system.

culture that they inherited, yet there is nothing like Anglo Saxon-like in their culture.

While not pretending that I can give an answer to these questions, I feel that the Anglophone problem is artificially created or invented by the powers that be in order to divide and rule the people according to their whims and caprices. Otherwise, how can we explain the fact that of the 58 Senior Divisional Officers, less than five come from the geographical region of Southern Cameroons?[167] The Betis with a population size that is less than some of the ethnic groups in the so called Anglophone regions have more than 35 Senior Divisional Officers. Worst still, Francophone *prefects* and *sub-prefects* posted in Anglophone Cameroon often do not speak a word of English and tend to disrespect the customs while relegating the Anglophone population to the position of subjects rather than citizens (Jua and Konings 2004: 15), just as Anglophone 'subversives' are regularly tried in Francophone rather than in Anglophone courts and are subjected to different treatment in Francophone cells than Francophone prisoners' (*Ibid: 15*). The situation is the same at the national oil refinery though situated in Southern Cameroons, all 24 recruited cadres employed in May 2009 were all Francophone; and this is the same with any other appointments or recruitments in the country.[168]

Furthermore, of the over 25 Army Generals, only three are Anglophones.[169] Usually, a few Anglophones are brought into the government as a smoke screen to please the people. These Anglophones who have the opportunity to dine with their 'superiors' are always quick to deny the existence of an Anglophone problem so long as they are allowed to pick the

---

[167] See list of Biya's appointments of new Senior Divisional Officers of 25/10/2012 www.crtv.cm accessed 27/10/2012

[168] This forced the South West Chiefs to mobilise for a strike action if the plight of Anglophones were not taken into consideration arguing that the refinery is found in Limbe; an Anglophone region and so they have a right to occupy top positions.

[169] They include, General Tataw, General Ivo, and General Tumenta

crumbs falling from the masters table. Francophones also refuse to recognise that there is any Anglophone problem because according to them, 'Anglophones freely voted to join la Republique du Cameroun and argued that the historical act of nation building was already sealed' (Nyamnjoh and Awasom 2008: 6). However, when they are booted out of office it is then that they admit and shout that there is an Anglophone problem. Within the party hierarchy, no Anglophone can become the Secretary General of the CPDM and a Francophone that of the SDF- the two leading parties in Cameroon. Tradition has shown that only a Francophone is capable of being the Secretary General of the CPDM and Anglophone the Secretary General of the SDF Party. This reveals that there is mutual mistrust and suspicion among Francophone and Anglophones. The systematic marginalisation of Anglophones and their institutions only seems to further radicalise this community through groups such as the Southern Cameroons National Congress (SCNC) (*Ibid: 5*).[170] Unfortunately, inter and intra Anglophone competitions have led to the emergence of several factions that have weakened their strength and legitimate claims to their marginalisation. Several splitter groups fighting for the same course have not yielded enough results.[171]

As I noted earlier, most Anglophones are reduced and seen as second class citizens, and are always appointed as assistants. As the Francophone says, '*Adjoints de ceci..., adjoints de cela...,*'-

---

[170] There are several splinter organizations fighting the Anglophone course from different fronts; sometimes with many and confused leaders. Some of these include the Cameroon Anglophone Movement (CAM), Southern Cameroon Youth league (SCYL), Southern Cameroons People Organisation (SCAPO) led by Dr Martin Luma, See Jua and Konings (2004) 'Occupation of public space: Anglophone nationalism in Cameroon' *Cahiers d'etudes Africaines* PP 14-51, Konings and Nyamnjoh (2003) *Negotiating an Anglophone Identity: A study of the politics of recognition and representation in Cameroon* Brill, Leiden-Boston PP 198-204

[171] For instance, there is SCAPO and they SCYL headed by Mola Litumbe and Nfor, respectively.

That is, 'Assistant for this…or assistant of that…The Anglophone Prime Minister is considered by most as a figure head and ever since Anglophones started occupying this post they have always been helmed by at least an assistant.[172] Given such treatment Anglophones have come to think of Cameroon more as a prison than a nation (Jua and Konings 2004: 3). As such, they prefer to be slaves elsewhere than to remain in Cameroon where there is out right discrimination (Tumi, 2006: 130).

After the launching of the SDF in 1990, it was embarrassing to hear the then Minister of Territorial Administration refer to Anglophones as *Biafra* (Krieger 2008: 28) and was even quick to say: *S'ils ne sentent pas Camerounais, ils peuvent aller allaires*. Translated to mean, *if they do not feel as Cameroonians, they can go elsewhere*. Also, Anglophones have always been reminded as *les enemies dans la maison* - enemies in the house (Jua and Konings 2004: 15; Konings 1999: 186). This has been re-echoed in another way by Foncha when he says that 'the constitutional provisions which promoted the Anglophone minority have been suppressed, their voices drowned, while the rule of the gun has replaced the dialogue which Anglophones cherish very much'. Because of the long standing phobia exhibited by Francophones towards them, most of the Anglophones feel that the arrest and imprisonment of one of theirs -Zachaeus Forjindam was a smoke screen meant to ridicule Anglophones. Most of them argue rightly or wrongly that the former Director of *Chantier Naval* did not deserve to be arrested given that he was the one who raised the revenue at the Port from less than 400 million to several billion in less than two years. 'They have gone further to contest his arrest and see it as a ploy by the powers that be to show to the

---

[172] When Achidi Achu became Prime Minister on the 9th of April 1992, the government instituted the idea of assistant Prime ministers and to date all Anglophone Prime ministers have had an assistant- sometimes more than one assistant.

international community that not only Francophone and especially Betis, Ewondos and the Fang embezzle state funds.'[173] In truth, of all those arrested for embezzling state funds, over 95 % of them come from one ethnic group alone. (See table in chapter 3 on list of embezzlers) Whichever side of the divide you may choose, it is clear that something is wrong somewhere in the Forjindam affair.

Cameroon and Canada have often been heralded as the only two bilingual countries in the world where French and English are considered official languages. Unlike in Cameroon where the minority is Anglophones, Francophones are in the minority in Canada. Since in both countries there is a semblance of majority and minority dichotomy in terms of linguistic divide, one might have expected the same (ill) treatment by the majority over the minority in both countries. Bilingualism in Cameroon and Canada appear to be very opposite in terms of conception and practice. The Canadian bilingualism is refined and real while that of Cameroon is crude and artificial. Firstly, the legal system of Canada recognises the unique characteristics of the Quebec French speaking Province. They are seen as equals and are protected by the law. It is a quasi-federal system which gives room for each state to administer its affairs within the ambit of the law. The rights of the Quebecois are respected and they have the freedom to live as Canadians, not strangers. The educational system of Canada encourages all Canadians to be bilingual.

In Cameroon, however, the situation is very different. First, Cameroon bilingualism is on paper only and is preached over the media. 'Even most Cameroonians have admitted that it is the country that is bilingual, not the people'.[174] This has even been manifested by top government officials including the Head of state who incarnates state institutions. The usage of English is restricted and reserved for the Anglophone regions

---

[173] Kum Joseph interviewed 12/10/2013 in Wum
[174] Chi Ngang Interviewed 23/10/2013 at Ntingkag Mankon

of northwest and southwest and French is a language belonging to the other eight Francophone regions. A Francophone can become bilingual only if he has crossed over the Mongo River into the Anglophone regions; that is the only moment he remembers that there is another official language known as English.[175] If he has nothing to do in the purported Anglophone regions, he or she could live a successful public service career without uttering a word in English. I have also seen this in the public addresses and official communiqués that the President of the Republic makes. As long as the Head of state is not in the northwest or southwest, he cannot include English as an item in his speech but once he is on a state visit to these regions; that is when he attempts to read a few words of his speech in English.[176] Although it is not written anywhere in the constitution, experience has shown that it is forbidden for the Head of state to read one of his numerous speeches or portions in English if he is in the former East Cameroon now considered as a Francophone region. The President has never addressed the nation in English but has persistently done so in French and each time he does it those Anglophones who care to know the content of the speech have to wait for an English translation from Peter Esoka.[177] Anglophones have come to consider Esoka not just as a translator but as their own President. Perhaps for once, the best way for Francophones to understand what it means to be marginalised would be for the

---

[175] The Mongo Bridge is a symbolic Bridge that seperates Former East Cameroon from the Southern Cameroons.

[176] See contrasts in the languages used in the speeches delivered in Bamenda during the celebrations of the 50th anniversary of Cameroon Armed Forces in 2010, and the one in Buea during the 50th anniversary celebrations of independence on the 20th of February 2014 against the speech in Douala during the laying of the foundation stone for the construction of the second bridge across River Wouri. See also the 2013 New Year speech delivered in Yaounde in which he uses English in Buea and Bamenda and French in Douala and Yaounde.

[177] He is a veteran journalist on retirement and is currently the Vice President of the National Communication Council appointed by President Biya.

Head of state to deliver his traditional New Year address to the nation in English. This could potentially result in the Anglophones feeling a sense of belonging, possibly for the first time. By segregating his choice and use of the official languages in the different regions, Biya has been accused by the so-called Southern Cameroonians as the person instigating the Francophone/Anglophone imbroglio. Therefore; he has continued to define Cameroon in geography and not as a social entity. Consequently, he has become a wedge to the national integration that he is purported to be preaching.[178]

The government has created bilingual schools in all the ten regions and divisions of the Republic but one barely understands how these bilingual schools operate. Just as bilingualism operates at the national level, it is the same way that the bilingual schools function. One might have thought that in a bilingual school, children are taught in their second language; that is French for English speaking children and vice versa. That is not the case in Cameroon. From the way they operate, a bilingual school is made up of two: (French and English schools) functioning on the same campus. There is nothing that unites them. They have different administrative set ups. There is a Principal for the French section and another for the English section. In government bilingual schools the language of instruction for the Francophone remains French and for the Anglophones, English. Bilingualism in Cameroon is politicised and used as a bet to cajole the international community and make personal gains from it. Bilingualism in Cameroon can be likened to an uneasy mixture of water and oil that superficially appears to be well mixed whereas no mixture has actually taken place. That is why an Anglophone could complete from a bilingual school without knowing a word in French and vice versa.

When Pope Benedict IV succeeded Pope John Paul II, he visited Cameroon which was the first country he visited on the

---

[178] Akom Vincent Yuh interviewed 12/10/2013, Ntarinkon

African continent. It was alleged that he chose Cameroon because of the bilingual nature of the country which other African countries do not enjoy. During his four days visit (from 17th -20th of March 2009), Christian faithfuls poured in from all the regions of the country and even from neighbouring countries such as Nigeria, Gabon, Equatorial Guinea, Chad, and Congo. They were not only Catholic Christians but those of other denominations such as the Presbyterians, Baptists and even Moslems. For those who were not familiar with Cameroon, particularly those coming from English speaking countries and regions, most were definitely disappointed when all of the speeches were in French. Right from the Nsimelen Airport when the Pope arrived, only French was used. It is the Pope who was giving us lessons and reminding us of our bilingual nature. I wonder what lessons and impressions the Pope took back to Rome. The way Cameroon is run in all spheres does not reflect the bilingual nature of the country that the government has been preaching.

At the higher education level, the situation is no different, examination questions are not translated or they are translated by Francophones who are not proficient in English. For example, in the University of Yaoundé 1, bilingualism is reflected in the language of instruction of the lecturer and it is the student who has to choose which language to use. Francophones believe that they know English even more than the Anglophones. Generally, most communiqués in the country such as decrees, press releases and ministerial texts are written and spoken only in French. It is the duty of the Anglophone to translate or understand. When there is the opportunity for a translation they (Francophone) are always eager to translate for the Anglophones. In so doing, they translate poorly and what comes out is not even English. I came across a sign post in Yaoundé that was probably translated by Francophones. It reads; *Ministere de condition feminine*. The French translated it as *Ministry of Women Condition* instead of *Ministry of Women's Affairs*.

In all this confusion and their close associations with Francophones, it has even become fashionable for Anglophones to end official letters with bad English, for example: *Accept the assurances of my highest esteem.* There are many of these types of translations. A statement like this: 'Students matching during 11th February celebrations' is easily translated by Francophones as 'children defiling on 11th February'. Defiling translated literally as *defilé* (which means to match) in French. Discrimination is easily visible everywhere in Cameroon. Francophones use different font sizes on all official documents, letterheads, sign posts, communiqués and those in English must be in smaller characters even if there is enough space. This is to show that they are not afraid of the Anglophones and do not hide their hatred or feelings towards the Anglophones. They make sure that if you cannot read you must see that there is a difference between Anglophones (English) and Francophones (French). When I visited the United States, I was surprised to note that Spanish is America's second official language. I recognised that all the billboard messages on public notices did not have different font sizes.

The much heralded communication forum that took place from December 12-16, 2012 to examine the problems affecting the media landscape in Cameroon turned out to be a drama and an opportunity for the Francophones to further legitimate the marginalisation and discrimination against Anglophones. First, Anglophone media experts were never invited for the forum and one would have thought that most of the Professors from the Department of Mass Communication at the University of Buea should have been major players at the Forum. Of the few that attended, such as Charly Ndichia, the publisher of the Herald Newspaper, the Minister never allowed him to speak.[179] Worse still, all the documents at the forum

---

[179] Cameroon Calling of 9/12/2012

were in French. The Minister of Communication, Issa Chiroma, could shamelessly say 'it was an oversight and that measures were being taken to translate these documents in English'. As the French would say; *Mais a quelle l'heur?* –Too late .Let us imagine what it would look like if Minister Issa Chiroma attended an international conference and the documents and the language were in Spanish- a language he does not understand, only receiving the proceedings in French afterwards. How would he feel and what would he do with the documents at that stage? Whatever apologies the Minister offered, Anglophones continued to play the usual peripheral role as second class citizens. Encouragingly though, such actions further confirmed that Anglophones are mere footnotes in the country. As Jua and Konings (2004: 14) have noted, 'Anglophones are daily reminded of their identity and homeland in language, in individual and collective experiences, and in stereotyping'. Also, during the 2014 World Cup that took place in Brazil, all broadcasts and the transmission of matches carried out by CRTV were only in the French language.

In my sense, if Cameroon had developed a good policy for its bilingualism, the country would have reaped maximum benefits from it, especially in a world that has become a 'global village'. We would have been more exposed than some of the countries that are monolingual. We would have had the advantage of running most of the international organisations and to even perform better at international or national conferences. When I was a student at Ahmadu Bello University Zaria in Nigeria the students of the Nigerian Sociological and Anthropological Students Association (NSASA) undertook an international field trip to Ghana by land transport. I was the only foreign student among them. When we crossed from Lagos into Benin Republic, I was the one commanding, interpreting and translating information from the Benin and Togo Police and Custom officers to my lecturers and colleagues. At that time, my knowledge of French was really rudimentary. In fact, the best I could was to hear a few words, but I could not make a sentence in French without a dozen mistakes. This was only known to me and no one else in the bus. As I come from Cameroon, however, all the Nigerians thought that I must be bilingual and even an expert in the two languages. Given the confidence bestowed on me by the Nigerians, I could not reveal my true self. I accepted the position and the role I had to play. With the little knowledge that I had in French, I managed to translate until we went to Ghana and came back to Zaria. From that day, I was held in high esteem by my class mates and venerated as well. Whether my French was good or not, the scenario that I have explained above shows how bilingualism can, create social space and give respect.

For some time now, Anglophones have used different means and tactics to draw the attention of the government to their 'invented problem' but the government has never accepted the existence of the problem nor has it created a forum for dialogue. This shows how irrelevant the Anglophones are in the eyes of the Francophones. They pretend not to recognise the problem they have created and so the only way for Anglophones to vent their cry has been through organisations such as the Southern Cameroon National Conference (SCNC). Continuous government refusal to recognise SCNC and other Anglophone Movements has led to several confrontations and arrests of their leaders (Konings and Nyamnjoh 1997).

Interestingly, one gets confused in this system that has relegated the importance of national languages to the background for so long. Until recently, only official French and perhaps English were recognised despite the 200 or so other languages that exist in the country. Because of this neglect, most children grow up not knowing their own first (national) language, whereas experience has shown elsewhere that those children who know their national languages are sharper than those who do not. With the disorganised and disoriented bilingualism that is in Cameroon, the children end up not speaking or writing English or French, but a strange and complicated language that one cannot understand. Most often pidgin[180] has taken centre stage and most Anglophones think in their national language and then translate it into pidgin before writing or understanding the English version of the text. The final text, then, is burdened with all sorts of grammatical errors. In schools, buses, taxis, everywhere, even at conferences you can easily become irritated when people communicate in pidgin instead of English language.

Ironically, Cameroonian families, for the most part, attribute the speaking of English or French by kids as a sign of enlightenment or modernity at the expense of mastering a national language. Yet what these children speak is neither English nor French; a few examples may suffice, such as: *you are doing what? You are eating what? Is who? You are going where? You are where? You are sick?* How do we expect our children to speak or write good English when the teacher or instructor also speaks this type of English? Even some university professors and students are not spared and so it is a jumble and jungle of a strange language. If there are any Africans who would be first to lose their identity, it would be Cameroonians who are too quick to dissociate themselves from their roots out of an inferiority complex.

Language is very crucial in any human endeavour and apart from being a communication tool, it is the means through which culture and knowledge are produced, stored and even transmitted from generation to generation. It is the source of our identity and heritage. Once a language is not understood or distorted as is the case in Cameroon, what is produced, stored

---

[180] Pidgin is a lingua Franca spoken predominantly in the northwest and southwest regions of Cameroon, sometimes referred to as 'broken English'

or transmitted is also distorted and the sequence continues as we become alienated from English itself. Today, English is the business language of the world and most countries are now paying greater attention to it. Poor English or the wrong use of English in branding or advertising can convey wrong messages and can even cause serious problems of huge magnitude. If we want to learn English (variations not withstanding) we should do just that or if we like to Cameroonise English it should be standardized but not drifting away from main stream English as an international language.

A colloquium organised on the 18th of February 2014 to mark the belated 50th anniversary celebrations of Cameroon at the Amphitheatre 750 University of Buea, was a fertile ground and an opportunity for some Anglophones to speak their minds. One such person was Mola Njoh Litumbe who is also the leader of the Buea based Liberal Democratic Alliance (LDA) and frontline Coordinator of the SCNC. When he took the floor and stood in front of Prime Minister Yang (an Anglophone) he lambasted at the regime. "I am happy because the Prime Minister is here. I want to sound here to the hearing of even his ministers who are sitting here that there is and there has never been any reunification between Southern Cameroons and La Republique du Cameroon."[181] Another eloquent speaker was Professor Ephraim Ngwafor- a former minister and seasoned lawyer who also took to the rostrum to disclose that the reunification of Cameroon still leaves many wounds to be healed given that section 18 of the Foumban Federal constitution was violated at the time of referendum. Southern Cameroonians have therefore continued to look back in nostalgia, especially when they hear or see projects being

---

[181] Litumbe's argument is pegged on a clause of the United Nations charter which stipulates that any two entities which agree to come together must put it down in a treaty and register it with the United Nations Organisation. Failure to do this renders the agreement null and void. In this regard, Litumbe holds that the union therefore remains null and void since nothing of the sort was registered with the UN.

launched everyday in East Cameroon, but very little happening in Southern Cameroons. However, this is not new as J.N Foncha lamented during the All Anglophone Conference (AAC) that took place in Buea in 1992.[182]

All the roads in West Cameroon my government had built, improved or maintained were allowed to deteriorate making Kumba-Mamfe, Mamfe-Bamenda, Bamenda-Wum-Nkambe... inaccessible by road. Projects were shelved even after petrol produced enough money for building them and the Limbe sea port. All projects of the former West Cameroon I had either initiated or held very dear to my heart had to be taken over, mismanaged and ruined, e.g. Cameroon Bank, West Cameroon Marketing Board, WADA in Wum, West Cameroon Cooperative Movement Tiko Airport and Warf, Bali Airport Besongabang Airstrip. Whereas I spent all my life fighting to have a deep sea port in Limbe (Victoria) developed, this project had to be shelved and instead an expensive pipeline is to be built from SONARA to Douala in order to pipe oil to Douala.

To conclude, this chapter has examined the so-called Anglophone problem in Cameroon. I start by admitting that the people now known as Cameroonians occupied this territory in pre-colonial times with only fuzzy and fluid boundaries and it was because of colonialism that artificial boundaries were created and people became tied to a fixed territory. That notwithstanding, I argue that the Anglophone problem is socially constructed (imagined) by the Francophone power elite as a means to have control over the resources of the country at the detriment of the Anglophones. There is absolutely no

---

[182]Wache,F'onMountMaryAnglophonesstand20yearsattheAAC http://www.franciswache.com/2013/04/on-mount-mary-anglophones-stand.html#sthash.2LC4jAWA.dpuf
Accessed 18/03/2014. Also see Foncha's resignation letter of 9th June 1990.

difference between the cultures and people of the Western grassfields of Cameroon. That is, the West (Francophones) and the Northwest (Anglophones) are culturally and socially the same, while the Southwest (Anglophones) and the Littoral (Francophones) have the same or similar cultures and forms of social organizations. Yet, the northwest and the southwest that have dissimilar cultures are glossed together as an ethnic group thereby concealing the identities of the ethnic groups in these regions. With increase social mobility, it is even difficult to separate or distinguish an Anglophone from a Francophone in Cameroon especially among the younger generations. Pointing blame at this point may not solve the problem because most of the architects of Cameroon's reunification have died.

It is enshrined in the constitution that French and English are the two official languages in Cameroon but unfortunately there are no legal provisions to enforce these constitutional provisions. Additionally, bilingualism is an asset that if well managed, can become a very useful tool at both national and within the international arenas. It is important to note that the grievances raised by Anglophones are legitimate though the Francophone regime does not want to create a platform for dialogue. That notwithstanding, it should be clear that separation from the union is not the best option at this point in time. What we need are structural reforms that should guarantee and reflect the principles of equity, equality and representation so that every Cameroonian should feel free as belonging. As Fo Angwafo notes 'I think the union is more like a mixture of garri in abundance (two-thirds), and water (one-third) but we need to add more water to it. Though disproportioned, we complement one another and we continue to hope for the better'.

Chapter 8

Insecurity, Disorder and Moral Decadence

Cameroon like most of sub-Saharan African countries is characterized by insecurity, disorder and moral decadence.[183] In this chapter, I try to present a panorama of case studies of incidences of insecurity in the country and also show how state corporations create situations of disorder and insecurity. Most of the cases cited in this chapter are first-hand accounts and newspaper reports of events that took place in Cameroon between 2008 and 2012. I start with the Cameroon Electricity Corporation (hence AES-SONEL) which is in charge of providing electricity to the country. I also use the water utility company- Cameroon Water (hence CamWater) to show how monopolistic tendencies can generate disorder and anxiety. Several organisations and institutions have also been used to support my arguments. The following anecdotes elaborate the way these corporations operate and the animosity that exists between the officials and Cameroonians.

In Cameroon, electricity supply is the monopoly of the Cameroon Electricity Corporation (AES-SONEL).I have decided to concentrate on this company because of the importance of energy to the socio-economic and industrial development the country. Unfortunately, the company has not been able to provide enough energy that is always in high demand, despite Cameroon's energy potential which is only second to that of the Democratic Republic of Congo (DRC) with 55.2 gigawatts (See Business in Cameroon 2012). On the other hand, Cameroonians consider the services that are rendered by the company as inefficient and highly exploitative,

---

[183] Majority of the countries involved in fraud and other crimes are in Africa 'Nigeria'419'Scams' http://en.wikipedia.org/wiki/419_scams accessed 8/7/2014

a situation which has often resulted in hostile working relationships with their clients. Worse still, many people have not only lost their property as a result of intermittent power cuts, but others have lost their lives. I argue that because energy supply is the monopoly of one company, inefficiency and power cuts will continue to exist and the socio-economic development of Cameroon will be stunted to a greater extent. I present some of the issues that Cameroonians are confronted with as clients of AES-SONEL.

Between 28th September and 1st October 2008 and from 4th February and 5th 2009, the inhabitants of the Bamenda metro pole suffered from continuous blackout. For the entire period that there was no electricity there was no explanation from the officials of the electricity company. What was even more disturbing was the fact that the people were in black out and did not consume energy, they received exorbitant electricity bills which did not take into consideration the black outs. On the contrary, the bills were inflated. It should be recalled that in the city of Bamenda with a population of over 180,000 customers there is only one centre where electricity bills are paid. This does not only make it difficult for people to pay bills easily but it also takes a lot of time since the system is done manually. Again, bills are arbitrarily accessed and there are instances where sometimes a small family unit of two with three bulbs could pay more than an industrial plant. When a client realises that a bill was not properly calculated and tries to complain, the client is expected to pay the amount before the complaint can be looked into. The principle is to 'pay before you complain'. Unfortunately, once the bill is paid, the complaint becomes irrelevant because there will be nobody to look into it nor will there be a reduction in the next bill. Many Cameroonians have the feeling that because of the monopolistic tendencies of the AES/SONEL, their workers are very rude and insolent.

First of all, they consider providing electricity to the population as a favour and a privilege, not a necessity. Often, when costumers are unable to pay bills on time the electricity supply is disconnected. The issue is not the disconnections but the fact that one has to bribe a member of the AES/SONEL staff before the supply is reconnected. Even new subscribers are not free from these corrupt practices. They also struggle to have their electricity meters installed. What is more worrisome with the situation in Cameroon is that in most capitalist economies, the bourgeois uses all methods and strategies to keep the clients "comfortable'. I mean that capitalism strives on subtle politeness, but in Cameroon, it is the client who runs after AES/SONEL. The decision to have energy in one's house entails a lot of patience and one has to make several trips to the AES/SONEL office before they will be heard. Finally, you are compelled to bribe if you really need electricity. 'I paid for a meter three months ago and up till now, the meter has not been installed. I go to AES/SONEL office every morning and they keep telling me to go and wait. This is really frustrating'.[184]

As it is with other state corporations in Cameroon, AES/SONEL is not efficient in the way they operate. It is common place to find AES/SONEL poles that have been erected and abandoned to rot in the bush while the people wallow in darkness. At Ngulung neighbourhood in Mankon one can still find electricity poles that were planted in 1998, yet the inhabitants have continued to live without electricity. This is not unique to a particular region or area in Cameroon but it is recurrent all over the country. Also, electricity supply is not always constant and there is always shortage of energy. There are crucial moments in the country that AES/SONEL has embarrassed everybody including the Head of state. For instance, AES/SONEL has always made it impossible for

---

[184] Pa Forngang Alphonsus Interviewed 12/7/2013 at Atuazire Mankon

many Cameroonians to watch live football matches, some involving the Indomitable Lions. This is particularly annoying to many Cameroonians considering that football has become an obsession and people cannot forgo watching the Lions play.

In 2007 and precisely on the 19th of May when the President of the Republic was addressing the nation on the eve of the National Day, lights went off in Yaoundé. Light failure is a normal occurrence in Cameroon and AES/SONEL has a track record of frustrating Cameroonians during such national events. During the Japan 2002 World Cup match between Cameroon and Austria, the northwest region could not watch the match live from their television screens because lights suddenly went out a few minutes after the match started. In that frustration, the population got annoyed and in a spontaneous move, attacked the AES/SONEL office and installations at SONAC Street causing enormous damages. It did not take long after these attacks for the lights to be reinstalled. On several occasions that the population has reacted angrily, the AES/SONEL has often responded promptly by bringing the lights back to the people. The question one is begging to ask is: are the cuts intentional or why is it that each time the people attack their installations, they are able to provide energy instantaneously?

Apart from the fact that these incessant light cuts cause much discomfort to the people, it also provides a good moment for thieves to carry out their nocturnal activities. It had been observed that most bandits break into homes during light cuts, especially at night and this also fosters insecurity. On the eve of 20th May 2009, there was power outage at Ntarinkon. On that night, bandits broke into a store just opposite the main entrance into Ntarinkon Market looting property and carrying away the sum of 1.2million Frs. Again, at the Ntarinkon neighbourhood, a gang of armed robbers invaded the home of one Mr Akenji during power outage and in a struggle, the son was killed.[185] There are so many of such incidences where people have lost their lives and property as a result of attacks by bandits during power outage.

Accidental deaths caused by power outage have also been reported in different parts of Cameroon for the past years. For example, a family in Douala lost three of their members because of these light cuts.[186] As the story goes, these three children were left at home by their mother who went for prayers in the Ndokoti neighbourhood and there were no lights. The children decided to use a candle in their bed room where they were doing school home work. The candle was placed on top of the bed cupboard and after a while, the children fell asleep. While they were sleeping the candle fell and the mattress caught fire. That is how the children lost their lives. In another instance, high voltage sparked fire in a house where there were two boys and a child. The child was sleeping and the two other boys rushed out and tried to disconnect the meter. Unfortunately, they were electrocuted and they fell dead on the spot. The baby in the house was also consumed by the fire while all the family property was set ablaze. So many people have lost their lives and property because of AES-SONEL and light cuts. On the 1st of April 2014, the entire Municipal building of the Menji Council in Lebialem Division was razed by fire caused by a short circuit.[187]

Pertaining to insecurity, we present a tragic case where on the night of 28th September 2008, a gang of 50 armed robbers, or as they say 'pirates', attacked three supposedly reputable banks in Limbe and operated for four hours and left incognito with a heavy booty of 228 million francs.[188] Until this operation took place in Limbe, I have always boasted that Cameroon has a good and effective security network. In all honesty, I was

---

[185] Name withheld, but he was a youth and Sports instructor in Mbengwi

[186] Crtv News cast of 12/10/2010

[187] CRTV 6.30a.m newscast of 3/4/2014

[188] Cameroon Tribune No of September 30/2008

wrong to think this. The attacks in Limbe were not only a disgrace to Cameroon but also revealed the weaknesses of the security network. Secondly, it taught Cameroonians a lesson that even though the Police, Gendarmes and Soldiers parade themselves and boastfully harass their own citizens with arrogance, they are mere pimps. It was alleged by government officials that the pirates came from a neighbouring country. This was shameful and more doubtful to hear a Minister accuse a neighbouring country whose name he did not know. Interestingly, the said Minister revealed that the gang had hinted that they would carry out attacks on Limbe. Having learned that Limbe would be attacked the question is: why was the government not on the alert?[189] Many questions remain hanging. For instance, where was the naval force? What went wrong with the army camp at *Man or war bay*? The SGBC, Amity and BICEC banks are in the same neighbourhood and are well guarded by police/soldiers and/or private security guards. Why was it not possible for them to alert the military and police barracks? With the abundance of cell phones, why was not phone call made to the appropriate military and administrative quarters in Limbe? The residence of the Senior Divisional Officer (SDO) for Fako is not very far from where the attacks took place, and one keeps wondering why he was not informed.

In a press briefing, the Minister intimated that the operations took three to four hours. This was a long enough time for reinforcement to come from anywhere, even including Douala. The drive from Limbe to Douala is only 25 minutes. On 28th August 2008, Cameroon soldiers were attacked in the Bakassi Peninsular by an unknown assailant and some were killed. The government media claimed that the attacks were orchestrated by a neighbouring country. The national television said that eight of them were captured. Until the next day, no

---

[189] Minister Amadou Ali in a press interview on the incident made the declarations

statement or identity of those alleged to have been captured were revealed to Cameroonians. Again, one wonders whether, as citizens, Cameroonians do not have the right to know who these assailants were. Another issue was the persistent reference to a neighbouring country. This made the government appear ridiculous in public eye.

I do not want to imagine the implications of such statements within the circles of international diplomacy. Instead of admitting that the security of the state failed woefully, the government decided to accuse its neighbour. The question that the Minister never provided answers to was: who was this neighbour? The minister raised more complaints than answers and it was difficult to know to whom he was complaining. The fact that the International Court of Justice (ICJ) helped us recover Bakassi[190] from Nigeria does not mean that the court will become the security force of Cameroon. The Limbe incident was a matter of internal security and was supposed to be handled by the government of Cameroon. It was even difficult to believe the story that the gang came in from a neighbouring country. As I continue to ask, what made the government think that the pirates were not Cameroonians? Furthermore, how could the government vindicate the Cameroon military and administration from the Limbe conspiracy? The journalist who anchored the news claimed that there were 40 pirates but it was difficult to understand how the journalist arrived at the number 40. A few days after the Limbe conspiracy the Cameroon Radio and Television (CRTV) announced that ammunitions were uncovered in a small locality around Maroua. I use all these instances to show how porous the Cameroon security is and it is no surprise that there are increasing numbers of maritime attacks.

---

[190] The Bakassi Peninsula has been occupied by Nigeria for over a century and slow due the negligence of Cameroon, but finally the matter was settled at the International Court of Justice (ICJ) at The Hague. Also see Sama and Johnson-Ross (2006)

If Cameroon was a country where moral values were respected or where people admitted failure, the top brass security personnel would have resigned. They had nothing to offer at that juncture but their resignation letters. The Senior Divisional Officer, the Commandant, and the Regional Delegate for National security would, by now have resigned. On the contrary a few days later, these same military officers in Limbe received epaulettes and were promoted to higher echelons in the army. In South Africa Thabo Mbeki resigned as the Head of state and stepped down because of accusations over corrupt practices. In Cameroon, workers of the taxation department enjoy undue privileges that give them the opportunity to manipulate state finances as they like. The taxation system therefore is very porous and there are no checks and balances. The officials have access to money at any time and also the powers to waive taxes and penalties. They also have the powers to give moratorium to customers according to his/her whims and caprices. In well organised societies, these powers and privileges to carry out such a waiver is made possible through the courts to ensure effective control. In Cameroon, the waiver is entrusted to the hands of individuals who, due to lack of control mechanisms, often manipulate the figures of state finances.[191]

According to the Cameroon's Criminal Code that was enacted into law in 2007, freedom of expression is the rule.[192] That is, the criminal procedure guarantees bail and freedom to all Cameroonians without exception.[193] In several instances, this has never been respected, especially with regards to some persons of high social standing. The former Director of the Cameroon ship yard Chantier Naval-Zacheaus Fornjidam was arrested for having embezzled 980 million francs, while the

---

[191] See Supreme State audit Report of July 2014
[192] Before 2007, Cameroon operated with two bi-jural legal systems but in 2007, the penal code was harmonised
[193] See Cameroon penal code

investigations were still going on, the suspect requested to be released on bail but the bail was never granted. According to the penal code this was seen as unlawful because the criminal procedure allows even a murderer the right to be released on bail. In the same country, others are released on bail, while others are refused bail.

On the 26ᵗʰ of October 2008, someone wrote to *Morning Safari*[194] complaining to the Minister of Finance about the incessant disappearance of state property from offices. The complaint stemmed from the fact that very often, civil servants who are transferred to new stations take along office equipment such as photocopiers, printers, and refrigerators. In such instances, the old offices are left empty while the new occupant finds it difficult working without these important equipment. Another boss was noted to have taken a table fan and window curtains. The implications of such attitudes show that state property is not protected and secondly, there are no control mechanisms to ensure that things are in order. Thirdly, it also reveals the level of moral decadence in the country.

Strikes over unpaid salaries are also a common occurrence in Cameroon. For example, the workers of the Cameroon Postal Service (henceforth CAMPOST) went on strike for the non-payment of salaries for over 35 months on 27th October 2008.[195] Another reason was the fact that ever since they were recruited into the public service, their salaries were not harmonised and their indemnities on secondment were not paid at all. As a result of the strike, there was a disrupture in the distribution of mails and people could not carry out the financial transactions through CAMPOST since the offices were paralysed. It took the Minister of Finance two months to

---

[194] Morning Safari is an early morning English program which allows people to participate through phone calls and make contributions on topical issues in the country. It runs from 4.30am to 6.30am from Mondays to Thurdays.

[195] Some of them work without clearly defined statuses while most have not been integrated into the public service.

resolve the problem before the workers could go back to work. During this period of strike, the consequences were enormous. As we have said, it is very common for civil servants to embark on a strike action for non-payment of allowances or salaries.

Yet in another example, in February 2014, the Syndicate of Cameroon Railway Workers threatened to go on strike because they had not received their salaries for 30 months.[196] It bid ones imagination how workers could work for close to three years without salaries and still be expected to carry out their duties effectively. The question we may ask is: Can the Minister also go without his own salary for such a time?

I move away from strikes and present some instances were cases of criminality that were recorded in some parts of the country. I note that shootings and killings by thieves have been recurrent in Cameroon for the past two decades. In Mayo Kani, thieves killed the Commandant of the Gendarmerie in the neighbourhood of Maroua when he was on patrol searching for *coupe de route*. In Tiko, the Second Assistant Gendarme officer shot his own boss on 18th October 2012 and successfully escaped with the gun. To date, the culprits have not been arrested. These criminal activities depict a high degree of social disorganisation and this may range from not respecting simple traffic rules to throwing dirt everywhere.

In 2009, armed robbers invaded the National Police headquarters in Yaounde and successfully escaped. This was more disturbing because this particular incidence was carried out at the police headquarters and this signalled the total collapse of the security system of the country. Nobody would have imagined that thieves could think of stealing from this particular office, given that it is the heart of the police force that is supposed to have tight security. Yet they visited the head office and left in their usual way without being caught. My worry should not be the thieves anyway, what puzzles me is the fact that no police officer was aware just as it was in Limbe

---

[196] See Cameroononline.org accessed February 20th 2014

when the banks were looted. As if that was not enough, they also successfully entered the cabinet of the Minister of Territorial Administration and Decentralization and left incognito. The question remains, what is wrong with the security system?

The financial law in Cameroon allows for individuals to set up financial establishments, businesses associations, schools and even universities. According to the law, any individual or group of persons intending to operate a financial cooperative credit union must submit the necessary documents to the competent authority. The law stipulates that once this is done and a receipt is issued the person or group can go ahead with the presumption that the authorisation has been granted.[197] Following this logic, thrift and credit schemes grew in Cameroon like mushrooms. Unfortunately, most of them were not genuine and immediately after enough money was saved in such financial institutions, the officials left with the money to unknown destinations. Several instances abound in Cameroon where proprietors of such financial institutions disappeared with money. I cite here some examples of such cases that took place in Bamenda within the past ten years. In Bamenda, Zion Credit, NISCAM and BIZBANK were all established under dubious circumstances and collapsed after the founders robbed their clients of their finances. It was the same approach that the fake organization FAMM Cameroon used to deceive people and got away with a fortune. All of this happened within a framework of business laws that were acclaimed to be very good but these laws turned out to be very porous without any checks and balances.

In 2004 a petrol filling station at Nsam Efolan in Yaounde was set ablaze after a petrol tanker fell nearby. The inhabitants of this community rushed there to take the fuel to their homes. Unfortunately, a man lit a cigarette and there was a huge explosion that killed and wounded dozens of people

---

[197] See the OHADA Law of 2007

(Geschiere and Nyamnjoh 2001: 163). The government decided to compensate the families of those affected. This gradually turned into a mad rush for money where everybody in the area claimed to have lost a relative in the inferno. People went to the mortuary and took corpses that did not belong to them just to receive an amount of 200,000 Frs. CFA that was intended to help families bury the corpses of their family members. It became difficult to understand how someone could decide to take away a corpse not belonging to his or her family.

Before the start of each academic year, the government publishes a list of schools and colleges that are authorized as operational for each academic year. Logically, it means that schools that are not found on the official published list are considered illegal and should therefore be shut down. In Cameroon, it is not the case. However, the schools that were considered illegal continued to operate and were even more pronounced than some of the schools officially authorised by the state. First of all, the law and procedure for creating schools is very complex and conflicting and once somebody or group of persons have gone through the difficult process it is not easy for them to close the school down. A school is made up of school children, staff, and the administration. Very often, the minister's decision is made at the time that schools are in session. It becomes frustrating to close down a school considering that there are already children attending such schools. It can also be difficult to enrol or relocate the children to other schools. What then becomes of these children in an event of a closure? It is also surprising that even state officials approve schools that do not have premises just as there are Non-Governmental Organisations without offices. Paradoxically, these same illegal schools and organizations pass in front of the administration of the state during national festivals.

At the level of higher education, there are universities that are tagged as illegal but interestingly they participate at the

National University Games organized by the government, holding graduation ceremonies at public places with state officials attending, presiding and even awarding degrees. Whatever the polemics, the text on the creation of higher educational institutions is caught in a web of entanglement that cannot close down a higher institute once the requirements are met. I continue to ask: why can the officials at each level not act promptly on the documents and give the final decision within the shortest possible time, and not allow proprietors to invest so much money before a closure is ordered? The answer is simple, - 'we cannot act very fast because we expect the proprietor to go through the rituals of bribery and corruption. In addition we are very lethargic as we need to take more time so that money can change hands'.[198] It is this exchange that makes it impossible for the state to stop the so-called illegal schools from operating.

Indiscipline in the country goes together with irresponsibility. All of this indicates that Cameroonians lack the sense of patriotism, national consciousness and nationhood. Cameroonians appear to be strangers in their own home land and most people are only Cameroonians because they have no other place to go to. Cameroonians exploit and exhaust the resources of the country with impunity and wickedness. They are like vultures that perch on their preys every time they have the opportunity. That is why it is difficult to explain the nonchalance and lukewarm attitude that are displayed by the civil servants as we saw in chapter 4. In the public sphere; there is no respect for public property. In a recent nationwide strike organised by transporters because of price hikes for petroleum products in 2008, most of the youth who joined went on rampage and carried out acts of vandalism, arson, killings, and the destruction of state and private property. The things that were destroyed had no direct relationship with the rising price

---

[198] That is the common mentality and the culture of corruption in Cameroon

of petrol. For instance, schools, private homes, and municipal offices were destroyed. Tires were burnt on major patchy tarred roads thereby destroying the little tar on the roads. Even innocent flowers and beds along the Mankon Commercial Avenue were destroyed. There was total moral decadence. This behaviour was contrary to what is found in civilized societies.

When I was a student at Ahmadu Bello University Zaria in the Federal Republic of Nigeria, the Student Union organised about fifteen strikes in four years. Yet, in none of the strikes was a nail removed or property destroyed. Each time the students made their point to the university administration and stood their ground. They were aware that the university property has done nothing wrong to them. They regarded this property as their own worth protecting. They knew that after them other students have a right to use the property. They were conscious that their problem was with the university authorities and not with immovable and inert objects. They knew that destroying these things would not help or solve their problem. They were aware that destroying property would instead impoverish them and the university. That was signified a civilised and mature student union.

In Cameroon the situation is very different because whenever students in Cameroon go on strike, they start by destroying their own classrooms, vehicles and anything that comes their way. They even get into the streets and harass innocent citizens. This is usually an opportunity for most of them to loot and steal from others. This raises concerns about the type of educational system that operates in Cameroon. Students of Cameroon universities have adopted the culture of destruction as way of life and the irony is that these very students who destroy their own property turn around and complain that the universities are not well equipped and lack basic study facilities. They behave like a wife who in the course of fighting with the husband destroys the television set or a radio and turns around to complain that there is no television set in the house.

The indiscipline in this country is a reflection of the type of leadership that we have. It is a laissez faire and insensitive leadership. A good leader who is well focused and committed can bring order even when everything appears not to be moving. Indiscipline manifests itself in a myriad of ways. In most of the cities, people throw waste anywhere even where a bin has been made available. Generally, it is not that they do not know how to use the bins, but it is a reflection of stubbornness. It is common to see even adults throwing dirt just outside the dust bin. Each time that you ask why they throw dirt carelessly, they always refer you to the workers of the municipal councils. People seem to be happy when they see council staff or someone else carrying dirt. Ironically, those who litter the streets are the first to complain that the town is dirty.

Every country has a National Anthem which is considered an identity marker for the country and each time it is sung, it instils patriotic feelings and a sense of belonging to citizens of the nation. An anthem is therefore not only seen as a national value but also as a sign of civic responsibility on the part of the citizens of the country.[199] Unfortunately, most Cameroonians consider their national anthem as an issue restricted to those in government and the elitist group of persons. That is why most of the people do not know whether an anthem even exists in Cameroon let alone being able to sing their own anthem. Usually when the anthem is being sung, most of the people go about their normal duties; some wearing their face caps and not standing at attention while others are busy making or answering phone calls. Our lack of morality has been manifested to a point where we do not have consciences. The churches have not been spared from this high level of moral

---

[199] The National Anthem is one of the national symbols of Cameroon which should be respected but hardly do people do that.

decadence. It has been discovered that even in our churches Christians give counterfeit money as offering. Instances of church ministers and elders embezzling church money have also been recorded. If we can become so dishonest even in front of God then where can we turn to for salvation?

In Cameroon, it is fashionable to say 'yes' when you really mean to say 'no' or to say 'I am coming' when actually you are going. In most organised countries there are national codes or policies on attributing titles to names of streets, state institutions, monuments and public places[200] ; but in Cameroon no such code or policy exists. Like any other thing or issues; names are attributed arbitrary and are based on the prerogative of a state official. Usually they do it even without consultations and these names may change as people change offices too. That is why the name Ahmadu Ahidjo Stadium can by mere pronouncements be changed to the Main Stadium or simply Omnisport Stadium. It is in this same manner that the Government Delegate to the Bamenda City Council can decide to change the name of the Mankon Main Market into Bamenda City Council Market. It is a system where as power changes hands so too are the names of public places and institutions. It is even in record that some names have been changed more than ten times. It is just normal in the country that an airport is located in Mankon for instance but named Bamenda-Bafut Airport or that the University of Bamenda is instead located in Bambili or Nkambe out of the administrative jurisdiction of Bamenda. There is absolutely nothing wrong with giving the name of the institution as the University of Bambili or University of Soa in the case of the University of Yaounde II Soa. Yet the institutions are located in entirely different towns with their own municipalities and administrative units. This mismatch and misrepresentations make the indigenous

---

[200] See Skare, O.K (2010pp) for details on the process through which the streets of Durban were renamed during the early years of post-Apartheid in South Africa.

communities feel that they are victimised, marginalised and socially excluded. From the foregoing; this "confusion" is systemic, intentional and creates tensions and competition. Writing on ethnicized politics in Nigeria, Orji (2010: 166) contends that 'such a confused system results in a highly contested public sphere, which has been made the arena of rhetorical confrontations between various ethnic groups in the country'. This becomes problematic, especially in Africa and Cameroon where ethnicity is still the most dominant form of identity and this is also enshrined in the 1996 constitution. Nigeria, for instance, has adopted an inclusive approach in the naming of Universities, Federal, State institutions and national monuments as a means of managing public sphere and power sharing amongst ethnic groups which Cameroon could emulate.[201]

Each time a government minister is appointed in Cameroon; he or she considers what the predecessor has put in place as obsolete and defines a new program for the ministry. A ministry can have as many programs as there are new ministers or change of government. Consequently, most of the time is spent changing or redefining things and policies as nothing is being done. For the past 50 years Cameroon has moved from a federal system at independence to a United Republic and is now simply a Republic; and also from provinces to regions. I am still expecting a change of name when the next Head of state takes over (if he does). Often, the new appointees do everything to condemn their predecessors for having done a bad job or embezzled funds and therefore give reasons as to why they should be prosecuted or why the offices should be refurbished and the furniture replaced. Everything of the past has no history except in situations

---

[201] Nigerians attribute the names of their heroes and local names to institutions, streets, Libraries monuments etc. See the names of Nigerian Universities and Libraries, for example. Also see Orji, N (2010) 'Governing 'ethnicised' public sphere: insights from Nigeria', *Africa Development* Volume, 1XXX. No 4

where the issue favours the incumbent. Any other thing of the past is condemned with vehemence and is obliterated. The poor state or destruction of archives also suggests the lack of importance that we give to history and research.[202] This is a country whose foundation is based on mistrust and pretence with a false historiography. Cultural identities are values that instead of preserving are being destroyed and eroded by the powers that be, whereas our strength as a nation ought to be based on the diversities of cultures in Cameroon.

In societies where the role of law prevails and is respected such naming and renaming is carried out through a parliamentary act, a municipal ordinance or a community or royal acts, but in Cameroon the powers are trusted or mistrusted and invested in the hands of individuals, be them ministers, Directors, Government Delegates, Senior Divisional Officers (SDOs), the Divisional Officers (DOs) who can just name or rename by mere pronouncements or the stroke of the pen. The system gives great powers to civil administrators who use and misuse the powers to appropriate and misappropriate community assets, especially land, for their own selfish interests. That is why these land grabbers popularly known here as '*chef de terre*' (land lords) molest people over land and stir ethnic conflicts and confusion as they create opportunities to sell the land.

Conclusion

In this chapter I have discussed, elaborately, the social problems of insecurity, disorder and moral decadence. As we indicated earlier in chapter six, insecurity is a crucial problem in Cameroon. This insecurity comes from the disorder that is characteristic of the system of governance in the country which finally gives rise to moral decadence of some sort. In reality,

---

[202] See for instance, the poor state of archival materials in the National Archives Buea and Bamenda regional archives.

Cameroon has very good laws but the problem is the enforceability of the laws or the arbitrary application of the laws. In some circumstances, the application is selective and there is no uniformity as the same law may be applied differently in some areas by different administrators. To overcome the problem of disorderliness in the country, the government should have harmonised programs that must strictly be adhered to by all citizenry. In addition, there is an urgent need for a moral code of conduct with particular reference to state institutions and government or appointed/elected officials. Since Administrative Courts were created, no government official has been brought to book for causing atrocities on the populations or individuals that they are supposed to serve. We would love to see Senior Divisional Officers and Subdivisional Officers convicted for their wrong doings. It is as a result of lack of morals that corruption, embezzlement, bribery and all other social vices are rampant in Cameroon. By this we mean that there is moral corruption which must be checked if the country is to fully develop its potentials.

Chapter 9

As the English people say, better late than never': Cameroon and the Waithood[203] Syndrome

'At last here we are in Buea! Here we are in Buea to celebrate the 50th anniversary of our reunification. As the English people say, "better late than never". In Fact, after a long period of preparation, we are finally glad to be here in this historic town of Buea, the town of legendry hospitality' (Paul Biya, 2014)[204]

On February 20th 2014, Cameroon celebrated' its fiftieth anniversary, following the reunification of French and British Southern Cameroons in 1961. The 'Golden Jubilee' celebration that was supposed to be celebrated in 2011 took place three years later than planned. That is why in his opening statement at the Buea ceremonial ground President Paul Biya referred to the delay of the event. In this speech made by the President one could see that it was embedded with insinuations of reluctance and uncertainty. As we trailed the President's speech which had the flavour of having patches of it delivered in English, one expected the President to highlight why the event was belated but he did not. Finally, the event ended without anybody knowing why 50 years turned out to be 53 years. While most Cameroonians expected the President to tender an apology or simply tell his audience that 'I am sorry for the delay in the 50th anniversary' as it is customary with Cameroonians, the President instead gave a big sigh of relief.

---

[203] Waithood is a term that I have borrowed from Honwana, A (2012) and to whom I give due acknowledgement.
[204] See speech delivered by Paul Biya in Buea during the 50th anniversary celebration on 20th February 2014

As it is with every other event in Cameroon, the delay and uncertainty surrounding the 50th anniversary celebrations of the reunification of Cameroon was not new to Cameroonians as it is traditional that things are never done on time. By conjecture, the reasons for the delay in the event are multifold. First of all, going down memory lane, when the Germans took possession of Cameroon, Buea was made the capital of German Kamerun in 1902. They saw the fertile Bakweri land situated between the slopes of Mt Cameroon stretching down to the Sea shore town of Victoria (now Limbe) suitable for the establishment of European plantations (Geschiere 1995: 158). The residence of the colonial governors was also erected in Buea, including the Bismarck Fountain that was constructed in Limbe. For the short period that Buea enjoyed the status of the capital city of German Kamerun, the Prime Minister's Lodge, Parliamentary Hotel and the Clerks' Quarters were constructed by the Germans. They also constructed the only road in Buea from Molyko up to the Clerks' Quarters which finally earned Buea the name of the 'one street town'[205]

After the Germans were defeated by the allied forces in 1916, German Kamerun was divided between the British and the French. Buea continued to serve as the capital of British Southern Cameroons until Southern Cameroons reunited with French Cameroon following the 1961 Plebiscite and became two federated states. Despite the structural changes and the creation of new administrative units in Cameroon[206], Buea has remained the capital of the southwest region of Cameroon to date. From 1972, when Buea became the Provincial capital of the southwest, no major infrastructural development has taken place. The town became an eyesore, so the President probably needed to carry out renovations in the city considering its

---

[205] Paul Mokoto Interviewed 11/11/2013 Buea

[206] For instance, after the 1972'Peaceful Revolution' Referendum President Ahidjo carved out the then northwest province and former Southern Cameroons into two provinces-northwest and southwest Provinces.

legendry role in the colonial history of Cameroon as far back as 1884 (see also Geschiere 1993: 153).

The choice of Buea as the venue for the 50th anniversary celebrations offered a sigh of relief to the inhabitants of Buea who saw it as an opportunity for the town to have a new face-lift. From 2009, many government initiated projects were announced for Buea. One such announcement was to widen the road from Molyko up to the Governor's office and to create feeder roads within the town down to Mile 17 and beyond. Some of the projects were awarded to contractors but delays were recorded at every stage of the execution despite the fact that government ministers paid regular site visits and held several meetings with contractors. It took three additional (50+3) years to celebrate 50th anniversary initially planned for 2011. By the time the celebrations took place, most of the projects were yet to be completed and some were still at the level of conception. Until the President visited and left Buea, one of the problems that have remained unresolved is that of perennial water scarcity in Buea just as it is the case in most towns in Cameroon. Elsewhere in the country, the same problem exists with other projects that have never begun on time. Some of these projects include; the much heralded tarring of the Kumba-Mamfe road and the Yaounde-Douala highways that were announced decades ago.[207] Another giant project that has just begun is the Bamenda Ring road that the President even swore in 1992; 'I will personally supervise the tarring of the road'.

While students from other parts of Cameroon were on their way for the Christmas vacation, those in Buea and environs were detained and kept on hold to carry out match

---

[207] 'Kumba-Mamfe road construction was to start May 5-a typical "419" case' http://www.cameroonjournal.com/KumbaMamfe%20road.html accessed 19/05/2014

pass[208] rehearsals. The match pass practices continued until it became clear by the 20th of December 2013 that the President could not be in Buea and parents decided to take their children home for the holidays. It was not only the students that were kept on hold, usually when the President or a government personality is about to make an official visit, everything, including other events, are disrupted and people are on hold, waiting indefinitely. Usually, uncertainty looms as nobody is ever informed or sure that the event will occur or that the personality will come. In such circumstances people find it difficult to plan their own events or programs since their reasoning faculties have been arrested by this 'waithood' syndrome.

Cameroonians are therefore not only generally confused about what to do but are also easily angered by the way they are being treated. Furthermore, many Cameroonians attributed the delay in the anniversary celebrations to threats that came from the Southern Cameroon National Council (SCNC), an Anglophone pressure group who saw the anniversary celebrations as an opportunity to make their voices that have been quarantined heard.[209]

Not having things done on time in Cameroon has become a way of life. As a result, Cameroon has become a country-in-waiting. I follow Mbiti's (1990: 19) 'African concept of time' as a mirror to understand why things are never done on time in Cameroon. Mbiti's concept of African time is also commonly known in Cameroon as 'Black man or African Time' that Cameroonians are so attuned with. *Black man time* is time that follows the lunar calendar and relies on individuals, events and natural phenomena. This has been captured by Mbiti (1990: 19) as follows:

---

[208] March Pass simply refers to public manifestations where groups or institutions file pass in front of authorities singing or follow the rhythm of music produced by an orchestra

[209] www.cameroononline.org accessed 22/02/2013

For example, the rising of the sun is an event which is recognized by the whole community. It does not matter, therefore whether the sun rises at 5 a.m. or 7 a.m., so long as it rises. When a person says that he will meet another at sunset, it does not matter whether the meeting takes place at 5 a.m. or 7 a.m., so long as it is during the general period of sunrise. Likewise, it does not matter whether people go to bed at 9.p.m or at 12 midnight: the important thing is the event of going to bed, and it is immaterial whether in one night this takes place at 10.p.m while in another it is at midnight. For the people concerned, time is meaningful at the point of the event and not at the mathematical moment... In western society, time is a commodity which must be utilized, sold and bought; but in traditional African life, time has to be created or produced. Man is not a slave of time; instead, he 'makes' as much time as he wants.

In the above excerpts, the *day* for instance in traditional life is reckoned according to its significant events and the same sequence is true for the week, month and year. This simply means that in two different African communities the rainy or the dry seasons are marked by events and not by dates, days or weeks insofar as the events take place. It is the same with the planting, harvesting, and cooking times. 'For instance, there is a planting season but not a planting time. Time also refers to events that took place in the recent past and people talk about the past by describing the memories of the past event. This is time that is simply a composition of events that have occurred, those which are taking place now and those which are immediately to occur. What has not taken place or what has no likelihood of an immediate occurrence falls in the category of "no time" (*ibid*). According to Eboh (2004: 22), the conception of time is cyclic based on the popularly observed cyclic movement of things in the universe.

The sun rises and sets, thus bringing day and night. Seasons of the year repeat themselves in their respective turns. Plants and animals have their cycles. Even human life is seen to flow in a cycle, from birth to puberty, through adulthood, ripe and death, it does not terminate. There is re-incarnation to rewind the process.

The traditional African therefore perceives time and sequence in the movement of things and the occurrences in the universe *(ibid)*. Eboh (2002), has also identified two distinctive forms of African time-*quantitative* (where time is seen as an opportunity) and *qualitative* where time is an abstraction.[210] This concept of African time where time has to be created or produced is now in conflict with the Western concept of time where time is a commodity which must be utilised, sold and bought (see also Honwana 2012; Mbiti 1990: 19). 'Man is not a slave of time; instead, he 'makes' as much time as he wants'. While most Cameroonians appropriate the Western concept of time through the use of (sometimes) the most expensive wrist watches and clocks, in practice they still adhere to this notion of 'blackman's time'. Therefore, they make mockery of watches on their wrists, clocks and calendars on the walls. The discourses and narratives presented above seem to be characteristic of President Biya's rule in Cameroon. Here, I present four case studies to help us understand how this works.

---

[210] In its quantitative form, time is the locus of all activities and events and there is also in time the fact of irreversibility and uninterruptibility. (I.e. time can never be stopped, not even for a moment). It is ever flowing. Time is for the human person to act in, and according to time as it unfolds itself in days and nights, via the sunlight and moonshines. It reveals life in its *rhythmic repetitions*. Qualitative is profane time, say a moment when rituals, for instance, take place and in which case the time lapse depends on when the mythical performances, incantations, or transformations that have taken place. Also see Eboh (2004: 24)

Case Study Number One

In 1996, Cameroon adopted another constitution and seventeen years later, the constitution has not yet been fully implemented and only selected portions that favour the regime in power are discretely put in place in a piecemeal manner. As a result, it took over fifteen years before the Senate was put in place. The stipulations of Article 66 of the same constitution warrant civil servants to declare their assets before and after leaving office. After a long wait, the President signed a decree in 2006 for the text of application but to date this has never been effected.[211] Enshrined in the same 1996 constitution is a Constitutional Council that is supposed to handle issues or conflicts arising from the abuse of the constitution and also to examine petitions on electoral (fraud) matters. The Council also has the responsibility to proclaim results of elections be them Presidential, legislative, municipal or regional. To date, the Constitutional Council has remained an issue of procrastination as the Supreme Court has continued to validate election results with all its shortcomings.[212] This is the same sequence with every other law, project, activity, event and festivities in Cameroon. The Regional Councils that are enshrined in the constitution have been kept in the freezer forever. It becomes inconceivable that after promulgating the 1996 constitution, Cameroon has been operating with two constitutions, mediating between the 1972 and the 1996 constitutions.

---

[211] See Cameroon online decree No/003/2006 of 25 April 2006, "Declaration des biens et avoirs:decretsd'application du President de la Republic   attendus' http://www.cameroononline.org/2014/04/22/declaration-des-biens-et-avoirs-decrets-dapplication-du-president-de-la-republique-attendus accessed 25/04/2014

[212] Since Cameroon returned to multiparty politics, petitions and complaints from election results have been in the hands of the Supreme Court. Alexi Bepanda has been the President of the court for over three decades and has often been accused of 'fixing' results in favour of the CPDM.

Case Study Number Two

In 2008, the CPDM created new Sections for the party as it became clear that some Sections had been outgrown in terms of population. Since then, the officials of the new Sections have never been elected and confusion has continued with a Section President controlling more than three new Sections.[213] By the statutory provisions of that party, an Ordinary Congress is supposed to hold after every five years. It is difficult to remember when the last congress of the party took place but has been a long time. In the same manner, elections into the basic organs of the party were supposed to have been organised in 2012 but that has not yet been done. The mandate of Parliamentarians and Municipal Councillors was prolonged for two additional years before elections finally took place in 2013. There is also no calendar for elections for the different elective positions in Cameroon, be them elections into the Presidency, Senate, Parliament, and Municipal elections amongst others. Regarding the Senate and the National Assembly, it is common knowledge in Cameroon that Senators and MPs spend half of the one month that they are expected to be in session waiting for texts, and instructions to come from somewhere before deliberations can take place. In this manner, bills and budgetary sessions are hurriedly done and bills without representation are passed. This is the same scenario with major state issues be them, the non-functioning of administrative and criminal courts, the switch over from analogue television broad band to digital, the non-respect of texts of implementation, the ban on traditional medicines, late and irregular convening of the supreme council of magistracy, and the delay in the writing of the Bar Council examinations.

---

[213] Following the creation of new sections of the party in 2008, three new sections, Mezam 1(A), Mezam 1(B) and Mezam 1(C), were carved out of Mezam I. This party has continued to be in the hands of the executives of the Mezam I that is considered by the new creations to be moribund and this has brought about much in-fighting and mistrust among militants who want to have their own section.

The above mentioned are policies that operate in Cameroon without a time frame and only according to the dictates of a few.

Case Study Number Three

In 2012, the President of the Republic appointed Senior Divisional Officers and Sub-divisional Officers. As it is customary in Cameroon, these appointments are expected to be followed by series of installation rituals. A typical installation ceremony in Cameroon goes thus: Cultural groups, school pupils, and students are mobilised. The official time for the start of the ceremony is 9am but the population and invitees are assembled as early as 7.30am at the ceremonial ground. The grand stand is strictly restricted for the 'big men'. The children and dance groups stand under the sun or are squeezed under a tree, with the rest basking under the scorching sun, waiting for the big man to come. The waiting begins and continues until the officials show up at 2pm. No apology is tendered and the installation is done. Different groups are compelled to carry out cultural animations. The official program then comes to an end. It is time for what is often referred to as 'refreshment' but strictly on invitation. The groups are allowed to wander about sometimes with a few hand-outs.[214] This is characteristic of all official or national events in Cameroon. Even when politicians have announced their campaign itinerary, they still often show up extremely late. It becomes difficult to understand how someone who wants to cajole others to vote for him or her does not know the psychology of voters and that once they feel annoyed, they will not vote for such a candidate. Again as it concerns elections, state officials (civil servants) abandon their offices to go for campaigns while the offices remain closed and anybody seeking service from them has to wait until campaigns

---

[214] An envelope with about 3000-5000 Frs. for a cultural dance group with a membership of at least 60 persons is given to the group as appreciation for taking part in the event.

are over.' As things are in this country, 'we will keep on waiting for manna to come from heaven one day'.[215] Even the installation rites have to wait for the Ministers and SDOs, except that the appointment of Ministers is often hurriedly done because of the juicy nature of the position.

Sometimes I am saddened by the way poor and old parents are treated by their very children in the name of a Minister, DO, SDO or 'August guest'. These people usually keep poor children and parents waiting for hours without food or even water to quench their thirst. I think our officials enjoy seeing people wait for them otherwise one cannot explain why these officials plan a visit several months ahead but always come late. One informant[216] had this to say 'Sometimes the people go home frustrated as the big man may fail to turn up and if he does, only those with invitations are expected to dine and wine with the guest as the rest are allowed to fend for them elsewhere'.

The social system in Cameroon is also characterised by this waithood syndrome with all its ramifications. Within the public sphere and even in private, things are done slowly and are never planned or executed on time. Things are easily conceived but they are never realised on time as one Cameroonian commented; 'we are like a baby, easy to be conceived but difficult to be delivered'.[217] One of the main reasons why things have to always wait is the fact that power is in the hands of a few and the system is over centralised and people are conditioned to wait for others/or orders and instructions from 'above'. For instance, the executive arm of government appoints everybody right down to the appointment of the University Dons, administrative officers and Divisional officers. This renders the legislative and judiciary worthless and

---

[215] Tumasang Peter, interviewed 12/1/2014 in Douala
[216] Anye David Ngang, interviewed 12/1/2014 in Douala
[217] Mercy Ngum Awah, Interviewed 14/1/2014 in Limbe

useless since their own arms have been clipped by the executive.

A project duly carried out in Cameroon has to wait for an official inauguration ceremony before it can be put into use. This could well be a hospital unit constructed to save lives but people may still die because the inauguration ceremony has not taken place. Inaugural ceremonies go along with huge financial expenses and this is money that could have been used to improve the social welfare services for the people. Also, the executions of projects that have been funded are sometimes delayed because the President or Minister has not laid the foundation stone. Laying of foundation stones at project sites in Cameroon have become not only arenas for the ostentatious display and squandering of wealth by the state, but also avenues for political campaigns and sloganeering with the ruling party appropriating the project conception and always taking credit for the realisations.[218]

Be it at private or in public events, time is never respected. Every time there is an occasion, it generally begins at least one hour behind time and never do occasions start before time. Although it is not often found on the agenda, it has become a ritual that whenever the event starts the first thing is an apology for starting late and the circumstances are usually claimed to have beyond control. Because we do not learn our lessons the cycle continues at the next event. Since time is not well managed, it also means that time is not a commodity.

On 8th June 2014, the national football team of Cameroon- the Indomitable Lions could not travel to Brazil

---

[218] For example Laying of the Foundation stone for the second bridge over River Wouri in Douala http://www.cameroon-embassy.nl/?p=1574 accessed 25/04/2014 and that of the Lompanga Dam project were done by the President of the Republic. http://cameroon-info.net/stories/0,36570,@,lom-pangar-cameroon-s-energy-revolution-begins-in-earnest.html accessed 25/04/2014. Upon completion, Cameroonians will have to wait for the President to do the inauguration ritual at his convenience.

for the World Cup tournament on time because the match bonuses of the players were not paid. An Angolan Airlines that was hired to take the team to Brazil was grounded in Yaounde for the whole day alongside other passengers waiting for the team. The 'Lions' were expected to leave at 9am but because an agreement to pay the match bonuses could only be reached at about 11pm, the team finally left at 5am the next morning.[219] This was not the first time that the team has had squabbles with officials over match bonuses and the situation has often degenerated into tensions and animosity. After a farewell match in which the Lions defeated Moldiva 1-0 on Saturday 7th, the players threatened to boycott the tournament and even refused to receive the Flag of Cameroon from Prime Minister Philemon Yang who was at the Ahmadu Ahidjo Stadium. The Prime Minister finally handed the flag to the German Born Coach Volker Finke and this raised much criticism from the public.[220] For the seven times that Cameroon's national team has participated at the final phase of the World Cup tournament, this problem of match bonuses has always shown its ugly head. Because of this perennial problem, the team arrived Japan in 2002 just a day before their opening match against Austria and their performances were dismal.[221] 'Money, money, money has been the refrain by the players and it is a pity that they allowed this to ruin our World Cup'.[222] It is a privilege to be selected to play for one's nation at a World Cup,

---

[219] 'Cameroon are now on the way to World Cup http://www.cameroononline.org/2014/06/08/cameroon-now-way-world-cup/ accessed 9/06/2014

[220] Most Cameroonians felt that handing over the Cameroonian flag to a German was not only an act of betrayal, but an indication that Cameroon sovereignty was being compromised.

[221] After the 1990 brilliant performances of the Cameroon National team in Italy, the country has participated at five World Cup finals. They have played 15 matches and won only two as their fortunes have dwindled.

[222] Ghana FA president Kwesi Nyantakyi was quoted as saying by the state-owned *Daily Graphic* June 2014.

but there is a duty on behalf of football associations to ensure that all players are respected.

The roar over match bonuses is not an isolated case of the Indomitable Lions of Cameroon but is endemic with African teams. For example, Ghana's players allegedly threatened to strike instead of playing against Portugal until they had their $3 million collective bonus flown to Brazil and paid in cash; that money was initially promised but not delivered. Nigeria's players reportedly refused to train until their bonus money for qualifying to the last 16 the second round was paid.[223] Cameroon's case was however pathetic because, they were the worst team in Brazil. They conceded eight goals and scored only one and came back with no point. Worst still, they were among the most undisciplined teams in Brazil.[224]

It should be recalled that FIFA usually provides financial assistance to every team that qualifies for the football tournament to ensure effective preparations. For the 2014 World Cup in Brazil, FIFA provided 1.5 Billion Francs to each participating team. Nobody in Cameroon knew how the money was spent. It was only known that the Normalisation Committee claimed to have spent 1.7 billion Frs. thus superseding the money they received. Apart from this deficit that they claimed to have incurred, the Angolan Airlines insisted that Cameroon must pay 200million Francs as damages for the delay.[225] In all of this, what is most worrisome is the fact that sport infrastructures in Cameroon, especially football stadiums remain underdeveloped and the few that exist are in poor shape. Cameroonians blame the situation on

---

[223] There are two sides to every story. "Why did our federation not invest some of the considerable amount of money in football? http://sports.yahoo.com/news/date-set-neymars-first-clasico-131800529--sow.html accessed 3/7/2014

[224] Alexander Song was sent out with a red card during the Cameroon-Croatia match and the Lions were defeated by 4-0. Worse still, indiscipline was very visible when Assou Ekotto and Benjamin Moukanjo fought in the field during this match.

[225] www.camfoot.com accessed 9/6/2014

mismanagement, corruption and embezzlement by football and government officials. In support of the players, the people insist that players have a legitimate claim to their bonuses because as they argue, the money is generated by the players. Others see footballers as commodities that are just like any other factor of production and must be considered as assets and not as mere liabilities. More importantly, players do not believe or trust those managing football in the country. 'It is convenient to paint the players as the bad guys as that keeps the focus off the football federation itself. These things are normally sorted out before the competition, you cannot keep telling the players the money will come'. One supporter lamented.

African regimes and the system in Cameroon have conditioned their youths to be on hold waiting for their own time or for their tomorrow. They have been arrested by the system to remain in what I refer to as *waithood* – a situation where biologically they are adults but are not socially recognised as adults. Following Honwana (2012: 22-23), 'historically in African societies, the socialisation of young people into adult life was traditionally marked by a series of symbolic and educational sets and was the responsibility of the entire community'. In these societies, initiation rituals generally conferred on young men the right to be accepted among adults, receive land, leave the parental home, and marry; they offered young women the means to become good wives and mothers. For both men and women, marriage was a crucial step in a ritualised journey to adulthood (*ibid*). Unfortunately, most African societies are faced with economic decline, high rates of unemployment, strained health care delivery systems, and insecure livelihoods which have made it difficult for the transition from youth to adulthood. The dilemma of the African youth has been summarised by (Honwana 2012: 23) as follows:

Although young Africans are forced to grow up quickly, they find it difficult to achieve social and economic autonomy- the existing markers of adulthood- getting a job or some form of livelihood; leaving their parents' house and building their own home; getting married; having children; and providing for the family- are no longer readily attainable under the socio-economic and political conditions that prevail in most countries.

Under the prevailing conditions cited above, adulthood eludes most of the African youths as they are deprived of its main building blocks: skills, jobs, housing, and marriage *(ibid)*. They, therefore, have no dignity in society. They are seen as adults but cannot play adult roles since they have been disfranchised by the system and prevented from growing into adulthood. And so everybody is struggling to survive at all costs and most of them have opted to migrate to the USA or Western European countries in search of greener pastures (Nyamnjoh 2011; Alpes 2012).

The youth find themselves in waithood, perpetually waiting to enter adulthood yet never getting there. Some have taken personal initiatives to come out of this waithood by establishing businesses and others have become armed robbers, since there are no clear path ways of becoming an adult. The situation has forced most of the desperate youth to prolong the period for marriage, building a house, buying a car, owning a plot, for example. This can be found in the lyrics of the popular song from Cameroon; *Fonction publique* by Beko Sadey. Today, delayed marriages in Cameroon are imposing new costs on society as young people end up being dependent on their parents for longer and children end up being taken care of by their grandparents. This situation places an enormous financial and even social burden on the families. It is very common to find a grown woman in her mid-twenties sharing clothes and make-up with her mother or young men quarrelling with their fathers over food.

The general political discourses in Cameroon assign the youth to the future leaders of tomorrow, whereas in reality young African people in waithood live mainly in the present (Honwana 2012: 30). The distant future is difficult to envision in the face of daily social and economic hardships. 'Adulthood as a destination in which they will settle into a secure job, a house, and a family appears remote and unachievable. Their everyday present becomes their life, and they focus on the here and the now. For many young people in waithood, daily life is a struggle' (*ibid*). Job opportunities in Cameroon are highly limited and the government is the main employer. One of the main criteria to be recruited in Cameroon is the age of the candidate and the age limit varies from one recruitment opportunity to another. Since most young people have to apply for these positions several times and over many years (because of limited places and corrupt practices), most young people have different ages and birth certificates. Records also show situations where children are older than their biological fathers and mothers; and it is very common to find a youth as old as 50 years and an adult as young as 30 years.[226]

In Cameroon, there are conflicting and contradictory ages for everything that is done depending on the interest and issue at stake. For example, the age to possess the national identity card is 18 years which is different from the voting age of 20 years, yet the same person is qualified to be recruited into the army at 18 years of age. To sit for public *concours* (examinations) the ages also vary from one *concours* to another. There is also no universal age to go on retirement. In some ministries, people go on retirement at 55 years while in others it is extended to 60 years. Also, there are some professions that do not have a

---

[226] Most of the Presidents of the youth wing of political parties in Cameroon are actually above the acceptable age for a youth which is 35- 40 years. Some are as old as 50 years but still considered as youths

retirement age; going on retirement is the prerogative of the powers that be. This is particularly true of the military corps where Army Generals hardly go on retirement. This disparity and confusion provides room for people to adjust many things by changing their ages very frequently.

The culture of waiting is so strong in Cameroon that architects design ministerial and government buildings *ab initio* with a whole apartment reserved as the 'waiting room' or *salle d'attendre*. It already signifies that in the public service, it is not normal to get into an office and be attended to without waiting in the 'waiting room'. Most of the waiting rooms are equipped with very expensive furniture, refrigerators, television sets, computers and many other luxurious gadgets. It is therefore, not surprising that much of the budget in Cameroon goes for running expenses than for investments. We have become a waiting people; waiting for the rain, for time, for others, for food, and waiting for everything that one can imagine.

The impact of the poor management of time is devastating in a global world where time has become a commodity. This does not only lead to economic stagnation but also hinders the social development of the country. This also makes it difficult for the country to have a development plan. Implicitly, this gives room for those at the corridors of power to influence the execution of projects in their own constituencies at the expense of those who have no political influence. It is even thought that the poor management of time is deliberate because after losing hope in a project that was announced for several years, the decision to have it done at a particular time is often politicised by the ruling party as a means to drum support.

In conclusion, I have tried to show how the waithood syndrome which has eaten into the social fabrics of Cameroon has had devastating effects not only on young people in Cameroon, but also contribute to the economic and social stagnation and rupture of the entire system. Time as the saying goes, 'waits for no one' and it would be important for

Cameroonians to regard time as a commodity that has a financial value and; not to look at time as something that is out there to be created or produced at will. While most countries are presently executing their development agendas, the government of Cameroon has postponed its own program to the year 2035. Cameroon, therefore, has to wait until it is the year 2035 to become an emerging nation.

Chapter 10

Cameroon in Search of Nationhood

What makes a country tick is the national identity or character that distinguishes that country from all others. Each country has developed certain values or codes that reflect the philosophy or ideology of the nation. Nationhood refers to the sense of belonging which transcends ethnic ambitions and cleavages. It is a phenomenon where there is patriotism and every citizen has the equal opportunity and access to the wealth of the nation, where there is no discrimination, nepotism and favouritism. It is a concept which depicts a people working for the nation and not the nation working for them. People sacrifice and die for a course and for the fatherland. In societies that have attained nationhood, there is no need for corruption and bribery. Public servants know that they are paid to render services to the people without requesting money, favours or rewards.

For many years, Cameroon has not yet evolved into a nation; we are yet to set our own value system which can propel this country to prosperity. Instead, we are, first of all, members of our various ethnic groups before we are Cameroonians. We think along ethnic lines and this is reflected in the way we are governed (see the constitution of 1996). Cameroonians cleave to their ethnic identity. They are, first of all, Mankon, Bayang, Bum, Fulanis, and Beti Bassa, for example, before they are Cameroonians. I can remember that when Sanjou Tadzong Abel Ndeh was dropped as the Government Delegate to the Bamenda City Council, those who hate everything Mankon sang 'Alleluya' and jumped into the air, rejoicing that at last the Mankon man has been sent off. Whether the then delegate worked well or not, he is first of all seen as protecting the interest of Mankon. And so when someone is appointed, the first question asked is where he is from (*Na wich contri man?*) This son of the soil syndrome is very devastating and makes it difficult for the appointee to work, especially if he is not from the main ethnic group within the area. The ethnic origin of the appointee will determine the nature of one's response. If he is from your ethnic group, then the president is hailed as a good man but if he comes from another ethnic group or that which you do not like, then the appointment is condemned and the Head of state is seen as a bad man. The Mankon, Bafut, and Beti on the other hand, feel that they have lost an opportunity to another ethnic group. This is the same with all appointments in Cameroon.

The public service is infested with quacks who know nothing but corrupt practices. So many unemployed youths are condemned with their families to misery because they lack money to bribe the recruiting agents. Many children die of neglect because they do not have the means to pay the nurse who should look after them (Tumi, 2006: 114). Doctors and nurses do not attend to patients even in times of emergencies such as accidents and deliveries. They stock pile drugs and release them to patients at exorbitant prices. Most of these drugs are stolen from the state pharmacies and in turn sold to patients. Material wealth has without our realizing it becomes the supreme and highest God for some of us. Perhaps, without our realizing it money has become the new idol (*ibid*: 114). By implication, we aspire to live beyond our means, beyond what our salaries or honest earnings warrant and so we decide to render services to our fellow citizens only when we are bribed.

Cameroonian youths have indulged in all sorts of malpractices so far as they fetch money for them. They have become notorious scammers. Young people use cell phones to deceive people and even dub well placed personalities in order to get money. Most of our youths cajole rich people to give them money to clear goods that have never been shipped. There are countless people who have been victimised in this way. Through this process of organised stealing, there are young boys and girls of less than 15 years driving very expensive cars, which their parents could never afford throughout their lives. As they say 'it is better to get rich and die than to be alive in misery'.[227] It is embarrassing to see young girls parading pornographic pictures over the internet in search of men and money.

The police have held road users throughout the country hostage. A bad road network can transform a journey that could have been completed in a few hours to the whole day. For instance, the distance from Mankon to Banso is just about 67Km but vehicles take longer than expected not only because of bad road networks but also because of harassment from the forces of law. Road blocks are mounted by police officers not for security reasons but to extort money from drivers and travellers. Sometimes I am saddened by the way that the wives of these police officers devour ill gotten money.

Each time one enters a shop and price a commodity, the shop keeper always reminds you that the article in question is 'original'. Most shops display a variety of goods, some of which are considered and preferred because of their 'originality', while others are disliked because they are 'fake' or are counterfeits. 'Original' in this sense simply refers to goods produced or manufactured overseas. Two strands come out clearly, superior quality goods from overseas and inferior goods produced in Africa. It is true that most of the things produced in the West are of superior quality than those we produce locally. The question now is how did the West arrive at this level of superiority? It is clear that they started by producing goods of inferior quality. Technological invention begins in a crude and rudimentary form and is then perfected upon until it develops into an advanced and desired stage. The textile machines, farm tractors used in Europe were invented during the era of the

---

[227] Nde Michael, interviewed 23/11/2013 at Ntarinkon

211

Industrial Revolution. Today, they are of high and superior quality and that is what we should emulate.

Most often we condemn drugs produced by our neighbours as mere cassava flour. Yet, they have advanced in more pharmacological sciences than Cameroon. We cannot even produce the cassava drugs if we continue thinking that we are inferior. How shall we then develop? If we are to develop, then we have to learn to accept our low level of development and come out with our own development strategy no matter how inferior it may be at the start. By looking elsewhere we are in essence lacking in self-pride and esteem as a people. Unless we believe in ourselves and accept our situation, we shall leach onto others as parasites forever.

The unfortunate thing is that a parasite is alive and continues to live as long as its host is alive and healthy. Its existence depends very much on the host. Once the host dies or is sick, the parasite is also in trouble. That is exactly the situation in which we find ourselves in. We depend totally on others, especially the West for our existence and have shown that our survival is dependent and dictated externally. We do not have a national culture, or call it character, for self-reliant development. We always look up to someone else to make things work for us. We do not even believe in ourselves. This partly explains why we are rejecting everything indigenous and accepting all that is foreign. We have abandoned some of our own cultural values that could have been very useful in fostering a development path for this country. We admire everything good in the West, yet we fail to copy their values of hard work, honesty, patriotism, discipline and respect for each one and national institutions.

Development is highly influenced and dependent on the cultural background of a people. While accepting that Europe and the USA are developed continents, we should however recognise that there are differences in their development patterns, which are highly conditioned and propelled by some cultural values. We have those values that can help us develop but we have refused to integrate these values in our development drive. The only cultural values we seem to appreciate are music, carving, dancing and even drinking.

To borrow from Amical Cabral[228], 'the culture of a people is not restricted to drumming and dancing, to carving of statues and calabashes and other inert forms associated the world over with some static entity named culture. Culture is a way of life. Culture is the sum totality of a people; their way of thinking, of doing things. It is an integral part of their struggle for economic production, political liberation and social development. People should not watch culture but be part of it'. From the analysis above, it seems true that we have a particular culture that is not geared towards our own development. We think foreign, eat foreign and rely on everything foreign. We consume what we do not produce and produce what we do not consume.

In Japan and China, their technological advancements developed from their cultural values of family hood. In these countries, one's family is very important. It is the nucleus from which Japanese or Chinese development radiates and builds the nation. These families are very crucial towards the technological advancement of the country. Companies take on family names. These include companies such as Toyota, Mitsubishi, and Suzuki, amongst others. In Cameroon, we are afraid to promote our families. Family hood was very useful in the pre-colonial era and was the basis on which communal labour was conscripted. It gave self-esteem and respect to

---

[228] Born on 12 September 1924, Cabral was a Guinea-Bissauan and Cape Verdean agricultural engineer, writer, a nationalist thinker and a politician. He led the nationalist movement of Guinea-Bissau and the Cape Verde Islands and the ensuing war of independence in Guinea-Bissau. Unfortunately, he was assassinated on the 20th of January 1973 before Guinea-Bissau's declaration of independence. http://en.wikipedia.org/wiki/Am%C3%ADlcar_Cabral accessed 28/01/2013

members of the family and was the foundation on which social relations such as marriages were established (Rodney 2012: 36; Ndege 2012: 43). Today, our families are disintegrating. There is no more unity in the family. The family name that was protected is now being soaked in mud. Family love has been replaced by hatred. We have adopted individualism as opposed to communalism. This is at a time that nations are coming together to form strong economic blocs. This is no different from what is in Japan and China.

By 1960, Cameroon was economically more advanced than China and Korea. The only difference was that while the Japanese and Chinese have maintained this principle, we have abandoned it. Instead, we treat every other family member with suspicion. We are also not happy to see other family members' progress. Those who progress would want to be on top, alone and forever. Any other person, then, is seen as a threat and must not be helped or trusted. The root causes of most of the problems in this country stem from the colonial encounter, especially the emerging elite that were trained by the colonialists in elitist foreign institutions. This has greatly influenced our perceptions about life and the way we function. In fact, Africans trained abroad are honoured even more than parents and the Traditional Rulers of Africa. The authority of these personalities is often ridiculed and challenged by their very children who feel that acquiring Western education means the abandonment of their own culture.

Colonial education appears in this context as a process of denying the national character, alienating the Cameroonian from his country and his origin and in exacerbating his dependence abroad, forcing him to be ashamed of his people and his culture. The education provided by the colonial government was not designed to prepare young people for the service of their own country; instead, it was motivated by a desire to inculcate the values of the colonial society and to train individuals for the service of the colonial state.

I continue to insist that moral decadence, disorder that prevails in Cameroon and most of Africa are partly caused by self-denial of one's culture. Colonialism, a system for the deprivation of an entire people's freedom is the greatest destroyer of culture that humanity has ever known. African society and its culture were crushed and when they survived they were co-opted so that they could be more easily emptied of their content. The African chief found himself hierarchically subordinated to the lowest European colonial civil servant. The people might prostrate themselves as he passed but his only role of note was the collection of taxes to hand over to the colonial administrator and the sending of men for forced labour (Wilmot 1982: 189). Africans whose ancestors created complex systems such as age grades, chieftaincies, powerful armies, mighty states and people are now thought incapable of creating structures suited to their present conditions. As Rodney (2012 48-53), notes, these were sophisticated and efficient organizations, with complex functional ideologies, ideally suited to their time, their environment and the level of technology. In 2013, five of the top ten fastest growing economies in the world were found in Africa[229] yet Africans are condemned to a life of misery, hunger, and disease in a land literally flowing with milk and honey. Ironically, war torn South Sudan occupied the first position with a GDP of 32.59 in percentage.[230] The leaders of most of the countries in Africa have continued to serve Western interests and seen as tools that are utilised by the white man in the interest of maintaining his high standard of living after which they are discarded and sent to pine away and die in the so-called homelands when they are no longer able to serve as beasts of burden (Wilmot 1982).

---

[229] 'Top ten countries with fastest growing economies' http:/ / www.mapsofworld.com/world-top-ten/world-top-ten-fastest-growing-economies-map.html. accessed 3/7/2013

[230] Ibid accessed 3/7/2013

It is over 50 years that most of the states in Africa achieved independence and to date, most of them have tried to imbibe Western style democracy and are yet to make progress. It is however, important to note that Europe or the Western world is different from Africa. While Africa needs to follow democratic principles, it should be noted that a European party structure is unsuitable to African social conditions not only because Europe is not Africa but also because Africa has its own cultural values which need to be protected and preserved. Put the other way round, while not refusing that democracy has become one of the most accepted forms of governance, we must also admit that the practice of democracy is not universal; because no two countries have the same historical experiences. Consequently, democracy as it is practiced in France does not fit squarely with what is obtained in the United States yet the basic democratic hall marks are there.

We can also emulate the example of the late Tanzanian President Julius Nyerere who refused to copy and paste Western European democratic models for his people and formulated his own style of democracy which he called *Ujamaa*. The main guiding philosophy of this system developed from the Tanzanian family organization. *Ujamaa* worked very well and helped Tanzania to develop in its own way even if it developed its own internal dynamics and contradictions.[231]

Yet, in Cameroon our own form of democracy is largely copied from Western concepts that do not reflect the local realities. That is why the voting patterns in the country are still dependent on ethnic cleavages and relations. This means that people in Cameroon still think and act along ethnic lines and not on any democratic values. It means that we have to, first of all, acknowledge the existence of these ethnic groups and then

---

[231] Ujamaa was the concept that formed the basis of Julius Nyerere's social and economic development policies in Tanzania after it gained independence from Britain in 1961. The Term has the meaning of 'unity', 'Oneness',-uniting with your countrymen as one extended family. http://en.wikipedia.org/wiki/Ujamaa accessed 3/7/2013

formulate our own system that incorporates these groups before trying to reject them. When you look at the electoral laws in Cameroon they are silent about the position and rule of traditional rulers; even at the local council level they are not recognised, yet it is from the traditional ruler that the state expropriates land for developmental projects. The Fon or chief is only there to receive orders from the SDO and with an ambiguous land tenure system the land offered to the state is never compensated. Governance means accountability, transparency, inclusion, and management but if we are in a system where there is social exclusion, it is difficult to practice good governance (Fisiy 1992).

One day I walked into an off license and got the worst treatment of the day. When I sat down I recognized a friend sitting near me so I turned and greeted him in my national language –Mankon. I do not know how irritating my language was, but two ladies sitting opposite me were really annoyed and furious. The two asked us the same question in succession why have you people decided to be talking here in Mankon, that is not good it's bad manners. I told them instantly 'No No!! Madam I think I have the right to speak Mankon wherever and whenever I deem necessary'. The issue then turned into a heated debate with two opposing camps. When I insisted on knowing what wrong we have committed they argued that we are not in the village. Then I told them that Mankon is not a language restricted for the village but that it is a medium of communication and is spoken in the village, in the city, in Africa and anywhere in the world. I wondered whether there is an urban language and a rural language. She insisted that speaking Mankon was a sign of disrespect and lack of manners.

These are the kind of issues that I am interested in because the two ladies were a replica of a typical Cameroonian. I told them that Cameroon has remained under-developed because of the type of mentality that they have; the love for anything foreign. When I inquired to know the appropriate language that

I should have used, I was told English was the best language. I recalled that she was speaking to me in Pidgin and not even in English.

When you analyse the episode you already see how the Cameroonian mentality has been eroded and is gradually being replaced with a foreign mentality. I went further to inform them that Nigeria is more developed because they believe in themselves. Nigerian languages are taught in the Universities. Language is the main medium through which culture and traditions are revitalised and transmitted from one generation to another. I told them that because we are ashamed to identify with our national languages we have tended to refuse using our own dresses. I insisted that there are elderly statesmen in Cameroon who have never appeared in public in their traditional attire. Then one of the ladies told me that even the Ewondos from where the President comes from do not have traditional attire, and so I should not expect the Head of state for instance to dress otherwise. She was even quick to inform me that Cameroon has no dressing pattern that the country can be identified with.

Indeed. I was embarrassed to learn that a Cameroonian in the 21st century could still hold the notion that our people do not have a traditional outfit. Cameroon and the northwest have one of the best traditional outfits. The outfit has even gained international recognition and is also cherished by the whites. After a careful look, I realised that there was no reason to blame her. Suddenly the ladies left. I noticed that one was driven in a huge Pajero vehicle with the German-DED written on it. Then it dawned on me that she was promoting and protecting her mentor, the Germans. To say that our people do not have a dressing pattern reminded me of the notion that the colonialists had about Africa before their penetration into the continent. They regarded Africans as people without a culture and that were very primitive, disorganise and living on tree tops (Crowder, 1970). Today Europeans should be very happy and

218

proud that there are still Cameroonians like the two ladies I met. She insisted that dressing is fitting and if the European suits fit anyone he should wear them. By so saying she meant that Cameroon attires are not good or do not fit. The question that one may ask is how can one admire the dresses that we refuse to wear?

For Cameroon to come out of these issues and gain its rightful position among nations there is a need for good policies to be formulated. The truth is that we do not have good policies and whenever we conceive a policy it is hardly implemented. It is usually very difficult to understand the basis on which social policy is formulated in Cameroon. The social problems that have been raised in this book need appropriate policies and if these social issues are not well articulated then it may be difficult to formulate appropriate social policy to solve the said problems. The prerequisite to policy formulation therefore, is that the issue must first of all be identified. It is unfortunate that the government of Cameroon has never taken any of these issues seriously and that is why only cosmetic solutions are given to some of these problems. Unfortunately, the few policies that are formulated are changed frequently by Ministers as they come and go. Each time a Minister takes over office, old policies are abandoned and new ones are put in place by the new Minister. Furthermore, these policies are not research oriented and do not follow any pattern or trend.[232]

In other countries such as Britain, there are institutions that have direct links with universities such that policies are designed and formulated with the collaboration of these higher institutions. Once they are formulated, they go through parliament or other legislations and once promulgated into law, they cannot be changed or violated by any individuals no matter what political position they may hold.

---

[232] For example, in Cameroon each time a Minister is appointed, a new program is designed and the old one is abandoned and there is no coherence in the programs.

Chapter 11

Concluding Reflections

Many issues have been raised in this work and it is intentionally designed to be that way. Raising these issues without coming out with some suggestions that can provide the way forward is not my approach to solving a problem. The country is endowed with many agricultural potentials yet a majority goes with empty stomachs on daily basis. According to the World Food Program (WFP) Report 2009, Cameroon is a low income and food deficit country where there are 4.6 million Cameroonians that cannot afford a balance diet a day. In July 2014, the government increased the prices for petroleum products and this led to a steady increase in the prices of food items; and with their meagre finances, people have continued to buy anything they see and so may eat the same thing every day –say corn, rice, and garri being the most popular options and belonging to the same food class.

Agriculture accounts for 23.3 percent of the total export earnings yet the country still relies heavily on the importation of food as up to 13.9 percent of food was imported in 2006 (FAO: 2007). This trend has continued to rise as the country still imported 291,380 tons of wheat in 2007 at the cost of US$ 90,693,000, and 203,137 tons of rice at the cost of US$ 63,169,000.[233] In 2011, the quantity increased as Cameroon shipped in 545,000 metric tons of rice estimated at 145 Billion CFAF (Business in Cameroon, 2012). These figures are disturbing because little has been done to empower and provide incentives to the rural women who are the main cultivators and food producers. Statistics from the Ministry of Agriculture and Rural Development indicates that of the

---

[233] See 'Business in Cameroon' 2012

240,000 hectares of cultivable land for rice, barely 25,000 hectares have been developed. This is largely insufficient considering that rice is a staple food for most Cameroonians with an annual demand between 600,000 and 650,000 metric tons and local production remains staggering at only 40 percent of this amount.[234]

Cameroon is one of the highest producers of export cash crops within the Central African sub-region. These crops constitute the main source of government revenue and according to the FAO (2007) report, 161,961 tons of cocoa were exported and it generated, US$ 261,224,000 while 224,546 tons of Banana earned US$185,927,000. A total of 72,791 tons of cotton fetched the government US$90,039,000. In all, total revenue generated from exports stood at US$ 962million, with average growth rate of exports from 2005-2007 at 17.7%; while the figures for imports were US$ 624million with average growth rate of imports from 2005-2007 at 11.7%[235]. The situation of food crops is deplorable as in 2007, only 2100, 000tons of cassava were produced and the yield per hectare was 60,000.This showed a -4.4% in yields from 1997-2007 (FAO 2007). The same scenario was also observed with cocoyam where 1200, 000tons were produced and the yield per hectare was 54,545. This showed a significant drop from 2.7% to -.3% from 1997-2007 (*ibid*). This raises fundamental questions as to the rationale of the Roots and Tubers sub sector programmes in the Ministry of Agriculture and Rural Development. This parity between cash crops and food crops already show the trend of food deficit. Despite the figures indicated above, the population growth rates continue to exceed the productive capacity of Cameroon's food reserves

---

[234] See www.cameroononline.org accessed 07/04/2013
[235] Other important cash crops are sugar and production stands at 60,000tons,palm oil 50,000tons annually see Cameroon Business (2012:) Also see (FAO 2012)

and agricultural transformation remains a fundamental development challenge.

Other factors affecting food insecurity include alterations in climate regimes. Frequent floods and drought in the Far North seem to be a result of worldwide changing weather patterns associated with global warming as observed elsewhere in the country (Perry, 1990). In 2012, the government of Cameroon declared an emergency situation in the Far North region of the country due to major drop in cereal production following poor rainfall. A crop and food supply assessment mission by the FAO of the UN, Ministry of Agriculture and Rural Development and the World Food Program (WFP) in the two northern regions of Cameroon concluded that the cereal harvest in the Far North is significantly below the previous year's production resulting in a 50000mt deficit. Over 400.000 people in the Logone and Chari division were affected by the decrease in food production, half of whom require immediate assistance.[236] Despite rainfall which supports production, and waterfalls and rapids which offer much hydro power potential, little agricultural land is irrigated-only 0.4 % of irrigated land is put in to use in Cameroon (FAO 2012: 3).Given the lack of irrigation, the unpredictability of rainfall implies high risks in agriculture (Collier et al 1999: 8).

A majority of Cameroonians do not eat meat while others depend on bread for sustenance. Because of hunger, children that ought to be in school can be found begging in the streets or going to garbage heaps to select whatever food they can find. At a glance, the Ministry of Agriculture and Rural Development has some of the best programs on paper. There is the plantain, maize, rice; root and tuber sub-sectors with huge financial allocations intended to help local farmers

---

[236]http://www.wfp.org/content/food-assistance-drought-affected-household-logone-and-chari-division-and-nutritionally-vulne accessed 08/04/2013
http://www.agrifeeds.org/en/filtered_rss/CMR/all/all/all/news accessed 08/04/2013

improve on their yields. Despite the enormous efforts, farmers have continued to wallow in misery. That is why irrespective of the efforts by the state to increase food production, food insecurity still looms in the country. One would have thought that the agricultural technician who works with the farmers every day in the field teaches them new techniques.

My personal experience has shown that for an agricultural officer to go to the farm and work with farmers he needs to be 'fed' and be given transport money. This, as they say, is motivation and failure to 'motivate' means they will also not work with farmers on their farms. All the rice farms such as UNVDA in Ndop, Logone Valley, and Menchum Valley that flourished in the 80s have been abandoned and the country now resorts to importing thousands of tons of rice. We can revert these importations if assistance meant for farmers gets to them and it would mean by-passing the Agricultural Officers and getting to the farmers directly.

The Hunger Task Force of the United Nations Millennium Development Goals program has identified 342 regions of the developing world with more than 20 percent of underweight preschool children (IAC 2004: 13). In Cameroon the situation is not much different as malnutrition[237] has continued to affect 30 percent of children under 5 years; high mortality rate under 5 years stands at 136.0/1000, far above the continental rate of 121.0/1000 and maternal mortality remains high at 690.0/100,000 per live births (IMF: 2012). The implications of inadequate food on the health care of the population and especially women according to the IAC Report (2004: 11) have been condensed in the following analysis:

Malnourished means a population that falls below an Adjusted Average Requirement of 2.600-2950 kilocalories per person per day depending on the country and its population structures (age, sex, body weight) see (IAC Report 2004:10)

Malnourishment leads to baby low birth weight and high mortality. This also impairs mental development of children, increases the risk of adult chronic diseases and results in inadequate catch-up growth. Another consequence is that malnutrition retards growth (child becomes stunted) and reduces the mental capacity of the child. The problem becomes more serious with malnourished women as it results in pregnancy low weight gain and consequently inadequate foetal nutrition leading to higher maternal mortality.

There is also high prevalence of Tuberculosis with 21 percent deaths recorded annually and 103 deaths/100,000 from malaria related illnesses. All these diseases affect the productive capacity, especially for women. The situation is deplorable as 600 women die from pregnancy related causes per year (UNDP, 2011). HIV/AIDS is exacerbating this situation further as the nationwide prevalence rate for women stands at 6.7 percent while that for men is as low as 4.1 percent.[238] This does not only reduce their nutritive intake but makes them vulnerable to disease, unhealthy lives and can lead to the slow growth of the economy (Collier and Gunning 1999: 7). Finally, when elderly women are malnourished it reduces their capacity to care for the baby which in turn affects the work force of the women adversely. Paradoxically, the steady economic recovery for the past five years with a growth rate from 3.1 percent in 2009 to 6 percent in 2013, has instead witnessed a drop in life expectancy from 57 years in 1995 to 52 years in 2012, while the standard of living has also fallen from US$1,739 to US$1.190 in 2012 (Collier and Gunning 1999: 5; FAO 2012: 1).

At the political level, other examples in Africa have shown that there is a need for a comprehensive constitutional review

---

[238] See Minister announces decline in HIV/AIDS Prevalence http://www.cameroon-info.net/stories/0,15516,@,minister-announces-decline-in-hiv-aids-prevalence.html accessed 29/06/2013

process which will bring about the reform of the electoral system and the judiciary amongst other institutions (Jerome 2010: 188). This will foster the accountability of elected officials. Given the current situation, the opposition lacks the institutional means to pressure the government effectively. For decentralization to be effective and trigger the development that Cameroonians have been yearning for, let individual states and regions elect their own local representatives from Governors, Mayors, local councillors, and Parliamentarians to senators. This will spark developmental competition amongst the states and within a few years the backwardness of this archaic system would be relegated into the dustbin; not the ubiquitous Government Delegates who only serve as town cleaners and cannot initiate any projects. All they rely on are building permits fees and extorting money from poor women in the name of market fees. It is difficult to pretend that you can develop someone else's area. Moreover, 'President Biya inherited a bad system from Ahidjo and made it worse. The problems of Cameroon are no longer at his level'.[239] There is an urgent need for the different voices including those in the Diaspora to sit together and come up with an acceptable system of governance for the country.

In Africa, there is a preference for the old over the young. That is why the continent is ruled by octogenarians. The longest serving President is Teodoro Obiang Ngeuma of Equatorial Guinea who came to power on August 3rd 1979, and has been there for the past 35 years. The second position is occupied by President Jose Eduardo Dos Santos of Angola nicknamed as the 'quiet dictator' and he has been there since September 1979. The next position goes to President Robert Mugabe of Zimbabwe who has been leading his country since February 1980. President Paul Biya of Cameroon is the fourth longest serving head of state in the continent. He took over

---

[239] Mishe Fon's postings on the internet on the need for Cameroon to be over hauled

from Ahmadou Ahidjo on 6th of November 1982. Finally, the fifth longest serving African leader is President Yoweri Museveni of Uganda who has been there since January 1986. Each of these leaders is not less than 80 years of age.[240]

They have made their own contributions towards the development of their respective countries but it is also good to leave and give chance to the young and energetic people to take over. I have raised the issue of power transition in this work and the idea is that we need to formulate a system through which the old relinquish power to the younger generation. These young people need to be schooled with party ideology and policy such that we can predict who can be elected into which office. Democratic governance is not a monarchical arrangement where the successor of the king is kept secret. The leaders of the political parties in Cameroon are tired and need enough rest. I was surprised to hear in an interview that Ni John granted in which he dabbled over his potential successor. He said, 'you are of the Tamfu Family and can the successor to your father be known while he is alive?[241] The Chairman's insistence that he will continue to be the presidential candidate so long as his health permits him does not suit in a democracy. So does it mean that if his health permits him, he will remain the party Chair until he is being lowered into his grave? Without mincing words, all the current leaders cannot deliver the goods and so can only be useful as points of references or archival material. The issue here is not Paul Biya or Fru Ndi, or Bouba Bello. We simply need a new kind of leadership in Africa and particularly in Cameroon. It is important that our much venerated leaders know that it is nice to leave the stage when the applause is loudest.

---

[240] 'Presidents for life' http://mycontinent.co/Ditactors.php accessed 17/01/2013

[241] Watch Presidents for life http://mycontinent.co/Ditactors.php accessed 17/01/2013

[241] Watch www.youtube.com interview with the 'Man Fru Ndi accessed 16/01/2013

Most readers may be tempted to say that this work is washing our dirty linen in public, but I also want to say that if the linen becomes too dirty, it must be taken even to the sea where there is enough water for effective cleaning. Again some may be wondering to which party I belong. I have and I am still a militant of the Cameroon Peoples Democratic Movement (CPDM).[242] I am convinced that belonging to a party does not mean that you subscribe to or agree with all the party does. I am sure that my party is strong enough to provide the next president of the third Republic. There are young and intelligent people in the CPDM that can lead. The table below gives an idea of the distribution of Board of Directors among a few selected major state Corporations, and the former positions they have held in government and their respective ages. They have been in these respective positions for at least a decade. They have, at one moment or another served as Ministers, Governors, Ambassadors or Members of Parliament as far back as Ahidjo's regime and they are still there. Little wonder that Cameroon's state companies are under-performing and many qualified young people cannot get jobs. Some have died and their positions have remained vacant while others hold cumulative positions.

---

[242] If membership to a party is considered through the possession of membership card, then I belong to the CPDM but I differ substantially with the party on ideological basis.

Table: Octogenarians and the political economy of Underdevelopment in Cameroon

Name	Corporation	Previous position held	Age
Ousmane Mey	CNPS	Governor	87 years
Chief Victor Mukete	Camtel/Senator	Member of Parliament/Senator	88years
Adolphe Pokossy Ndoumbe	ADC	Government Delegate DUC	89years
Rene Ze Nguele	IRAD	Several ministerial portfolios	83 years
Paul Pondi	Civil Aviation Authority	Ambassador	86 years
Robert Mbella Mbappe	SOCAPALM	Several Ministerial portfolios	82 years
Achidi Achu	SNI/Senator	PM, Minister	79 years
Adolphe Moudiki	SNH	Minister	75 years
Charles Metouck	SONARA GM		
Peter Mafany Musonge	Grand Chancellor /Senator	PM, General Manager (CDC)	67 years
Eteki Mboumoua, William. A	President Red Cross	Minister	80 years
Robert Mbella Mbappe	Telecom Regulatory Agency	Minister	77years

Source: http://www.cameroon-info.net/stories/0,40774,@,inertie-gouvernementale-ces-laquo-vieillards-raquo-qui-gerent-les-societes.html accessed 30/01/2013

But irrespective of the issue that strikes you in this book, the fundamental one remains the leadership crisis. All the problems raised can be eradicated or at least reduced to acceptable ways if we have a committed leadership. Leadership should be understood as an aggregate of those in positions of leadership and not referring to the Head of state alone. The family head, the head teacher, the Traditional Ruler, the Municipal authorities, administrators, legislative, judiciary and all those who occupy positions that exert power and influence in society. Good governance entails people who are transparent, accountable, disciplined, have managerial skills and are easily approachable. It has become fashionable in Cameroon for people to look at the President and his cohorts as the only people who are inefficient. Someone who embezzles money raised through a *Njangi* scheme by a group is as corrupt as one who swindles billions from the state. My argument is that old habits are difficult to abandon and all we learn is internalized and gradually becomes the norm or a way of life. If you can deprive the small *Njangi*[243] group of their savings, there is no doubt that if you have the opportunity to control lots of money you will refrain from such abuses. What Cameroon do you think we would have if everybody in his or her own sphere did his or her work judiciously? If each of us plays the assigned role well, then we will not have reason to complain about the other person. As I said earlier, complaining has become a way of life and we do not assume responsibility for our failures but always push the blame on someone else. I however, admit that those at the head should be the first to bear the brunt because they have been chosen to guide, to coordinate, to supervise and to control the resources. These resources should be allocated in a fair and equitable manner so that all the people and regions should not feel cheated or marginalized.

One of the main problems we are facing is that of bad institutional structures. There is the need for a total over haul of the institutional arrangements in the country. For instance, it sounds strange that the regime behaves as if the Anglophone problem that they have socially created is not there (Rangers 2010: 123). They also turn a blind eye to the fact that Ministers, Directors, and DOs are predominantly selected from few regions. The office of the President of the republic is invested

---

[243] Njangi simply refers to a financial thrift and loan scheme run by people with common objectives and basic rules. This is a common feature of the informal banking sector in Cameroon. Also Nyamnjoh 2013a,pp 2

with a lot of power without checks and balances and so he can use them to his advantage. There is therefore, the need to transfer or redistribute most of these powers with the Senate, Assembly, Judiciary Regional Assembly, Councils and traditional Authorities. There is a need to deregulate and decentralize the entire system and to allow local councils to present their indigenous development plans that will enhance development. The present arrangement rather stifles development because of the conflicting and overlapping roles of the Government Delegate, the SDO and the DO who are presiding over the destiny of a small city. Certain institutions such as the School of Magistracy and Administration need to be scrapped because for corruption to have taken place in Cameroon, the major corrupter must have been a graduate from ENAM[244]; be it the Custom, Administrators, Magistrates, tax Assessor, or financial controllers. It gives me the impression that ENAM is the production centre of corruption and bad governance in Cameroon.

The tenure of office for the President of the republic should be reduced to one term of five years, two terms maximum. When we have alternate governments, there is more development because every new Head of state brings in a new idea (good or bad). Bad ideas are sometimes useful because they influence better outcomes when someone else takes over. After all, the existence of evil is to serve good. It becomes unimaginable that for over 50 years Cameroon has had only two Heads of state, which means that their two ideas have been implemented and exhausted. Yet, the USA, from the same time that Ahidjo took over in 1960, has been governed by eleven Heads of state.[245] If each president has his own

[244] 95 percent of all those charged with corruption and those who have access to state resources are graduates from ENAM.

[245] 'Who are the past 10 US Presidents? From J.F Kennedy in 1961 to Barack Obama in 2009, America has been governed by eleven Presidents. http://wiki.answers.com/Q/Who_are_the_past_10_us_presidents accessed 3/7/2014

ideology, it means that America has had eleven different ideas while we stagnate on two outdated ideas.

It may be difficult for some people to accept that there are senior ministers in government today who got their first ministerial and ambassadorial appointments at the age of 28 years. These elderly statesmen have been in power for over 40 years and are still thirsty to remain in power for ever. I have insisted and will continue to insist that the country needs a new breed of leaders. I am against a system which is run by the old. The political panacea in Cameroon has often referred to the youth as the 'leaders of tomorrow' and we know very well that tomorrow shall never come. What sense do we make of a youth who saw Mr Biya being sworn into office on 6 November 1982 as the President of the Second Republic? Such a youth in 'waithood' must have realised that his tomorrow has been forfeited. In order to come out of the doldrums, it would be nice for the youth to forcefully engage in the political agenda at different levels because if they remain 'obedient' waiting for tomorrow, they will be forgotten as usual. As I said, you could effect change in your small corner, be it at the village or at the municipal levels. The population distribution of Cameroon is youthful with over 58 percent made up of youths between the ages of 18 and 40. Curiously, they also produce the highest number of votes but are hardly heard or represented within the decision-making process. So whatever decision they make has a great influence on the outcome of elections. The motorbike riders, (Bensikin) *Buyam Sellams, taxi men*, for instance, are cajoled with few gifts and food stuffs and used by politicians during political campaigns, yet in no council do you find them as Councillors. It becomes difficult for someone else to articulate and negotiate for solutions to problems that these categories of people are facing. Unemployment remains one of the most acute problems in this country. It is the main route from which other social problems originate. Therefore, if this particular vice is thrashed or minimised, then most problems should automatically be solved.

The entire African continent seems to be suffering from leadership fatigue because the leaders hang on to power for too long. If we juxtapose the level of development in the continent today and the contributions of the founding fathers of African nations we would notice that the pioneer Presidents performed better than their successors. The former were leaders and nationalists who had the continent at heart and some even gave up their lives for the liberation of their people from the vestiges of colonialism. Patrick Lumumba of the then Zaire, Amical Cabral, Sekou Toure of Guinea, Abdel Nasser of Egypt, and Kwame Nkrumah of Ghana laid a solid foundation for the continent. We cannot over emphasise the contributions of these great leaders to the liberation struggles in Africa and the match to independence. Almost all of these first generation leaders have left the scene and a few still live comfortable and respectable lives in their respective countries. In their time, it was impossible to hear of corruption and/or embezzlement as it is the sing song all over Africa today. Some of them died or lived as paupers. I am thinking of Rt Kenneth Kaunda of Zambia, Julius Nyerere of Tanzania and Ahmadou Ahidjo of Cameroon. To this list I would like to add the exemplary Former Prisoner and President Nelson Mandela of South Africa of blessed memory.[246] The second generation Presidents who were the first to receive Western education appear to be more educated than their predecessors, yet they have performed worse than the former. Most of what the founding fathers put in place have been obliterated and mismanaged, with corruption, nepotism, favouritism and ethnicity taking centre stage. All the structures that were realised at

---

[246] Born on 18th July 1918, Nelson Mandela became the first black President of South Africa in 1994, serving until 1999. Before becoming President, he was imprisoned by the Apartheid regime for 27years. Mandela died on the 5th of December 2013. He remains Africa's most venerated Idol and political legend.

independence are all dilapidated or crushed and now exist only in history.[247]

We need to give certain considerations when selecting the leaders of this country. It should be borne in mind that experience is the best teacher and most of our realizations are informed by the experiences that we have lived through. It is unthinkable to expect much from a leader who has not known what it means to trek for kilometres to attend school or who has never been jobless for years. It is even unacceptable to choose persons who have never spent weeks to cover the 158km of road from Mankon to Ekok. Neither will it be good to pick someone who has not had the pains or sufferings from lack of medical services. How can we entrust a nation to people who do not know what it means to live without electricity or have never travelled to such places like Nkang in Furu awa subdivision? Complaining to such leaders is not useful because they do not know what you are saying since they have never lived the experience! We should avoid selecting people who are not in touch with the local realities and understand the sufferings of the people.

The Anglophone problem is one of the burning issues in the country though the Yaoundé regime deliberately refuses to recognise and has adopted the culture of silence. However, to avoid an inferno in the future, there is the need to examine this problem and come out with equitable power-sharing and resource distribution mechanisms that will not only ensure a balance development but will make all Cameroonians have the feeling and sense of belonging and citizenship. 'Although the present regime has rejected federalism as alien and synonymous with fragmentation and secession, federalism remains the best option; in which there should be the transfer of power to a lower level of jurisdiction, legal status, specified functions, fixed financial resources and autonomous personnel' (Konings

---

[247] Many structures in Cameroon bank, such as Credit Agricole and WADA, are now mere appendices

and Nyamnjoh 2003: 205). The form of such a Federation should be decided upon by the people of Cameroon. If we admit that there are over 250 ethnic groups in Cameroon and the constitution reaffirms this assertion, we should ensure that power is devolved and reflected through equitable representation of some sort. To foster national unity in diversity, a one year National Youth service Corps (NYSC) reminiscence to that in Nigeria could be formulated. This provides the opportunity for graduates to adapt, get to know the country better and through which they can become socially integrated. While doing the youth service, the state should be able to provide a monthly allowance to each graduate. Such allowances will help some of them to plan and kick start their own businesses without necessarily looking for the state to provide jobs.

Linked to the Anglophone problem is the language disparity between French and English as official languages in the country. The constitution of Cameroon recognises French and English as official languages and that is only how far it can go. There is no law that enforces bilingualism in the country. A few Prime Ministerial directives have been made towards the use of French and English in government offices but nothing is said about sanctions for defaulters or noncompliance with the texts. There is therefore, the need for a law on enforceability of bilingualism. The continuous dominance of the Francophones and French does not only bring about imbalanced power relations but also stifles the occupation of the public sphere by Anglophones. The problem of the total control and monopoly of the state media by Francophones and the French language programs (audio and print) can be solved through the creation of two national channels as Ngwane, Mwalimu has suggested below:

... the present lopsided state of biculturalism in our state media has had a toll on our nation building project,

235

broken the communication mirror that is supposed to reflect our bicultural image to the world, [and] stifled the mental production of Anglophones. It has atrophied the creative space of cultural professionals both as producers and consumers of [the] English language. Deprived a critical mass of taxpayers of their legitimate information rights and benefits, distorted the prism of Cameroon's historical trajectory, closed the doors on employment, limited the marketing and sale of their products and thrown a large segment of their customers into the international market of Cable network. I concluded that the solution could be found in a number of options- sharing equitable broadcast time in English and French programs with alternative broadcast periods during the day, creating 2 National Channels, 1 in English and the other in French language and/or creating Regional TV stations after the pattern of our Regional Radio Stations as well…[248]

The creation of two national T.V channels and even regional television channels provides the opportunity for the regions to cater for local interests given the diversity of the country. The communication council forum that took place in 2012 seemed to have raised more problems than it could solve and so there is yet a need for a forum where both Francophones and Anglophones are involved in the planning and execution.

It would be important for Cameroonians to know that political parties are not religious bodies and one's decision to militant in a party can change as party policies change as well. We seem to have transformed political parties into occultist movements and clinch on the parties even when the parties are waning and become irrelevant. Political parties should function based on well-defined ideology and not just exist for the sake

---

[248] 'a conversation with Anglophone entrepreneurs ahead of and after the Cameroon communication forum 5-7 December 2012 (unpublished)

of it. If political parties have well defined ideology, we can explain the conditions under which a militant can switch camps not just for the sake of money. There are over 250 parties in Cameroon yet we are unable to say with precision the ideological leaning of a single party in Cameroon.

Finally all that has been discussed in *Cameroon's Predicaments* can have meaning only if there is the political will of the present leadership of the country. All is not yet lost as there is still a glimmer of hope. As it is often said, those at the top are accountable for the management of the state and its resources. For instance, corruption always starts from those at the top. If they ask or give bribes, those below will do same. After all, the fish starts to rot from the head and so if we need to clean the house we must also start from the top. Similarly, one starts bathing from the head. So if we have to clean this country of corrupt practices then we must start with those at the head.

Bibliography

Abbink, J. and DeBruijn, M (2011), eds, *Land ,law and politics in Africa: mediating conflict and reshaping the state*, Brill, Leiden

Adebanwi, W. and Obadare, E (2011),' When corruption fights back: Democracy and elite interest in Nigeria's anti-corruption war'. *Journal of Modern African Studies* Volume 49 Number 02 pp 203

Albert, I.O, (2005),'explaining 'godfatherism' in Nigerian politics, *African Sociological Review* Volume 9 Number 2 pp79&81

Alpes, M. (2011), *Bushfalling: how young Cameroonians dare to migrate*, PhD Thesis, Kiel

Alpes, M. (2012), 'Bushfalling at all cost: the economy of migratory knowledge in Anglophone Cameroon', *African Diaspora* 5 pp

Anyangwe, Carlson (2009), *Betrayal of too trusting a people; the UN, UK and the Trust Territory of the Southern Cameroons*, Langaa Research and Publishing CIG Mankon-Bamenda

Appadurai, A. (2008), 'Disjunctive and difference in the global cultural economy' in Inda and Rosaldo, eds, *The anthropology of globalization: a reader* Oxford, Blackwell publishing

Arthur, J. A. (2010), *African Diaspora identities: negotiating culture in transnational migration*, Lexington Books, Rowman &Littlefield Publishers, Lanham-Maryland

Asiwaju, A.I (2001), *West African Transformations: Comparative Impacts of French and British Colonialism*, Malthouse Press LTD, Lagos, Benin, Jos, Oxford, Port-Harcourt, Zaria

Ayee, J.R (2011),'Manifestos and elections in Ghana's fourth republic', *South African Journal of International Affairs* Volume 18 Number 3 pp372

Balogun, M.J (2007), 'Enduring clientelism, governance reform and leadership capacity: a review of the democratization process in Nigeria', *Journal of Contemporary African Studies* Volume 15 Number 2pp248

Bayart, J.F, (1973),'one-party government and political development in Cameroun', *African Affairs* Volume 72, Number 287pp128

Bayart, J.F (2009), the state in Africa: the Politics of the Belly, Polity Cambridge

Carrier, N (2009), 'The Hilux and the body thrower: Khat transporters in Kenya' in Gewald, J. Luning, S and van Walraven, K, eds, *The speed of change: Motor vehicles and people in Africa, 1890-2000*, Brill Leiden-Boston

Chanock, M .(1985), *Law, custom and social order: The colonial experience in Malawi and Zambia* ,Cambridge University Press, London, New York, New Rochelle, Melbourne, Sidney

Che, C. (2011), *Kingdom of Mankon: Aspects of history, language, culture flora and fauna*, Langaa Research and Publishing, Mankon

Chem-Langee, B. (1995), slavery and slave trade marketing in Nso' in the nineteenth century, *Paideuma,* 41 pp180

Chem-Langee, B (1999) 'Anglophone-Francophone divide and political disintegration in Cameroon: a psychohistorical perspective' in Nkwi, P and Nyamnjoh, F, eds, *regional balance and national integration in Cameroon: lessons learned and the uncertain future*, Yaoundé/ Leiden &ICASSRT monograph 1

Chilver, E. and Kaberry, P. (1970), 'Chronology of the Bamenda Grassfields', *The Journal of African History* Volume 11 Number 2 pp255

Chilver E.M and Kaberry, P.M (1971), 'The kingdom of Kom in West Cameroon' in Forde, D and Kaberry P.M ,eds, *West African Kingdoms in the Nineteenth century,* Oxford University Press, Oxford, London

Crowder, M (1970), *West Africa under colonial rule*, Hutchison, London

Collier, P and Gunning (1999), 'why has Africa grown slowly?' *Journal of Economic Perspectives* Volume 13 Number 3 pp5-13

Dafinger, A. and Pelican, M. (2006), 'Sharing or dividing the land? Land rights and farmer –herder relations in Burkina Faso and Northwest Cameroon', *CJAS/RCEA* Volume 40 Number 1 pp127-151

Davidheiser, M and Luna, A.M (2008),'From complementarity to conflict: a historical analysis of farmer-Fulbe relations in West Africa', *African Journal on Conflict Resolution,* Volume 8, Number 1 pp 98

Davidson, B. (1963*) Guide to African history,* George Allen and Unwin Ltd, London

De Bruijn, M. Nyamnjoh, F.B, and Angwafo, T. (2010), 'Mobile interconnections reinterpreting distance, relating and difference in the Cameroonian Grassfields', *Journal of African Media studies* Volume 2 Number 3 pp271

De Bruijn, M and van Dijk, R (2012) 'Connecting and change in African societies: examples of 'ethnographies of linking' in Anthropology', *Anthropologica,* 54 pp50

DeLancey, M.W. (1988), The political economy of Cameroon: Historical perspectives, the expansion of coffee production in Bamenda and banana in the Southwest' African Studies Centre, Leiden

Dolby, N (2006), 'Popular culture and public space in Africa: the possibilities of cultural citizenship', *African Studies Review,* Volume 49, Number 3 pp 38

Eboh, S.O. (2004), *African communalism: the way to social harmony and peaceful co-existence,* IKO-Verlag fur Interkulturelle Kommunikation, Frankfurt am Main-London

Ebune, J (2004), 'The making of the federal system' in Ngoh, V, eds, *Cameroon: from a federal to a unitary state 1961-1972, critical study,* Design House Limbe

Enloe, C (1980), *Ethnic soldiers: the state security in a divided society,* Penguin books, Harmondsworth

Eckert, M. A. (1999),'Slavery in colonial Cameroon, 1880s to 1930s'in Miers et al, eds, *Slavery and colonial rule in Africa*, Frank CASS, London-Portland, OR pp133-148

Egbo, O.et al (2010), *Legitimizing corruption in government: security votes in Nigeria*, ASC Working paper 91, Leiden

Ekpo, M.U (1979), 'Gift giving and bureaucratic corruption in Nigeria' in Ekpo M.U, eds, *bureaucratic corruption in Sub Saharan Africa: Towards a search for causes and consequences*, University Press of America

Etahgonop (2004),'Federalism in a one-party state' in Ngoh, V, eds, *Cameroon: from a federal to a unitary state 1961-1972, a critical study*, Design House Limbe,

FAO (2010),'Assessing progress in Africa towards the Millennium Development Goals: Section II', *Tracking progress*, Rome

Fisiy, C.(1992), *power and privilege in the administration of law: land law reforms and social differentiation in Cameroon*, African Studies Centre, Leiden

Fo, Angwafo. S.A.N (2009), *Royalty and politics: The story of my life*, Langaa, Mankon.

Fonjong, L.N (2004), 'Changing fortunes of government policies and its implications on the application of agricultural innovations in Cameroon', *Nordic Journal of African Studies* Volume 13 Number 1pp 14

Geschiere, P. (1993), 'Chiefs and colonial rule in Cameroon: inventing chieftaincy, French and British style', *Journal of the International African Institute* Volume 63 Number 2pp

Geschiere, P. (2005a), 'Autochthony and citizenship: new modes in the struggle over belonging and exclusion in Africa', *Quest: African Journal of philosophy* XVIII: 9-24 pp15

Geschiere, P. (2005b), 'Funerals and belonging: different patterns in South Cameroon', *African Studies Review* Volume 48 Number 2 pp 46-47

Geschiere, P and Nyamnjoh, F. (2001),'Capitalism and autochthony: the seesaw of mobility and belonging' in

Comaroff, J and Comaroff, J.L ,eds, *Millennial capitalism and the culture of neoliberalism,* Duke University Press Durham& London pp163

Gewald, J.B (2002) 'Missionaries, Hereros, and motorcars: mobility and the impact of motor vehicles in Namibia before 1940',*International Journal of African Historical Studies* Volume 35,Number 2-3 pp 261

Glassman, J. (1995), *Feasts and riots: revelry, rebellion and popular consciousness on the Swahili coast* 1856-1888 Portsmouth, N.H.: Heinemann

Goheen, M. (1996), *Men own the fields, women own the crops: gender and power in the Cameroon grassfields,* The University of Wisconsin Press, Madison Wisconsin

Gros, J. (2003), 'Cameroon in synopsis' in Gros (Eds) *Cameroon: politics and society in critical perspectives,* University Press of America, Lanham Maryland pp 23

Honwana, A. (2012), *The time of youth: work, social change, and politics in Africa,* Kumarian Press

Horton, P.B and Hunt, C.L (1982), *Sociology* Mc Graw-Hill, New York

IAC report (2004), *Realizing the promise and potential of African agriculture: science and technology strategies for improving agricultural productivity and food security in Africa,* Amsterdam pp10-15

IMF (2010),'Cameroon: poverty reduction strategy paper', *IMF Country Report No 10/257,* Washington D.C

Jerome, Y. B. (2010), 'The Anglo-leasing corruption scandal in Kenya: the politics of International and domestic pressures and counter-pressures', *Review of African Political Economy* 37:124 pp 124

Joseph, R.A. (1975) 'National politics in post war Cameroon: the difficult birth of the UPC', *Journal of African Studies* 2:2

Joseph, R. A (1976),'The Gaullist legacy: patterns of French Neo-colonialism', *Review of African Political economy,* Number 6 PP4, 5 & 12

Joseph, R, A. (1983)' Class, state and prebendal politics in Nigeria, The Journal of Commonwealth and Comparative Politics Volume xxi pp 26-29

Jua, N. and Konings, P (2004), 'Occupation of public space: Anglophone nationalism in Cameroon', *Cahieres d'etudes Africaines* 175 pp 3-15

Konings, P. (1995), *Gender and class in the tea estates of Cameroon*, African Studies Centre, Leiden

Konings, P. (1998), *Women Plantation workers and economic crisis in Cameroon*, Berg, Oxford pp151

Konings, P. (1999), 'The Anglophone problem' and chieftaincy in Anglophone Cameroon' in E.A, B.van Rouveroy Nieuwaal and R.van Dijk, R, eds, *African Chieftaincy in a new socio-political landscape*, Hamburg: LIT Verlag pp 181-206

Konings, P. (2001), 'Mobility and exclusion: conflicts between autochthons and allochthons during political liberalization in Cameroon' in De Bruijn, M.van Dijk and Foeken, D, eds, *mobile Africa: the changing patterns of movement in Africa and beyond*, Brill, Leiden

Konings, P and Nyamnjoh, F.B (1997), 'The Anglophone problem in Cameroon', the *Journal of modern African studies* 35: 2 pp 270-220

Konings, P. and Nyamnjoh, F.B (2002), 'President Biya and the Anglophone problem' *in* J Takougang and J.M Mbaku ,eds, *the leadership challenge in Africa; Cameroon under Paul Biya*, African World Press, Trenton New York

Konings, P. and Nyamnjoh, F.B (2003), *Negotiating and Anglophone identity, a study of the politics of recognition and representation in Cameroon*, Brill Leiden-Boston

Krieger, M (2008), *Cameroon's Social Democratic Front: its history and prospects as an opposition political party (1990-2011)*, Langaa Research and Publishing (CIG) Mankon-Bamenda

Le Vine, V. (1963),'The Cameroon federal republic', in Carter, G. M , eds, *five African states: responses to diversity*, Cornell University Press, Ithaca, New York

244

Mbah, E.M (2009), 'Disruptive colonial boundaries and attempts to resolve land/boundary disputes, in the Grassfields of Bamenda Cameroon', *African Journal of Conflict Resolution* Volume 9 Number 3 pp 11-32

Mbiti, J.S. (1990), *African religions and philosophy*, Heinemann, London

MDG (2012), *Indicators*, UNDP, Washington D.C

Medard, C and Golaz, V. (2013),'Creating dependency: land and gift-giving practices in Uganda', *Journal of Eastern African Studies* Volume7, Number 3 pp550-552

Moritz, M. (2006), 'The politics of permanent conflict: farmer-herder conflicts in Northern Cameroon', *CJAS/RCEA* Volume 40 Number 1 pp107 & 118

Mung'ong'o, C.G (2002) 'the right to food, land and democracy: an analysis from a grassroots perspective in three semi-Arid rural districts in Tanzania', *Nordic Journal of African Studies* Volume 11 Number 1 PP 78-88

Mwangi, Oscar. (2008), 'Political corruption, party financing and democracy in *Kenya' the Journal of Modern African Studies* 46 pp 269 & 272

Neba, A. (1987), *Modern geography of the republic of Cameroon,* Neba Publishers, Camden

Ndege, P.B.(2012),*From accumulation of women and children to 'land grabbing: agrarian kleptocracy and the land question in Kenya.* Moi University Press, Moi University

Ndi, A, (2013), *Southern West Cameroon revisited 1950-1972; unveiling inescapable traps* Vol 1 Paul's Press Bamenda

Ndjio, B (2008), *Cameroonian feymen and Nigerian'419' scammers: two examples of Africa's 'reinvention' of the global capitalism*, ASC Working paper, Leiden

Ngoh, V. J. (2004), 'Introduction', eds, in *Cameroon: From a Federal to a Unitary State 1961-1972: A Critical Study,* Design House, and Limbe

Ngum, A. A (2013), *Gender and politics: Women of the Bamenda Grassfields in the struggle for independence and reunification 1958-2011*, Master Thesis the University of Ngaoundere

Njoku, O.N (1977), 'The burden of imperialism: Nigeria war relief fund, 1939-1945', in Were, G.S and Muriuki, eds, *Transafrican Journal of History* Vol 6 and 7 Gideon .S and Were Press

Njeuma, M and Awasom (1988), 'The Fulani and the political economy of the Bamenda Grassfields, 1940-1960' *in* Geschiere, P and Konings, eds, *the political economy of Cameroon: historical perspectives,* edited by African studies Centre, Leiden, The Netherlands pp1-11

Njeuma, M. (1995), 'Reunification and political opportunism in the making of Cameroon's independence' *Paideuma* No 41 pp 30-34

Nkwi, P. and Socpa, A. (1997), 'Ethnicity and party politics in Cameroon: the politics of divide and rule' in Nkwi and Nyamnjoh, eds, *regional balance and national integration in Cameroon: lessons learned and the uncertain future*, Yaoundé/ Leiden &ICASSRT monograph 1

Nkwi, W.(2011),*Sons and daughters of the soil: land and boundary conflicts in north west Cameroon,*1955-2005,Langaa Mankon-Bamenda

Nnam, N.(2007),*Colonial mentality in Africa*, Hamilton Books, Lanham, Maryland

Nyamnjoh, F.B and Awasom, N (2008),'Introduction 'in Percival, John, eds, *the 1961 Cameroon Plebiscite: Choice or Betrayal*, Langaa RPCIG, Mankon

Nyamnjoh, F.B (2011), 'Cameroonian bush falling: negotiation of identity and belonging in fiction and ethnography', *American Ethnologist* Volume 38 Number 4 pp 707-711

Nyamnjoh, F.B (2012), 'Potted plants in green houses: a critical reflection on the resilience of colonial *education* in Africa', *Journal of Asian and African Studies* pp134

Nyamnjoh, F.B, (2013a), 'Politics of back-scratching in Cameroon and beyond' in Drulak, P and Moravcova, S ,eds, Non-Western reflection on politics, Frankfurt am Main: Peter pp

Nyamnjoh, F.B (2013b), The nimbleness of being Fulani, *Africa Today*, Volume 59 Number 3 pp111-114

Nyamnjoh, F.B. and Page, B. (2002),'Whiteman kontri and the enduring allure of modernity among Cameroonian youth', *African Affairs*, 101 pp 607-628

Nyamnjoh, H (2008),*'We get nothing from fishing': fishing for boat opportunities amongst Senegales fisher migrants,* Langaa and African Studies Centre, Mankon-Leiden

Obuah, E. (2010), 'Combating corruption in Nigeria: the Nigerian Economic and financial crimes', *African studies Quarterly* Volume 12 Number 1 pp 10-25

Orji, N. (2010)' Governing 'ethnicised' public sphere: insights from Nigeria, *Africa Development* Vol. XXXV. No 4 pp 166-168

Parkins, N.C (2011), Push and pull factors of migration, *American Review of Political Economy,* Volume 8 Number 2 pp12-15

Percival, J. (2008), *The 1961 Cameroon Plebiscite: Choice or Betrayal,* Langaa RPCIG, Mankon-Bamenda

Parry, M (1990) *climate change and world agriculture,* Earthscan/ UNEP/IISA, London

Rangers, T. (1994), 'The invention of tradition revisited: the case of colonial Africa' in Kaarsholm et al, eds, *inventions and boundaries: historical and anthropological approaches to the study of ethnicity*, Roskilde University

Rodney, W. (2012),*How Europe underdeveloped Africa,* Pambazuka Press and CODESRIA ,Cape Town &Dakar

Roth and Wittich (1978), eds, 'Economy and society: an outline of interpretative sociology' in *Max Weber and idea bureaucracy*, University Press, California

Sama, M. Cand Johnson-Ross (2006),'Reclaiming the Bakassi kingdom: the Anglophone Cameroon-Nigeria border', *Afrika Zamani*, Number 13&14

Schler, L. (2002), 'Looking through a glass of beer: alcohol in the cultural spaces of colonial Douala 1940-1945, *International Journal of African Historical studies* Vol.35, No 3-2 pp

Schler, L. (2005),'History, the nation-state, and alternative narratives: an example from colonial Duala', *African Studies Review*, vol 48, No 1pp102

Sender, J. Cramer, C and Oya, C. (2005), *Unequal prospects: disparities in the quantity and quality of labour supply in sub-Saharan Africa*, ASC Working Paper 62/2005 pp46

Skare, O. K. (2010), 'The road to renaming what's in a name? The changing of Durban's street names and its coverage in the Mercury, *Journal of African Media Studies* Volume 2 Number 3

Stock, Robert. (2004), *Africa South of the Sahara: A Geographical Interpretation,* the Guilford Press, and New York London

Szeftel, M. (2000),'Clientelism, corruption and catastrophes' *Review of African Political Economy* Volume 27 Number 85 pp437

Tanyi, L.M (2010), *HIV/AIDS disease burden and the elderly population in the Northwest Region of Cameroon,* PhD Thesis, University of Nigeria Nssuka PP4

Tumi, W. (2006), *The political regimes of Ahmadou Ahidjo and Paul Biya, and Christian Tumi* University of Michigan, Michigan

UNDP (2011), *Sustainability and equity: a better future for all,* Washington D.C

Van Beek (2012), 'Cultural models of power in Africa', in Abbink, J and De Bruijn, M eds, *land ,law and politics in Africa: mediating conflict and reshaping the state,* Brill, Leiden

Warnier, J.P (1975), *Pre-colonial Mankon: The development of Cameroon Chiefdom in its regional setting,* University of Pennsylvania, PhD Thesis in Cultural Anthropology

Warnier, J.P and Fowler, I (1979), 'A nineteenth century Ruhr in central Africa': *Journal of the International African Institute,* Volume 49 Number 4 pp331

Warnier (1995) 'Slave trade without slave raiding in the western grassfields of Cameroon' *Paideuma* Number 42

Wilmot, P.F (1980), *Ideology and National Consciousness,* Lantern Books, Ibadan, Ikeja and Lagos

Wilmot, P.F (1985), *Sociology: a new introduction,* Collins International Textbooks London

____ (1968), *Surveys of African economics,* International Monetary Fund Volume 1 Washington D.C pp 14-29

World Food Program 2009 country report- Cameroon

Wynchank, A.(2013), 'German and French colonizers in the words of a Cameroonian witness', *Mount Cameroun,* Number 8/9,pp 49-56

Websites

See Effa tambe Ncham (2012) A man's head receives bullet in Baffia http://allafrica.com/stories/201211010852.html Accessed 02/11/2012

Mosima   Elizabeth http://allafrica.com/stories/201211020157.html   accessed 02/11/2012 Automatic pistols of mark valtro, a charger and nine bullets see

http://allafrica.com/stories/201211020024.html   accessed 02/11/20

Njila, Hinsley Chia Innocent [eds] a guide to understanding Cameroonian-Immigrants in the USA «Cameroonian-American Filmmaker Shoots compelling film on Spousal Abuse | Main | How much I miss my mother! » Accessed 13/12/2013

The   World   University Rankings:http://www.timeshighereducation.co.uk/world-university-rankings/2012-13/world-ranking/region/europe accessed 18/01/2013

Also see World University rankings: http://www.webometrics.info/en/Africa/Cameroon%20 Accessed 18/01/2013

Vakunta, P. Cameroon: unravelling the leadership conundrum in Cameroon http://allafrica.com/stories/201211021100.html?viewall=1, accessed 02/11/2013

www.cameroononline.org accessed 16/11/2012 and 22/01/2013

Agendia, Aloysius: Cameroon 2005 census results: smack of diabolic geo-political planning. http://agendia.jigsy.com/entries/blog/cameroon-2005-census-results-smack-of-diabolic-geo-political-planning accessed 19/01/2013 also see Tande, D (2010) Cameroon:2005 census results finally published http://www.dibussi.com/2010/04/cameroon-2005-census-result-published.html accessed 19/01/2013

http://www.indexmundi.com/g/r.aspx?c=cm&v=74 accessed 18/01/2013

The World University Rankings http://www.timeshighereducation.co.uk/world-university-rankings/2012-13/world-ranking/region/europe accessed 18/01/2013

Also see World University rankings http://www.webometrics.info/en/Africa/Cameroon%20 Accessed 18/01/2013

See UNDP (2011) Explanatory note on Human Development Report, sustainability and Equity: a better future for all http://hdrstats.undp.org/images/explanations/CMR.pdf Accessed 28/01/2013

Africa, in NewAfrican, an IC Publication http://www.newafricanmagazine.com/blogs/money-talks/multinationals-steal-$50bn-per-year-from-africa accessed 28/01/2013 http://en.wikipedia.org/wiki/Crime_statistics accessed 28/01/2013

https://www.osac.gov/Pages/ContentReportDetails.aspx? cid=12083accessed 28/01/2013

Effa tambe Ncham (2012) A man's head receives bullet in Baffia http://allafrica.com/stories/201211010852.html accessed 02/11/2012

http://allafrica.com/stories/201211020024.htm accessed 02/11/2012

See letter of Fo Angwafo addressed to the Administration of Mezam http://cameroonlatest.blogspot.nl/2012/09/bamenda-on-time-bomb-fon-angwafo-iii.html accessed 28/01/2013

See list of Biya's appointments of new Senior Divisional Officers of 25/10/ 2012 www.crtv.cm accessed 27/10/2012

http://en.wikipedia.org/wiki/Am%C3%ADlcar_Cabral accessed 28/01/2013

Ngome, S. (1985), 'change in Cameroon, ARC publications, Alexandria, Virginia www.cameroon-tour.com

Watch Presidents for life http://mycontinent.co/Ditactors.php accessed 17/01/2013

Watch www.youtube.com interview with the 'Man Fru Ndi accessed 16/01/2013

Presidents for life http://mycontinent.co/Ditactors.php accessed 17/01/2013

Tedonkeng, E Country pasture/Forage resources profile Cameroon www.fao.org accessed 1/10/2o12

Cameroon: migration profile (2009) http://www.iomdakar.org/profiles/content/migration-profiles-cameroon accessed 30th /01/2013

http://www.cameroon-info.net/stories/0,40774,@,inertie-gouvernementale-ces-laquo-vieillards-raquo-qui-gerent-les-societes.html

Wache, F On Mount Mary Anglophones stand 20 years after the AAC http://www.franciswache.com/2013/04/on-

mount-mary-anglophones-stand.html#sthash.2LC4jAWA.dpuf
accessed 18/03/2014

http://capam-cam-ltd.imexbb.com/ accessed 3/7/2014.

'United   States   Presidential   elections   2012'
http://en.wikipedia.org/org/wiki/United_States_predidents_e
lection accessed 3/7/2014

'Who are the past 10 US Presidents? From J.F Kennedy in
1961 to Barack Obama in 2009, America has been governed by
eleven   Presidents.
http://wiki.answers.com/Q/Who_are_the_past_10_us_presid
ents accessed 3/7/2014

There are two sides to every story. "Why did our federation
not invest some of the considerable amount of money in
football?   http://sports.yahoo.com/news/date-set-neymars-
first-clasico-131800529--sow.html accessed 3/7/2014

Alexander Song was sent out with a red card during the
Cameroon- Croatia match and the Lions were defeated by 4-0.
Worse still, indiscipline was very visible when Assou Ekotto
and Benjamine Moukanjo fought in the field during this match.
www.camfoot.com accessed 9/6/2014

Ujamaa was the concept that formed the basis of Julius
Nyerere's social and economic development policies in
Tanzania after it gained independence from Britain in 1961.
The Term has the meaning of 'unity', 'Oneness','-uniting with
your   countrymen   as   one   extended   family.
http://en.wikipedia.org/wiki/Ujamaa accessed 3/7/2014

'Nigeria 419 Scams' the number "419" refers to the article
of the Nigerian Criminal Code dealing with fraud. The scam
has been used with fax and traditional mail and is now used
with the internet http://en.wikipedia.org/wiki/419_scams
accessed 8/7/2014

El Dorado is used here metaphorically to mean any place
where wealth can be rapidly acquired. It also represents an
ultimate prize that one might spend one's life seeking. It could
represent love, heaven, happiness or success. It simply refers to

something much sought after that may not even exist, or, at least, may not ever be found. http://en.wikipedia.org/wiki/El_Dorado._ accessed 3/7/2014

'Crime rates in Cameroon' http://www.numbeo.com/crime/country_result.jsp?country=Cameroon

Accessed 3/7/2014

See Report of National Anti-Corruption Commission (CONAC) http://www.conac-cameroun.net/en/index_en.php accessed 25/6/2014 Also see list of ministers convicted of embezzlement in chapter 3

'Cameroon Police and Gendarmes, Crooks in government: in the case of the Bamenda Ring Road, they operate like toll gates' http://www.cameroonjournal.com/Cameroon%20Police%20and%20Gendarmes.html accessed 14/7/2014

Newspapers/ Magazines

Cameroon Tribune No 9090/5289 of April 30th 2008
The post No 0946 of Monday April 21st 2008
Business in Cameroon

9 789956 792382